Moral Ambition

THE ANTHROPOLOGY OF CHRISTIANITY

Edited by Joel Robbins

Moral Ambition

Mobilization and Social Outreach in
Evangelical Megachurches

Omri Elisha

UNIVERSITY OF CALIFORNIA PRESS
Berkeley · Los Angeles · London

Parts of chapter 5 appeared in different form in "Sins of Our Soccer Moms: Servant Evangelism and the Spiritual Injuries of Class," in *Local Actions: Cultural Activism, Power, and Public Life in America,* ed. Melissa Checker and Margaret Fishman, 136–158 (New York: Columbia University Press, 2004). Chapter 6 appeared in slightly different form in "Moral Ambitions of Grace: The Paradox of Compassion and Accountability in Evangelical Faith-Based Activism," *Cultural Anthropology* 23, no. 1 (2008): 154–189. Parts of chapter 7 appeared in different form in "Evangelical Megachurches, Racial Reconciliation, and the Christianization of Civil Society," in *Politics and Partnerships: The Role of Voluntary Associations in America's Past and Present,* ed. Elisabeth Clemens and Doug Guthrie, 269–296 (Chicago: University of Chicago Press, 2011), and "Taking the (Inner) City for God: Ambiguities of Urban Social Engagement among Conservative White Evangelicals," in *The Fundamentalist City? Religiosity and the Remaking of Urban Space,* ed. Nezar AlSayyad and Mejgan Massoumi, 235–256 (London: Routledge, 2010).

University of California Press, one of the most distinguished university presses in the United States, enriches lives around the world by advancing scholarship in the humanities, social sciences, and natural sciences. Its activities are supported by the UC Press Foundation and by philanthropic contributions from individuals and institutions. For more information, visit www.ucpress.edu.

University of California Press
Berkeley and Los Angeles, California

University of California Press, Ltd.
London, England

Library of Congress Cataloging-in-Publication Data

Elisha, Omri, 1972–
    Moral ambition : mobilization and social outreach in evangelical megachurches / Omri Elisha.
        p. cm. – (Anthropology of Christianity ; 12)
    Includes bibliographical references and index.
    ISBN 978-0-520-26750-3 (cloth : alk. paper)
    ISBN 978-0-520-26751-0 (pbk. : alk. paper)
    1. Big churches.   2. Church work.   3. Missions.   4. Church and social problems.   5. Evangelicalism–Tennessee.   I. Title.   II. Title: Mobilization and social outreach in evangelical megachurches.
    BV637.9.E45 2011
    253.09768'09045—dc22   2010053747

Manufactured in the United States of America

20 19 18 17 16 15 14 13 12 11
10 9 8 7 6 5 4 3 2 1

This book is printed on Cascades Enviro 100, a 100% post consumer waste, recycled, de-inked fiber. FSC recycled certified and processed chlorine free. It is acid free, Ecologo certified, and manufactured by BioGas energy.

For my parents, Haim and Rina Elisha

Contents

Acknowledgments

Writing this book has been a labor of love, but a labor nonetheless. I am tremendously thankful for all of the support, encouragement, and insight I have received from people and institutions along the way. I alone take full responsibility for the content, but I am proud to acknowledge the company I have kept in the process. As I believe the subjects of this ethnography would readily agree, the most worthwhile achievements in life, personal and professional, are those that allow us to absorb the presence and talents of others into what we do.

Research for this book was funded by a research grant from the Social Science Research Council's Program on Philanthropy and the Nonprofit Sector, a dissertation fellowship from the Louisville Institute, and a summer travel grant from the Department of Anthropology at New York University. A vital stage in the writing of the book took place at the School for Advanced Research in Santa Fe, New Mexico, where I was a Resident Scholar in 2007–2008, with a fellowship funded by the Social Science Research Council.

It is no exaggeration to say that this book would not have been possible without the cooperation and goodwill of evangelical pastors and churchgoers in Knoxville who agreed to participate in my research. Almost all the individuals and local organizations described in this ethnography, including churches and faith-based ministries, appear under pseudonyms. For this reason, obviously I cannot properly acknowledge specific individuals using their real names. Those who have worked closely with me as consultants, facilitators, hosts, and interviewees should know that I am indebted to them for their hospitality and enthusiasm. I hope that in reading this ethnography they will find value in the fruits of their participation.

While conducting fieldwork in Knoxville, I benefited from institutional support from the Religious Studies Program of the University of Tennessee–Knoxville, including access to the university's resources and an academic community with which to share my work. I am especially grateful to Rosalind Hackett, for her extraordinary personal and intellectual generosity, and to Mark Hulsether and Charlie Reynolds, who took time to meet with me and help me get oriented to the local environment. My appreciation of the culture and history of the region was further enriched by conversations with Matthew T. Everett, a local journalist, friend, and guide to all things Knoxville.

This project began in graduate school at New York University, under the tutelage of my doctoral advisors, T. O. Beidelman and Faye Ginsburg, both of whom inspired me with their commitment to rigorous and original ethnography and raised the standards of what I expected from myself. I received additional guidance from the rest of my Ph.D. committee, Bambi Schieffelin, Angela Zito, and Diane Winston (of the University of Southern California), as well as from Karen Blu and Fred Myers. I am also grateful to the members of my dissertation writing group, who read and critiqued early versions of chapters with diligence and a spirit of true solidarity: Jessica Cattelino, Julie Chu, Jong Bum Kwon, Kathe Managan, Ayse Parla, Elizabeth Smith, and Winifred Tate. For several years I was incredibly fortunate to be affiliated with NYU's Center for Religion and Media, codirected by Faye Ginsburg and Angela Zito, and I thank all the scholars and staff for their friendship and intellectual stimulation.

In the transition from dissertation to book, I received invaluable feedback from Joel Robbins, who, as editor of the Anthropology of Christianity series, read the manuscript thoroughly and helped me to discern its core ethnographic and narrative themes while generously agreeing to include the book among the distinguished titles in the series. The incomparable Stan Holwitz, of the University of California Press, ushered the book through its initial stages of preparation before passing it to the capable hands of Reed Malcolm, Jessica Moll, and the production staff. I am grateful to Madeleine Adams for her superb copyediting and conscientious contributions to the final manuscript.

Few opportunities in my academic career so far have been as pleasant or productive as the nine months I spent as a Resident Scholar at the School for Advanced Research. It was in that idyllic and nurturing environment that the first full draft of the book manuscript was written, thanks in large part to support from SAR scholars and staff, including James F. Brooks, Rebecca Allahyari, Nancy Owen Lewis, and John Kantner. In addition, I was honored to be part of a collegial group of scholars-in-residence, with whom I shared countless stimulating conversations and hikes through the southwestern wilderness. Thanks to Peter Redfield, Silvia Tomášková, Joseph P. Gone, Tiya Miles, Angela Stuesse, Tutu Alicante, James Snead, Monica Smith, and Malena Mörling. A special shout out to Zoë Tomášková Redfield, who made a habit of knocking on my front door whenever she suspected I was sleeping in too late.

Portions of this book have been presented in draft form at conferences and seminars held at various academic centers. These include the Department of Anthropology at Queens College–CUNY, the Social Science Research Council, the Center for Religion and Media at NYU, a workshop on ethnography and American religion led by Alan Wolfe and Nancy Ammerman at the Boisi Center at Boston College, the Interdisciplinary Christianities Workshop at University of Chicago, the Religion in America University Seminar convened by Randall Balmer at Columbia University, and the Religion and Public Life Seminar led by Robert Wuthnow at Princeton University's Center for the Study of Religion. I am fortunate to have had such opportunities to share my work with distinguished colleagues across academic disciplines, and I thank these scholars for extending their invitations.

Over the years, a number of individuals have offered useful comments on different sections of this book, or discussed other relevant issues with me that informed the development of my work. They include John Bartkowski, Courtney Bender, Jon Bialecki, Mario Bick, James Bielo, Erica Bornstein, Diana Brown, Megan Callaghan, Elizabeth Castelli, Melissa Checker, Scott Cormode, Tanya Erzen, Maggie Fishman, Robert Hefner, Brian Howell, Jeffrey Jurgens, Laura Kunreuther, Tanya Luhrmann, Jennell Williams Paris, Gretchen Pfeil, Nina Schnall, Jeffrey Sharlet, Yuka Suzuki, Joe Tarr, and Peter Wosh. I am particularly thankful to Simon Coleman, a constructive reader and most genuine interlocutor, and R. Marie Griffith, whose suggestions regarding the tone and structure of the book were extremely helpful at a critical juncture.

I wish to extend heartfelt thanks to close friends, including Paulo Campos, Aaron Glass, Ann Neumann, Nejem Raheem, and Laura Terruso, for their unwavering reliability and humor, and to Adam Becker, both for his sharp analytical instincts and for reminding me that being one's own worst critic isn't always the most productive use of one's time. Finally, I cannot imagine a better companion in the final months of writing this book than Francesca Bregoli, who provided brilliant insights on several chapters, and, most important, inspired me with her wisdom, comfort, and encouragement.

Having been raised in New York City in a family composed of artists and educators, I grew up with a deep sense of appreciation for the creative and quixotic aspects of the human condition, and an awareness of what it means to pursue ambitious goals that others may not understand and lofty ideals that others may not share. I believe that this was a significant factor in how I was led to study conservative evangelicalism in East Tennessee, a world of engagement so vastly different from that of my upbringing yet strangely familiar in its aspirational overtones. Were this the full extent of my gratitude to my family, it would already be considerable. But the credit they deserve is far greater than this. For their emotional support and tireless optimism, in all things and in every way, I thank my brother, Ehran Elisha, and my parents, Haim and Rina Elisha. I further dedicate this book to my parents, for their love and sacrifice, and for demonstrating that working hard for the people and things we love is really no sacrifice at all.

CHAPTER 1

Introduction

Do not merely listen to the word, and so deceive yourselves.
Do what it says. Anyone who listens to the word but does
not do what it says is like a man who looks at his face in a
mirror and, after looking at himself, goes away and immediately forgets what he looks like.

—James 1:22–24

Religious postulates can come into conflict with the "world"
from different points of view, and the point of view involved
is always of the greatest importance for the direction and
for the way in which salvation will be striven for.

—Max Weber

There are many ways to be ambitious, and many different objectives
that ambitious people aspire to aside from wealth and power. For those
we call "people of faith," the life of religious commitment is a relentless,
often challenging pursuit of virtues that—like fame, fortune, or artistic
genius—are perceived as elusive yet ultimately attainable. Whether such
virtues are enacted in everyday life or conceived in other-worldly terms,
the ambitions that propel religious people toward lofty ideals are rooted
in cultural practices that allow sacred pursuits, including the triumph of
righteousness over mediocrity, to appear not only desirable but always
close at hand. The ambitions of religious faith, and for that matter all
personal aspirations that we often misrecognize as expressions of radical
individuality, are inherently social in their inception and saturated in
moral content.

  This book is about evangelical Protestants affiliated with megachurches and faith-based ministries in the city of Knoxville, Tennessee,

and the ambitious efforts of some pastors and churchgoers to increase their faith community's investments in various forms of altruistic social engagement. Based on nearly sixteen months of ethnographic research carried out between 1999 and 2002, my study focuses on cultural practices and individual experiences related to organized benevolence and social outreach, areas of ministry that are fraught with ideological tension. In describing how conservative and predominantly white evangelicals navigate the shifting and contested boundaries of social engagement, I offer an in-depth perspective on important aspects of North American evangelicalism—including the complexity of evangelical moral and political attitudes at the congregational level—about which there has been much speculation but little concrete analysis.

Central to my overall argument is the concept of *moral ambition*, which I have coined to highlight two key points. First, as socially engaged evangelicals work to attain religious virtues associated with grace and compassion, they simultaneously work to inspire others to adopt the appropriate moral dispositions necessary to enhance volunteer mobilization. In other words, their aspirations pertain not only to what they desire for themselves but also what they have come to expect of others, including those who share their religious outlook as well as the larger secular and nonevangelical public. Second, I argue that moments of creative agency triggered by these aspirations are at once fueled and constrained by the ideological demands of the institutional contexts in which they emerge. They are also complicated by multiple and at times conflicting historical, cultural, and theological influences that coexist within those contexts. Far from having a singular motivational source, evangelical social engagement is animated by diverse traditions of Christian missionization, revivalism, social reform, and fundamentalism. Socially engaged evangelicals struggle with a whirlwind of competing imperatives that they have inherited from these traditions. This is particularly true of perennial debates about the character of evangelism (from the Greek *euangelos,* or "bringing good news"). Disagreements abound, for example, over whether the Christian gospel should be viewed as a blueprint for making the world a better place or strictly as a mandate calling on individuals to repent as humanity heads toward its imminent demise.

Through my discussion of the moral ambitions of evangelical social engagement it will become clear that in the process of assuming an activist orientation, conservative evangelicals position themselves to renew and even redefine the terms of Christian evangelism—the project of "spreading the gospel of Jesus Christ"—in ways that reflect changing personal, social, and political circumstances. In so doing they also experience shifts, however subtle, in their ideological and even theological perspectives, which can at times put them at odds with other members of their home congregations and the prevailing cultural politics of the Christian Right. Nonetheless, their ambitions remain roughly consistent with a broad ideological agenda that underlies most instances of grassroots activism and institutionalization in modern evangelicalism. That agenda is the Christianization of culture, or "the reformulation of social relations, cultural meanings, and personal experience in terms of putatively Christian ideals" (Hefner 1993: 3–4). In the case of conservative evangelicals, those "putatively Christian ideals" are closely linked to a morality rooted in biblical fundamentalism and premillennial apocalypticism. They also stem from more or less articulated notions of public theology, which for contemporary evangelicals entail collective efforts to redefine civil society as a space of missionary intervention, efforts that have been well served by recent national trends such as the proliferation of evangelical megachurches and the political currency of "faith-based initiatives" in the wake of federal welfare reform.

At the center of my field research were two suburban megachurches, which I refer to as Eternal Vine Church and Marble Valley Presbyterian Church.[1] I also observed and interviewed representatives from local faith-based organizations, social service agencies, and informal ministries initiatives with ties to the megachurches. A megachurch is typically defined as a Protestant congregation with an average of two thousand or more worshippers attending weekly services (Thumma and Travis 2007). Eternal Vine and Marble Valley Presbyterian each had an average of thirty-five hundred to five thousand worshippers at Sunday services during the period of my fieldwork. This is moderate compared to massive megachurches in major cities, some of which boast more than twenty thousand or even forty thousand attendees, but the numbers are significant for a midsized city like Knoxville. Both congregations are made up of predominantly white, middle- to upper-middle-class churchgoers, including many who live in affluent suburbs in or around Knox County. Some members are among the region's political and economic elite, which is noteworthy for a study of this kind, given my emphasis on how megachurch ministries construct points of social intersection with the community at large. Megachurches are extremely resourceful organizations, capable of implementing bold strategies of social engagement and institutional networking. As such, they represent potential exceptions to the norm among conservative Protestant churches, which tend to be less directly engaged with their social and civic environment than mainline Protestant and Catholic churches (Ammerman 2005).[2] Insofar as megachurches are institutions where high concentrations of social and economic capital are put to the service of religious ideology, they are also sites of power, reproducing dynamics of class and racial privilege that prevail in stratified urban-suburban landscapes.

When I began fieldwork in the summer of 1999, I intended to study the social impact of affluent megachurches on a local religious ecology (Eiesland 2000), focusing on how emergent outreach ministries sponsored by large suburban churches affected the dynamics of welfare in a regional culture known for its religious and social conservatism. Although I do address this issue to some extent in the chapters that follow, there is another story at the heart of this ethnography. Almost as soon as I started attending services and outreach events in Knoxville, I observed a tendency among pastors and churchgoers to call themselves to task, almost routinely, for having failed yet to maximize the human and material resources at their disposal in order to achieve "real" cultural and spiritual transformations in the greater Knoxville area. They praised the achievements of the megachurches they were affiliated with, including the quality of the worship, the scope of foreign missions, and the opportunities for spiritual growth afforded by numerous congregational ministries. But they frequently lamented the lack of sustained commitment to ministries that targeted poor, distressed, and needy populations in the surrounding region. Such ministries were viewed by some as integral to the fulfillment of the "Great Commission," in which Jesus Christ commands his followers to "make disciples of all nations" (Matthew 28:19). The complaints were justified to a certain extent, since relatively few pastors and churchgoers were actively involved in the outreach ministries that the megachurches supported at the time of my research. And the fact that it was only a small but vocal segment of conservative evangelicals in the suburbs who took it upon themselves to change the situation suggests that the critique amounted to more than mere rhetorical flourish.

Early on in my fieldwork I was advised by members of the evangelical community to get in touch with a man named Paul Genero, who was then a staff pastor at a small suburban church with close ties to Eternal Vine Church. They told me that he too was "writing a book" about churches and faith-based ministries in Knoxville. I later learned that he had recently completed a fairly comprehensive survey of faith-based social services in Knoxville, with an emphasis on Christian community organizations and church programs. He circulated the findings in a self-published report full of regional statistics on problems such as poverty, homelessness, at-risk youth, and domestic violence, combined with moving biographical sketches of social workers and clients whose stories of despair turned to hope were meant to inspire local churchgoers to take action. When I finally contacted Paul in the fall of 2000, our initial phone conversation had that remarkable spark of serendipity, that moment when individual pursuits (in this case, his and mine) are forever changed by the fact that their paths have fortuitously converged.

The first thing that struck me about Paul was his infectious enthusiasm. "You're blowing my mind here!" he kept saying, as I explained that I was a doctoral student from New York studying the social outreach efforts of local megachurches. He could hardly believe it, and relished the fact that someone other than himself was interested in studying "what God is trying to do in Knoxville," as he phrased it. Wasting no time at all, he immediately pointed out that we would surely benefit from one another's work, and he recommended that we meet in person as soon as possible so he could tell me about a new Christian faith-based organization that he was creating to improve the state of social ministries in Knoxville. Two days later I met Paul in the parking lot of a barbecue restaurant on Kingston Pike, Knoxville's main commercial artery. He was a slim, energetic man in his midthirties with an athletic stature and a warm, slightly mischievous grin that seemed never to leave his face. As soon as I arrived Paul suggested that we go to a different location, where it would be easier to talk. I got in my car and followed his pickup truck to a small café by the railroad tracks about a half mile away. It was an artsy spot, popular among local hipsters and college students, where poets and folk musicians performed and artists displayed their work. I had been there already several times by myself to read or write field notes, but I had never gone there with any of the evangelical churchgoers I knew, nor had I seen many customers who looked like the churchgoing type. At first I didn't understand why Paul decided that we should meet there instead of the barbecue joint, but as I got to know him it made more sense. Paul Genero is a man who is committed to the idea of embracing the unfamiliar and the unknown. His life as a Christian—which has included short-term missionary work abroad and extensive charity work—has been guided by the motivation to push the boundaries of his "comfort zone" and meet cultural strangers wherever they live. It may have been that Paul moved our meeting to the café because he imagined it was the kind of place where I would be comfortable. It is equally likely that he chose it because the very act of being there signified for him a core value of his faith. At one point he picked up a copy of an alternative local newspaper and, flipping aimlessly through music reviews, liberal editorials, and lurid classified ads, smiled and said that these are exactly the kinds of people Jesus Christ would make sure to get to know if he lived in Knoxville.

With muffins and cappuccinos to sustain us, we sat down facing each other armed with yellow notepads. Paul asked me to explain again the purpose of my research, which I did in a somewhat labored manner. He took notes furiously while I spoke and kept reacting aloud, much as he did on the phone: "You're blowing me away here," "This is amazing!" Every now and then he interrupted me to recommend specific books or people I should make sure to consult. When it was his turn to speak, and my turn to take notes, Paul started with a frank acknowledgement of my status as an outsider and as a non-Christian (he assumed correctly that I am Jewish, without asking). He said he looked forward to hearing my observations about his work, adding that my "objectivity" would help him to keep things in perspective and prevent him from letting his "definite spiritual bias" affect his judgment in unproductive ways. He pointed at me excitedly with the tip of his pen and said, "You are the one studying it, we are the ones creating it." *Creating what?* I wondered, as the scope of my fieldwork took shape before my eyes.

With little prodding on my part, Paul launched into a lengthy but eloquent commentary ("Now you get to hear my soapbox!") enumerating his complaints, aspirations, and strategic intentions with regard to local churches and faith-based ministries. He argued that one of the biggest problems with Christianity in "middle-class America" was a general lack of commitment to addressing the problems facing poor and needy people "in our own backyards." He said that evangelical churches have become woefully inadequate in their mission to relieve suffering and offer hope to the distressed and have lost sight of the fact that compassion is a theological imperative, equal in importance to other components of Christian evangelism. "We've always been good at proclamation evangelism—preaching sermons and handing out pamphlets and such—but we're terrible at loving people." He added that conservative churches in the Bible Belt have "atrophied" with regard to "the social action part of Christianity," and that this was particularly ironic in a region known for its religious fervor.

Paul tore a clean sheet of paper from his notebook, drew a series of small circles randomly on the page, and twisted the paper around for me to see. The circles represented individual churches, dispersed and isolated like desert islands. This, he explained, was the current state of affairs in Knoxville: evangelical churches stubbornly refusing to work together and having little impact on the greater region. Paul then drew one large circle encompassing the others and said that this represented the spirit of unity and cooperation that will exist once churches are convinced of the need to work together to address pressing social and spiritual concerns. Conservative evangelical churches, he explained, tend to be "extremely ignorant" of social issues beyond their sanctuary walls "because they are too busy taking care of the flock." The first step toward fixing this was to educate people, and then to create organizational networks for communication and collaboration that will allow congregations to be more effective at social outreach. "We can love the city better together than on our own," he said, "and that's why we need structures for high-impact mobilization." This was the impetus behind Paul's plan to form a coalition of like-minded churches and faith-based ministries, and he would soon resign from his staff position at church in order to coordinate the effort full-time. The purpose of the resulting organization, which I will refer to as the Samaritans of Knoxville, was to streamline informational and material resources for church pastors, ministry professionals, social workers, and lay volunteers who were eager to increase the levels of outreach and volunteerism among Knoxville's churchgoing evangelicals. The Samaritans of Knoxville would also facilitate training workshops and distribute materials such as sermons and study guides that were meant to inspire and educate churches that were less than wholeheartedly committed to social ministries. Paul's ultimate vision, however, was even grander and resonated with the broad, seemingly utopian visions expressed by many of the evangelicals I spoke with: "We're after a cultural transformation. We're asking Christians to be Christians. If Christians would live like Christians, the aroma—the sweet smell of Jesus—would just overpower everything!"

My ethnography draws special attention to the impassioned and often quixotic efforts of people like Paul Genero, individuals whom I refer to collectively as *socially engaged evangelicals*. This is my own label to describe evangelical pastors and churchgoers who draw strong associations between religiosity and social conscience, and are notably active (either professionally or as volunteers) in promoting and participating in various forms of organized benevolence.[3] The charitable activities I observed among socially engaged evangelicals—whom I distinguish from occasional volunteers and seasonal donors to charitable causes—were directed at local populations such as the urban poor, the homeless, racial and ethnic minorities, and the sick and elderly. They included volunteering at soup kitchens and crisis shelters, mentoring inner-city youths, sponsoring immigrant refugee families, and providing charitable assistance to health clinics and halfway houses. In some cases, they involved working with state agencies and private nonprofits on urban community development initiatives and other social enterprises.

Many socially engaged evangelicals dedicate a considerable amount of their volunteer time to the work of mobilizing others to participate in and support their outreach initiatives. Such efforts involve building interest and momentum through sentimental appeals, theological argumentation, and other techniques of moral suasion. For a variety of reasons, outreach mobilization was a major source of exhaustion and frustration among socially engaged evangelicals in Knoxville, who believed that by struggling against the tides of social apathy, isolationism, and materialism in their churches, they were fighting against an almost indomitable status quo. In addition, they confronted traditions of cultural separatism and social conservatism that have left many evangelical churchgoers deeply resistant to social ministries that appear to promote progressive, secular, and humanistic agendas. This surely does not mean that conservative evangelicals are categorically opposed to helping people in need; far from it, in fact. But in the midst of trying to serve the needs of their communities, conservative evangelicals face what they see as palpable risks, including the risk of becoming unduly concerned with altruistic deeds as vehicles for salvation, at the expense of a theology that traditionally privileges confessions of faith over the performance of "good works." They also fear the risk of opening up their churches to liberal social influences, the likes of which Christian conservatives have denounced for many decades.

In order to get their messages across despite such hindrances, the socially engaged evangelicals I observed in Knoxville—not unlike Christian social reformers of the nineteenth and early twentieth centuries—always portrayed charitable social outreach as a legitimate and necessary component of evangelism. They demonstrated that ministries of social outreach were basically meant to achieve the same goals as most highly regarded revivalist and missionary enterprises, namely, to spread the Word of God and "make disciples" by religious conversion. The discourse of outreach mobilization was rife with tales of personal, cultural, and spiritual transformation, filled with alluring tropes of faith, compassion, redemption, and sacrifice. The tendency among many conservative Protestants to insist on a firm distinction between humanitarian effort and religious proselytization (privileging the latter) was rejected by those who favored a more integrative, holistic approach, the kind that prioritizes "words *and* deeds" and regards both as equally crucial for effective evangelism among society's poor, distressed, and marginalized populations.[4] Making the case for holistic evangelism in the evangelical churches of Knoxville—whether this meant arguing for broader conceptions of the church's role in society or simply arguing that, as one pastor put it, "You can't talk to an empty stomach"—was a vital strategy by which the socially engaged evangelicals I observed appealed to their conservative base (Elisha 2008b). Their appeals consistently upheld religious virtues that are commonly valued among conservative evangelicals, drawing on existing cultural repertoires informed by authoritative theological and pastoral discourses within the evangelical movement. Yet the socially engaged evangelicals in my study represented a surprisingly small and frustrated minority relative to the megachurches they belonged to—I encountered barely more than one or two dozen such individuals in each congregation—and the local evangelical community as a whole.

Part of the aim of this book is to explore what happens when religious actors of a certain aspirational persuasion—people like Paul Genero— pursue moral ambitions that are recognized as virtuous by others and simultaneously regarded with ambivalence and aversion. I examine how such moral ambitions are shaped within specific cultural and institutional milieus that define, authorize, and constrain their actual potential. Moreover, I analyze the mobilization strategies employed by those who, in claiming these moral ambitions, seek to inspire others to follow suit. The strategies usually involved identifying and critiquing deficiencies in the faith community, and then proposing socially relevant methods of counteracting those deficiencies. My ethnography works alongside other recent ethnographies in exploring the role of institutionalized narratives, concepts, and motifs in framing religious interventions in the modern world (Coleman 2000; Harding 2000), the ways that everyday religiosity is shaped by disciplines of ethical self-cultivation, especially in urban settings (Deeb 2006; Mahmood 2005; O'Neill 2010), and the significance of religious activism as a form of social action and cultural critique (Coutin 1993; Ginsburg 1989). All told, this book portrays a localized cultural arena where I found conservative evangelicals engaged in modest yet meaningful activities akin to what Sherry Ortner has called "serious games": a concept that helps us think about "the way in which people are defined and constrained by the intersections of culture, power, and history in which they find themselves, and yet at the same time are active players in making (and sometimes remaking) those worlds that have made them" (1999: 35).

WAVES OF ENGAGEMENT

The term *evangelical* has become such a media buzzword that its specific historical and cultural meanings are often misunderstood or ignored. The general lack of clarity about whom or what it actually refers to is exacerbated by the fact that so many churchgoing Protestants claim the label for themselves, but not always for the same reasons. This variability complicates most efforts to establish clear parameters and leads to striking inconsistencies among statistical surveys that try to determine (especially in election years) the size, demographics, and political influence of this undoubtedly significant portion of the U.S. population.[5]

Aside from its long-standing clerical and liturgical usages, the word gained renewed public prominence in the West as a cultural designation around the middle of the twentieth century. Hoping to reclaim the mantle of "authentic" Christianity, a broad segment of North American and European Protestants assumed the label on the premise that it accurately conveyed the spirit of Christian piety as mandated by scripture. They upheld the belief that to be a "true" Christian means embracing one's faith with deep personal commitment, doctrinal stringency, and evangelical fervor, which includes the apostolic (and often stigmatized) work of proclaiming the power of the gospel to the nonbelieving world. Despite the confidence of such claims, the category of "evangelical" is a source of debate and contention within Western Protestantism, and it remains a subject of relentless media speculation and scholarly inquiry.[6]

Woodberry and Smith (1998: 26) describe modern evangelicalism as the "moderate wing" of the larger category of conservative Protestantism. Conservative Protestants are defined as self-identifying Christians who "emphasize a personal relationship with Jesus Christ, believe in the importance of converting others to the faith, have strong view of biblical authority, and believe that salvation is through Christ alone"(1998: 36).[7] Like other conservative Protestants, including Pentecostals and fundamentalists, evangelicals adhere to a theology in which biblical orthodoxy, personal piety and missionary zeal are held paramount (Shibley 1996). Evangelicals also lean heavily toward the conservative end of the ideological spectrum on political and social issues, but in this respect they are by no means uniform. Many mainstream evangelical churches, seminaries, and parachurch organizations in the United States emerged into prominence as a result of the revivalist neo-evangelical movement that developed after World War II, a movement that not only strengthened the cultural relevance of evangelical religiosity in modern life but shaped its outward, relatively accommodating character for decades to come (Balmer 2006; Carpenter 1997; Stone 1997). In light of this influence, evangelicals today can be generally classified as a "moderate wing" because they remain committed to what Christian Smith calls "engaged orthodoxy," meaning that they are "fully committed to maintaining and promoting confidently traditional, orthodox Protestant theology and belief, while at the same time becoming confidently and proactively engaged in the intellectual, cultural, social, and political life of the nation" (1998: 10).

The congregations of Eternal Vine and Marble Valley Presbyterian exemplify many of the characteristics that follow from these definitions and, perhaps more important, my interlocutors identified themselves explicitly as evangelical Christians. Since the prevailing moral and ideological discourses in both megachurches (and throughout East Tennessee) are rather conservative in tone, I take the added measure of referring to the subjects of my research as *conservative* evangelicals, thereby distinguishing them along the wider spectrum of North American evangelicalism, which includes groups that would describe themselves as progressive or left-wing. I hasten to add, however, that a plurality of opinion exists not only in evangelicalism writ large but even within individual congregations. This is especially true for megachurches, which as a consequence of growth necessarily cater to a fairly diverse range of attitudes and dispositions. I do not mean to say that the evangelical megachurches I attended were full of closeted liberals (although there were a few). My point is simply that evangelical pastors and churchgoers are complex social actors, capable of holding multiple perspectives on pressing social concerns and as susceptible as anyone to shifts in temperament, even when faced with incentives to conform to principles of unwavering certainty.

The main portion of my fieldwork coincided with the first year of the George W. Bush administration. This was an auspicious time for conservative evangelicals. The election of 2000 brought one of their own into the White House and inspired confidence that their political priorities—including the appointment of conservative judges, the "defense" of heterosexual marriage, and policies limiting access to legal abortions—would be advocated from the seat of governmental power. Even the campaign leading up to the election was promising for evangelicals, as candidates from across the political spectrum engaged in what the media referred to as "God talk," speaking openly about their personal faith and the importance of religion in public life. The major candidates expressed support for what had come to be known as "faith-based initiatives," a seemingly innocuous phrase that heralded the expansion of government funding for religious organizations that provide social services and rehabilitative programs in local communities. Building on a controversial legislative provision known as Charitable Choice, part of the Personal Responsibility and Work Opportunity Reconciliation Act signed into law in 1996, faith-based initiatives were central to the GOP platform of "compassionate conservatism," and were touted as a primary policy agenda under the Bush administration in the months preceding the 9/11 terrorist attacks.[8]

Few of the churchgoers I met at the time talked about Bush's faith-based proposals with any specificity, and barely any of them spoke of Charitable Choice at all (with the exception of paid social workers). Their apparent indifference to the specifics of faith-based initiatives was initially surprising but not implausible. The affluent megachurches they belonged to were hardly in need of federal grants to support their ministries, and studies have shown that conservative evangelical churches are among the religious institutions least likely to apply for government funding (Bartkowski and Regis 2003; Chaves 1999). Moreover, conservative Christian leaders were, at best, cautiously optimistic in supporting federal faith-based initiatives. Commentators and pundits cited their concerns that the government would start regulating how faith-based organizations function, particularly their hiring practices. Prominent figures such as Pat Robertson and Jerry Falwell complained that taxpayer dollars would be made available to religious organizations they saw as dangerous or illegitimate, such as the Church of Scientology, the Hare Krishna movement, and the Nation of Islam.

Despite these concerns, evangelicals were emboldened by the new levels of political currency and cultural respect afforded to the role of religion in civil society. Conservative evangelicals in Knoxville were excited that religiously inspired notions of charity and community service were penetrating the mainstream. They relished the prospect of secular society catching on to the idea that social problems require spiritual solutions rather than "wasteful" government programs that, as they see it, enable welfare dependence, corruption, and social dysfunction. The regnant politics of neoliberalism, supported by popular themes of civic voluntarism, welfare privatization, and personal responsibility, resonated with force and clarity for conservative evangelicals, who tend to endow neoliberal trends with theological import.

At the same time, the optimism expressed by pastors and churchgoers during this period was indicative of another recent trend: the gradual broadening of evangelical social consciousness. The years leading up to the new millennium witnessed a rise in published critiques by Christian authors and activists challenging evangelicals—especially middle-class evangelicals in affluent suburban churches—to become better informed about structural issues that affect the lives of the urban poor, and to overcome their resistance to systemic social reform (e.g., Bakke 1997; Perkins 1993; Shank and Reed 1995; Sider 1999). Although hot-button issues such as abortion, same-sex marriage, and the teaching of creationism in public schools continue to galvanize religious conservatives, many evangelicals have started to turn their attention to issues of poverty, human rights, and the environment. Veteran left-leaning and centrist evangelicals such as Jim Wallis of the organization Call to Renewal (and editor of the magazine *Sojourners*) and Ronald Sider of Evangelicals for Social Action have begun reaching wider evangelical and general audiences as a result of renewed interest in social ministry at the grassroots, while prominent megachurch pastors such as Rick Warren of Saddleback Church have made headlines promoting international ministries dedicated to poverty relief and HIV/AIDS prevention.

Evangelical social ministries, relief agencies, and humanitarian organizations are nothing new historically, but the circumstances that implicated them in a more general shift in the focus of conservative evangelical activism are significant. For one thing, this shift was made possible by a concerted effort on the part of public evangelicals to distance themselves from the harsh, combative tone of engagement that characterized the old guard of the Christian Right. By the 1990s, even as conservative evangelicals still agreed with the moral and political agendas represented by the Christian Right, they saw the reactionary intolerance and rhetorical excesses of culture warriors like Robertson and Falwell as counterproductive and embarrassing. The angry exhortations of famed televangelists, often mired in controversy or scandal, weighed heavily on the hearts of evangelical pastors and churchgoers who increasingly doubted whether such provocations truly amounted to an effective public witness. For all the political gains that religious conservatives had made since the 1980s, there was a growing sense that the culture wars had achieved more in the way of vitriol than policy, and little in the way of cultural change.[9] Alongside the usual chorus of moral protest and indignation (which, if anything, has intensified in recent years), a growing segment of the evangelical population—including pastors, activists, ministry leaders, and theologians—started to advocate the virtues of social and civic engagement (Cromartie 2003). Pastor Tim, the senior pastor of Eternal Vine Church in Knoxville, spoke to this issue from the pulpit one Sunday morning and drove the point home by stressing that Christians must learn not only to preach the gospel but to exemplify it in their daily lives, for everyone to see. "To others," he said, "Christians should look like people who are extravagantly loving each other, not like people who are getting all upset over prayer at football games, or Ten Commandments in offices. We should look like a community of little platoons that are known for loving each other, and for loving the poor."

Much as contemporary evangelicals hope to improve their public image and establish a more proactive presence at the frontlines of social welfare, the history of social engagement among conservative Protestants in United States in the last two hundred years has not been straightforward, and it has produced enduring fissures within the evangelical movement. I begin my brief historical overview in the mid-nineteenth century, in the years following a period of intense revivalism known as the Second Great Awakening. During this time there was a steep rise in Christian activism and mobilization around antebellum issues such as abolition and temperance, with evangelical reformers leading the charge and drawing explicit links between individual salvation and the salvation of society as a whole (Young 2006). The appearance of a united evangelical front was accompanied by home missionary societies, parachurch organizations, and Christian charities and philanthropies that were established to address domestic humanitarian concerns, especially in rapidly industrializing cities where social reformers sought to root out poverty and all the disease and moral vice that came with it.[10] Activists and historians recall the energetic spirit of Christian interventionism and reform in the Victorian era as "muscular Christianity," and contemporary socially engaged evangelicals yearn to recreate that cultural moment as they position themselves to tackle the social concerns of the present day.

At the dawn of the twentieth century, public debates raged over issues of poverty and social dysfunction and how best to address them. Religiously inspired notions of redemption and moral worth figured prominently in these debates, reinforcing perceptions of the poor as either "worthy" or "undeserving," even as institutions of charity and social welfare became increasingly professionalized, bureaucratic, and secular (Hall 1990; Katz 1986). This period also witnessed the rise of the Social Gospel, a progressive movement that emphasized the need to combat economic injustice and improve society through structural reforms. Its leading proponents, including Walter Rauschenbusch and Charles Sheldon (author of the popular 1897 novel *In His Steps: What Would Jesus Do?*), combined theological reasoning, prophetic rhetoric, and socialist critique in their efforts to rally the faithful against industrial capitalist exploitation. They interpreted the teachings of Jesus as revolutionary and argued that all living Christians have an intrinsic obligation to redress structural inequities and fight on behalf of the poor and disadvantaged (Rauschenbusch 1907). Although the Social Gospel was basically orthodox in its religious orientation, its greatest influence is tied to subsequent liberal theological trends in mainline Protestantism and the evangelical left. Indeed, because of its liberal connotations the Social Gospel during its heyday provoked hostility from ultraconservative Protestants, who by the 1920s were mobilizing under the banner of Christian fundamentalism.[11]

Antipathy among the early fundamentalists toward the Social Gospel and other modern cultural trends and institutions was fueled in part by the ascendance of an eschatology (or end-times theology) known as dispensational premillennialism. Developed in Great Britain in the middle of the nineteenth century by John Nelson Darby and later popularized with the publication of the Scofield Reference Bible in 1909, dispensational premillennialism offered a grim assessment of the future of humanity and stressed the ultimate inevitability of messianic intervention. According to Darby's reading of prophetic scriptures, the history of the world is a sequence of discrete stages or "dispensations" marked by continual moral degeneration and alienation from God. The Second Coming is presented in this apocalyptic scheme as the necessary precursor to the anticipated thousand-year reign of Christ on Earth following the defeat of Satan in the battle of Armageddon (Weber 1987), and the sole purpose of the church is to spread the message of salvation to as many people as possible before Christ's return. For the many conservative theologians and churchgoers who embraced Darby's interpretation, Christian social reform movements were deemed suspect because they relied on a progressive humanist worldview that was out of line with what was revealed in the Bible. Premillennialism remains to this day the predominant eschatology of North American evangelicalism. While not all conservative evangelicals wholeheartedly follow every detail of Darby's elaborate end-times narrative, its basic tenets regarding the evangelistic mission of the Church and the circumstances of worldly demise prior to the Second Coming (including the rise of the Antichrist) are widely upheld. Significantly, the premillennialist influence remains especially salient in the skepticism and even hostility that contemporary conservative evangelicals still harbor toward social movements and initiatives that appear to suggest that humanity is capable of redeeming itself on its own through social and political reforms. This is the source of much of the resistance that socially engaged evangelicals face as they struggle to garner support in steadfastly conservative churches.

The story does not end there, however. As already noted, another major influence in modern evangelicalism was the neo-evangelical movement of the postwar era. Championed by the likes of Billy Graham, Charles Fuller, Harold Ockenga, and Carl Henry, neo-evangelicalism challenged the entrenched separatism of the fundamentalists and represented "a movement away from dispensationalism and the sectarian, culturally alienated position that it suggested" (Carpenter 1997: 203).[12] Although theologically conservative and staunchly anticommunist, the "new evangelicals" set out to revive the ethos of compassion and social responsibility that they believed was essential to Christian faith. Carl Henry, a cofounder of Fuller Theological Seminary and the evangelical magazine *Christianity Today,* made the case for renewing evangelical social engagement in his treatise *The Uneasy Conscience of Modern Fundamentalism* (1947). By abandoning Christianity's social message, Henry argued, fundamentalists abdicated moral authority in society and prevented churches from realizing their redemptive potential. A similar emphasis on the interdependence of evangelism and social engagement was expressed in later missives, including the landmark Lausanne Covenant issued by the International Congress on World Evangelization in 1974, the Chicago Declaration of Evangelical Social Concern of 1973 (which was linked to the founding of Evangelicals for Social Action), and a recent document titled "For the Health of the Nation: An Evangelical Call to Civic Responsibility," released in 2004 by the National Association of Evangelicals.

The waves of evangelical engagement took yet another turn, however, in the 1970s–1980s with the emergence of the Christian Right. This was a broad yet organizationally synergetic movement of moral protest and political action that drew on antiliberal, antifeminist, and antigay sentiments among increasingly discontented and mostly white religious conservatives. The movement emulated the cultural savvy of neo-evangelicalism but used it in the name of fundamentalist rancor. Controversial government actions—notably, Supreme Court decisions legalizing abortion, banning prayer in public schools, and upholding the state's authority to enforce racial integration at Christian colleges—galvanized fundamentalists to enter the political fray, inspiring a reactionary and largely unprecedented wave of grassroots activism and church mobilization. Political action groups such as Jerry Falwell's Moral Majority and Pat Robertson's Christian Coalition pursued aggressive strategies of public influence, while parachurch organizations such as James Dobson's Focus on the Family and Beverly LaHaye's Concerned Women for America advanced right-wing cultural politics with powerful symbolic and affective dimensions (Kintz 1997). Consequently, matters of private morality became inseparable from the field of public policy, and movements for progressive social reform were increasingly associated with "godless liberals," from whom conservative evangelicals were keen to distance themselves.

The gradual softening of tone and the broadening of evangelical social consciousness since the 1990s highlights the fact that although the cultural politics of the Christian Right continue to hold sway through much of the evangelical subculture, evangelicals are once again considering new strategies of engagement in light of changing historical and political circumstances. As demonstrated in this brief overview, the ideological contours of conservative Protestantism are constantly in flux. A history of continuous ebbs and flows, with progressive and reactionary styles of engagement competing, as it were, to direct the currents of social engagement, has produced lingering tensions within North American evangelicalism. This is a reminder that contemporary evangelicals are far from monolithic in their political orientations. At the local church level, evangelical pastors and churchgoers wrestle with ambiguities they have inherited from a mixed legacy of engagement and retrenchment, of worldly accommodations and renunciations. Evangelical skepticism about the politics of social reform stands in conflict with an abiding "optimism about the perfectibility of society" (Shibley 1996: 101). Sectarian impulses to withdraw from affairs of "the world" routinely clash with an imperative toward worldly activism, one of modern evangelicalism's defining characteristics (Bebbington 1989).

There is no doubt that conservative evangelicals today are represented among the highest echelons of U.S. politics, business, and media, and in many cases they assert their presence with confidence and purpose (Lindsay 2007; Sharlet 2008). Before assuming too much about the social and political implications of such ascensions, however, it is necessary to recognize that the evangelical imagination is informed by a plurality of moral visions of what constitutes a "good society" and how Christians should go about achieving it (Williams 1999). Similarly, to assess the implications of evangelical social engagement in local communities it is necessary first to recognize that the altruistic and evangelistic commitments of socially engaged evangelicals are informed by a complex amalgam of religious imperatives and sentiments. We must consider ideologies of conversion and social change that guide their efforts to Christianize culture, and the conflicts and contradictions that evangelicals, like all missionary actors, face in creating institutions and social networks intended to carry those ideologies forward (Beidelman 1982). My concept of moral ambition offers an analytical idiom with which to assess a particular style of religious subjectivity, one that manifests in moments of concerted action and mobilization and yet reflects a range of personal desires, theological and cultural norms, historical circumstances, and social opportunities. The concept is an entry into the conditions that shape the lives of individuals who aspire to stretch the boundaries of what is imagined possible through practices of religious virtue.

MORAL AMBITIONS

Ambitions are always moral in that they are rarely detached from the norms and expectations that govern social behavior and direct individuals toward sacred virtues, life goals, and status achievements. They are technologies of the self in the Foucaultian sense, based in culturally situated ethics regarding what is and what should be humanly possible. Ambitious individuals, even rebels, "mavericks," and other nonconformists, actively negotiate the terms of human possibility when they aim to maximize personal wealth, power, virtuosity, or piety. By framing my ethnography as a study of moral ambitions I draw attention to the intrinsic sociality of such aspirations, that is, their inexorable orientation toward other people and their inalienability from social networks and institutions in which standards of personhood are constructed. Furthermore, the concept of moral ambition is helpful for analyzing individual aspirations that involve persuading and recruiting others to do likewise, as is often the case with evangelists and social activists. For socially engaged evangelicals, the process of enacting religious virtues in novel and compelling ways—that is, the work of moral action in a milieu where orthodoxy and ethical self-cultivation are explicitly linked (Mahmood 2005)—involves casting strategies of mobilization and moral suasion within the purview of evangelical piety, which is not as thoroughly individuating as is often assumed.

The subject of morality is a critical area of inquiry in the anthropology of Christianity. This is especially borne out in work on societies that have undergone some form of Western evangelization, where non-Christian moral traditions contend with Christian conceptions of personhood, meaning, and temporality (e.g., Keane 2007; Robbins 2004; Schieffelin 2002). Although Christian thought and practice are often strikingly recontextualized in postconversion cultures, there are many instances where the advent of Christianity produces religious movements that introduce radical breaks with prior ritual traditions and moral orders (Engelke 2007; Meyer 1999). The theme of social discontinuity runs through the ethnographic literature, relying on "the common claim that in cultures that have recently adopted Christianity, conversion often triggers a partial abandonment of social and cultural forms oriented toward the collective in favor of individualist models of social organization" (Bialecki, Haynes, and Robbins 2008: 1141). Such shifts in the nature of social organization entail consequences for morality as well. Based on his research in Melanesia, Joel Robbins (2007) has observed the potential for conflict between competing "moral-value spheres," namely, the conflict between an individuating "morality of freedom" inspired by Western Protestantism and a "morality of reproduction" rooted in normative local traditions in which personal agency is contingent on social hierarchies and relational calculations rather than individual moral autonomy.

In the Christianized West it stands to reason that what Robbins calls the "morality of freedom" reigns supreme, reinforcing capitalist ideologies that assign paramount value to individual autonomy and free will (Dumont 1986). Indeed, the "moral narrative of modernity" (Keane 2007), with its conspicuously Protestant salvationist overtones, hinges on the ideal of an interiorized, self-determining moral subject who is "purified" of social and material entanglements on the way to becoming truly liberated. However, in recognizing the prevalence of this ideal in Western thought, do we not risk accepting too readily the proposition that Western Protestants, including evangelicals, are narrowly driven by moral individualism, to the exclusion of salient counternotions? Can't we identify cultural values of relationalism and intersubjectivity embedded (albeit less explicitly) in the social fabric of Christian capitalist modernity?

The evangelical tenet that each and every believer can (and must) attain a direct personal relationship with Jesus Christ is essentially individuating, in that it ostensibly distinguishes one's path of salvation from socially determinative factors in one's life. But it is worth noting that this tenet is fortified by a comparable stress on the importance of human social relationships as vehicles of redemption. Evangelicals "seek to imitate the close, intimate bond they desire with God in their expectations for relating with each other and with those outside their community of faith" (Bielo 2009: 76).[13] Communion with the divine is conceived as a personal intimacy that is deeply spiritual and individually embodied (Luhrmann 2004); it is not strictly dependent on social relationships, but evangelicals readily acknowledge that this sense of intimacy is effectively facilitated and mediated by human intersubjectivity. Religious conversions are understood to be triggered by relational interventions of one kind or another, and the "fruits" that follow one's spiritual rebirth as a Christian are substantiated by evidence in people's lives; that is, their interactions—real and envisioned—with spouses, friends, coworkers, and believers and unbelievers alike, both at home and abroad. Social relationships are conceived through rituals and conversion narratives that are meant to reinforce links of spiritual fellowship, encompassing local communities as well as an imagined global ecumene (Coleman 2000; Stromberg 1986). The ubiquitous theme of "relationship" in church sermons and devotional books is instructive for churchgoers in maintaining their sense of being in a covenant with God and of belonging to a universal "Body of Christ."

The concept of "relationship" is so fundamental in evangelical churches that it also serves as an organizational principle suited to institutional as well as ritual functions. In the megachurches I attended in Knoxville, churchgoers are repeatedly encouraged to join "small groups," groups of usually ten to twelve members who gather together on a weekly or semiweekly basis for informal Bible study, group discussions, and prayer. The small-group meetings—which typically take place in members' homes—are idealized as spaces of relational intimacy, where religious commitments are forged through interpersonal bonds built on faith, love, humility, and mutual accountability. Given that large-scale worship services offer little in the way of direct interaction among congregants, small groups are meant to bring such relationships into being. Though informal and lay driven, they are usually supervised under the auspices of pastoral authority and therefore help to maintain a measure of ideological and doctrinal consistency in megachurches. Thus the small group is a social mechanism by which churchgoers indoctrinate and monitor one another and reinforce the moral premiums of evangelical subjectivity (Elisha 2008a). The primary stated purpose of intensive small groups may be to bolster individual faith, but as evidenced by their use in evangelical churches (Bielo 2009) and parachurch ministries (Erzen 2006; Griffith 1997), they also exist to reform individuals by making them into properly oriented and disciplined subjects of a collective body whose standards of religiosity are determined by authoritative institutions and discourses (Asad 1993). It is through relational practices that sinners are saved, and born-again selves are collectively socialized and sanctified within an enveloping framework of biblical interpellation (Crapanzano 2000; Harding 2000).

My general point is that American evangelicalism cannot and should not be reduced categorically to notions of individualism, as though the individuating aspects of Protestant theology and practice were the only aspects worth noting. Evangelicals go to great lengths to encourage (and enforce) relationalism as a collective ethos that complements and at times complicates individualism rather than merely receding under its hegemonic force. The story of individualism in modern America is not straightforward, in that it is rarely accepted without qualification and reflexive contemplation (Bellah et al. 1985). Even as evangelicals embrace individualism as an essential component of Christian identity, born-again spirituality, and democratic citizenship, they routinely evaluate the consequences of radical individualism as a way of life, entertaining alternative coexisting ethics and conceptions of the self in the process. Cultural tensions between individualist and communitarian ideals in the United States more generally are accentuated in evangelicalism. This is not surprising when we take into account the evangelical belief that true spiritual fulfillment is contingent on an individual's willing submission to the Kingdom of God, a concept that transcends the social but is also signified through human relationships (including bonds of fictive kinship) and cultural institutions where relational ties are formed (including churches and parachurches).

This observation is relevant to my ethnographic study because insofar as evangelical social engagement and outreach mobilization are framed in the rubric of Christian evangelism, they effectively build on existing conceptions that orient the faithful toward a lifestyle of immersion and implication in the lives of others, rather than one of atomized faith. As socially engaged evangelicals in Knoxville cultivated relationships with local faith-based organizations, social service agencies, and poor and needy populations, and as they sought to convince others to join their efforts, they complicated the preeminence of moral individualism as a cultural paradigm without ever going so far as to subvert or reject it. They drew on critical sentiments that were familiar to local evangelicals and extended them to avenues of ministry that were meant to convince middle-class suburban churchgoers to become better Christians by "sacrificing" their time, comfort, and social insulation for the purpose of sharing God's love with others. Although a fair number of their fellow churchgoers found these avenues of ministry disconcerting, intimidating, or just not sufficiently worth their valuable time and energy, the concern to break down the barriers of intersubjectivity resonated powerfully. And yet, such challenges to the status quo were equally limited by the fact that they remained subjected to the conservative social attitudes of the affluent communities with which the evangelicals in my study primarily identified.

The concept of moral ambition offers a window to examine the interplay of individualist and relationalist paradigms in modern religious communities, and the tension between the creative agency of individuals and cultural norms to which individuals are expected to conform. It also sheds light on an important dimension of evangelicalism as a lived religion. The idea of "lived religion" has gained currency among religion scholars who understand religious practices and experiences to be embedded in specific social contexts and realities of everyday life (Hall 1997; McGuire 2008). By shifting the focus of study from doctrine to practice and experience, lived religion is a "hermeneutical tool that corrects past privileging of intellectual, institutional, and theological studies" (Winston 2009: 5). It allows us to address "what people *do* with religious idioms, how they use them, what they make of themselves and their worlds with them, and how, in turn, men, women, and children are fundamentally shaped by the worlds they are making" (Orsi 2003: 172, original emphasis). This approach is useful for studying popular religious idioms that draw on a plurality of cultural resources other than those explicitly sanctioned by religious institutions, hierarchies, and conventional ritual frames (e.g., Bender 2003; Schmidt 2005). It is also useful for analyzing the experiences of lay churchgoers, especially women, who through various forms of religious participation discover opportunities to refashion themselves ethically and spiritually, exercise moral agency in the lives of others, and negotiate the conditions of their submission to (male) pastoral authority (Frederick 2003; Griffith 1997). In accounting for religious practices that perform cultural work outside normal institutional parameters, the study of lived religion also accounts for the role of power in people's lives, and the extent to which religious practices that facilitate self-transformation are simultaneously defined by forces and conditions beyond individual control (Orsi 2003).

Applied to evangelicalism, the notion of lived religion further highlights the fact that religious orthodoxy often reveals varying degrees of *plasticity* as well as constancy. This does not mean that evangelical beliefs and practices lack coherence or consistency, but simply that as a lived experience evangelicalism entails a host of quotidian dilemmas, aspirations, innovations, and frustrations that are not always easily explained (or dismissed) by a single, cohesive, uniformly authorized system of doctrine. To appreciate the complexity of the things that evangelicals do when they are "being religious" we must remember that they, like all religious people, act and react in a world where they are inevitably faced with diverse experiences and sentiments. Purists and "true believers" may seek to prevent unfamiliar elements from compromising doctrinal integrity, but many are just as likely to assimilate new influences and circumstances to a preexisting religious worldview that, at the end of the day, still presents itself as uniform and coherent.

The plasticity of lived religion can also have destabilizing effects in people's lives, as they contend with ambiguities that prove hard to reconcile. I have already indicated that for some socially engaged evangelicals in Knoxville, immersion in the field of organized benevolence brought about meaningful shifts in their knowledge and experience regarding matters connected to social welfare. The social outreach ministries I observed often involved communication and reasonably sustained interaction with agencies and individuals located beyond the cultural boundaries of the communities represented by suburban megachurches. The relatively few conservative evangelicals who ventured across these boundaries with regularity were exposed to alternative perspectives on the lives and life-dominating circumstances of poor and distressed people, and alternative insights into the roots of poverty and social dysfunction. In some cases the discrepancies between expectation and experience led to feelings of cognitive dissonance and eventual withdrawal. In other cases they led to broadened perspectives and adjustments in attitude, introducing a whole new set of quandaries, especially in relation to outreach mobilization. Understanding the moral ambitions of evangelical social engagement thus requires more than merely documenting the desires and motivations of individual actors. It involves recognizing that the desires and motivations of individual actors are formed by, and in response to, an array of overlapping and at times contradictory influences. The versatility of evangelical faith is neither a sign of hypocrisy nor evangelicalism's eventual undoing; it is rather evidence of a style of religiosity that compels its own adherents to pursue the ambitious and sometimes agonistic work of evangelism in innovative ways while also directing them to uphold moral and ideological traditions that resist radical innovation.

ACTIVIST ORIENTATIONS

Most of the socially engaged evangelicals I knew would hardly be called activists in the common sense of the word. In fact they would reject the characterization outright, preferring to identify as humble servants of God and purveyors of Christian love. Conservative evangelicals are no strangers to political action, nor do they ignore the political significance of even the most understated forms of public (or for that matter private) religiosity. Direct political action for the average churchgoer, however, is typically limited to activities like signing petitions and distributing voter guides rather than sustained activism (see Chaves 2004). Conservative evangelicals take pains to distance themselves from the very idea of "activism" as a personal commitment, which they associate with left-wing causes like socialism and radical feminism. As followers of a stern theocentric and moralistic worldview, in which humans are inherently sinful and salvation requires total submission to the will of God, evangelicals are keen to avoid claims of willful agency. They want to believe that when they take action in the world it is purely in the name of God's kingdom, not merely for the sake of action.

Yet there are good reasons to analyze evangelical social engagement in terms of social activism. Pastors and churchgoers who invest their time and energy in ministries of social outreach are engaged in purposeful, coordinated actions explicitly aimed at "making a difference" in the world. Knoxville's socially engaged evangelicals, in their capacities as ministry workers, volunteers, and mobilizers, demonstrated a high level of intentionality in their efforts, as well as a preoccupation with having an "impact" on the wider culture. In pursuing a lifestyle of Christian piety through organized benevolence, they operated as apostles advancing the cause of Christianization, a cause greater than themselves. As activists often do—including, for example, social reformers, environmental activists, and community organizers—they confronted what they perceived to be indifference, ignorance, and lackluster participation among their like-minded peers. They created new faith-based ministries and tried to improve existing ones, and in the process hoped to inspire levels of civic participation and spiritual revitalization that would profoundly transform local churches and the city as a whole. And like many activists, they sometimes felt compelled to go against the grain, pushing the boundaries of what was considered appropriate or practical, and pursuing ideals that almost all of their fellow pastors and churchgoers readily affirmed but few were willing to undertake.

Even though socially engaged evangelicals (as portrayed here) do not represent a singular social movement or political constituency, and do not adhere to a specific "activist identity" (Jasper 1997: 87), they do share what I call an *activist orientation*. They gravitate toward ideologically significant social commitments and for a variety of reasons prioritize those commitments at the center of their religious lives. Not all of them do so to the same degree or with the same outcomes, but in so doing they raise the stakes of their own religious participation, increase the likelihood of coming into meaningful (if at times problematic) contact with people outside their home congregations, and create opportunities to perform altruistic and evangelistic acts that are regarded by others as signs of uncommon virtue.

As Faye Ginsburg (1989) has demonstrated in her research among women activists on both sides of the abortion debate, when people assume what I call an activist orientation they become invested in the cultural work of identifying as well as renegotiating the terms of social action and personal fulfillment. Moreover, as Susan Coutin (1993) has shown in her ethnography of the U.S. sanctuary movement in the 1980s, the effects of activism in people's lives are expressed in the formal and informal ways that individuals reorient their lives around new social values and elements of cultural critique that they internalize in the process of becoming socially active. Reinforced by cultural institutions and voluntary associations that mediate civic participation, activist orientations allow individuals to become self-conscious conveyers of group values and interests, as different cultural groups vie for recognition, power, and moral authority in an increasingly diverse and competitive public sphere (Checker and Fishman 2004).[14]

Evangelical social outreach and mobilization reinforce activist orientations because the expressed purpose is to enhance the cultural relevance of what Lara Deeb calls "public piety" (2006: 34). Socially engaged evangelicals aim to demonstrate that it is possible for faithful Christians to be personally pious and committed to community service at the same time, and that to do anything less would effectively weaken the visibility of evangelical churches and their power to promote Christian conceptions of the public good. Their emphasis on personalized virtues connected to outreach—compassion, benevolence, humility, sacrifice, etc.—is expansive in its theological and social implications because these virtues are suggestive of the social aesthetics by which Christians distinguish a good society from an indecent, immoral, or unjust one (Brown 2005). As with Christian revivalists and missionaries, the moral ambitions of evangelical social engagement are never just about helping or converting individual people. When evangelicals in Knoxville like Paul Genero spoke of "cultural transformation"—or, as Paul put it, "the sweet smell of Jesus" overpowering everything—they envisioned something diffuse and totalizing. Although they tended to prioritize "face-to-face" and "one-on-one" approaches to social outreach over other approaches, their outreach practices and mobilization strategies hinted toward broader ideological potentialities, making the habits of social engagement all the more activist, and yet all the more precarious.

Adding to these qualities was the vigorous tone of critical reflexivity that suffused the discourse of mobilization. The actions and sentiments described in this ethnography proceeded almost uniformly from a baseline of evangelical self-criticism, ranging from concerns about whether Knoxville's megachurches were living up to a true evangelical mission, to preachers declaring an urgent need for citywide and regional revival, to the anxieties of suburban evangelicals fretting about the spiritual hazards of living comfortable middle-class lifestyles. These and other objects of consternation bolstered the mobilization efforts of socially engaged evangelicals, for whom the values of civic responsibility and social entrepreneurship—hallmarks of what Alan Wolfe calls "middle-class morality" (1998)—merged almost instinctively with the ideals of evangelical faith. At the same time, the social outreach initiatives that were pursued or sponsored by Eternal Vine and Marble Valley Presbyterian produced some unintended effects, the most notable of which was the reproduction of regional power dynamics based on disparities of wealth and racial privilege. The resources and prestige that megachurch-affiliated evangelicals relied on were applied in ways that reinforced the very boundaries of race and class that they were meant to overcome. At times evangelicals were conscious of this, which exacerbated their penchant for self-criticism, but often their political sensibilities did not allow structural logics to figure in their own accounting of such dynamics. As a result, there was a tendency among white conservative evangelicals to misrecognize some of the factors that augmented rather than diminished the structural and cultural alienation between them and the disadvantaged communities they wanted to serve.

Evangelical social engagement leads pastors and churchgoers to a level of concerted and strategic engagement with "the world" beyond the symbolic boundaries of their own congregations. A study like this might then well include the perspectives of relevant people who inhabit that world, such as social service workers and clients, recipients of charitable aid, and representatives from minority communities in Knoxville. Although some of my data come from interviews with service providers from state and secular agencies, inner-city black pastors and community organizers, and members of Knoxville's private nonprofit sector, the voices of those most dependent on social services are virtually absent from my ethnographic account. Though regrettable, this omission reflects a combination of practical and methodological concerns, including issues around gaining access to social service clients, and my interest to avoid creating an added level of awkwardness in the interactions between aid recipients and outreach volunteers. I was further concerned to convey to ministry workers and volunteers that I was not interested in verifying the effectiveness or sincerity of their efforts to help people in need. I frequently reminded them that my primary research interests revolved around their own beliefs, motivations, and experiences. Nonetheless, my conversations with local individuals who worked or interacted with socially engaged evangelicals gave me added insights into how social outreach initiatives emanating from evangelical megachurches and faith-based organizations were received, accommodated, or in some cases resisted by the community at large.

STRUCTURE OF THE BOOK

The theoretical and topical themes laid out in this introduction are meant to provide an overture to the analytical and narrative scope of the ethnography that follows. The chapters highlight different aspects of the lived social worlds, cultural habits, religious ideals, and moral sentiments of the people at the center of my research. As the chapters progress, I delve further into the social, emotional, political, and theological implications that follow from conservative evangelical forays into specific kinds of outreach activity. The crucial significance of evangelism, the desire to enact virtues that transcend the limitations of willful egoism and secular humanism, and the recurrence of motivational concepts associated with Christian revivalism and missionization are themes running through all the chapters. They are, moreover, themes that perpetually occupy the thoughts and actions of socially engaged evangelicals.

Chapters 2 and 3 provide institutional and geographical context, not merely to "set the stage" but in order to establish the extent to which the moral ambitions of evangelical social engagement correspond to the very fabric of the social worlds that the evangelicals in my study were busy constructing, inhabiting, and simultaneously questioning. In chapter 2 I describe the two megachurches where much of my fieldwork was based, Eternal Vine Church and Marble Valley Presbyterian Church. The chapter highlights major characteristics, principles, and controversies surrounding U.S. megachurches and the modern church-growth movement, including the concerns of socially engaged members who worry about whether megachurches live up to their potential for community service and social impact. In chapter 3 I explore aspects of local history and regional culture that have shaped the way many Knoxvillians think about their city, with its paradoxes and ambiguities, and how they approach issues of urban revitalization. I relate this to the spirit of revivalism that Knoxville's conservative evangelicals invoke as they aim to inspire higher levels of public religiosity in the wider region, which they believe only superficially earns its reputation as the "Bible Belt."

Chapter 4 is composed of four ethnographic profiles of socially engaged evangelicals who were among my most valuable interlocutors in the field. The profiles, which are not biographies so much as portraits based on sustained interactions and in-depth interviews, illustrate how moral ambitions are conceived and pursued in the lives of actual people. The chapter reveals the range of actions, expectations, and frustrations that accompany the activist orientation assumed by these individuals, each in his or her own distinct way, as well as subtle changes they experienced in their social and even theological priorities. Chapter 5 delves into the evangelical discourse of antimaterialism, a pervasive and self-reflexive cultural critique that carries strong significance in suburban megachurches, where affluent churchgoers routinely worry about the spiritual consequences of middle-class comfort and consumerism. Socially engaged evangelicals build on such sentiments in their efforts to mobilize churchgoers to commit themselves to the selfless and "risky" work of charity and social outreach.

Chapter 6 addresses one of the more puzzling challenges that socially engaged evangelicals in Knoxville experienced in their interactions with poor and distressed individuals who received (or solicited) charitable aid. The problem of "compassion fatigue," as they described it, was the result of a fundamental paradox between the competing imperatives of compassion (an unconditional gift) and accountability (a reciprocal obligation). The imperatives are conceived as mutually supportive but prove hard to reconcile in practice. The chapter explores the reasons for this difficulty, including the influence of relational power dynamics and the underlying logic of exchange in evangelical theology, which informs all ministries and especially those that emphasize charitable giving as a redemptive transaction. Chapter 7 examines various meanings and moral visions tied to the concept of the Kingdom of God as a temporal ideal, with a focus on the linkages between kingdom theology and the significance that white socially engaged evangelicals attach to the black inner city, particularly with regard to issues of racial reconciliation and urban community development. The chapter looks at specific outreach initiatives undertaken by suburban megachurches and faith-based organizations on behalf of inner-city communities, and concludes with a discussion of the larger implications of the resulting moral and political economy of altruism for the evolution of civil society infrastructures in the postwelfare era.

FIELD NOTE: DID THEY TRY TO CONVERT YOU?

When I talk about my fieldwork with friends and acquaintances, and even some evangelicals, I am frequently asked whether evangelicals in Knoxville made efforts to convert me to Christianity. It is a reasonable question, motivated by genuine curiosity and perhaps a hint of cynicism on the part of nonbelievers who take offense at people with proselytic dispositions. Owing to their penchant for missionary zeal, evangelicals have earned a negative reputation as glassy-eyed religious predators intent on luring unsuspecting strangers into a life of blind, intolerant, authoritarian faith. For the most part, such stereotypes are heavily exaggerated and a bit ridiculous. Evangelicals do proselytize, and some are quite brazen and insistent about it, taking their mission to evangelize to zealous or insensitive extremes. However, the average evangelical churchgoer is just as uncomfortable knocking on his or her neighbor's door, pressuring friends, or haranguing coworkers as anyone else would be. Furthermore, negative stereotypes often reflect a flawed assumption that when evangelicals act sociably it is only because they are hiding an ulterior motive to "trick" potential converts into thinking and acting exactly as they do. This is a simplistic and uncritical way of evaluating the complex factors and motives that define social relationships in this or any context.

In response to the question, "Did they try to convert you?" my answer is yes and no. Evangelical pastors and churchgoers in Knoxville were keenly aware of my identity as a non-Christian and endeavored to "witness" their faith to me on numerous occasions, but they rarely did so in a manner one might expect. Without a doubt, the possibility that I might come around to "accept Jesus Christ" as a result of my research was foremost in the minds of many of my interlocutors. It was not an ulterior motive but one that was readily apparent and explicit. They even acknowledged as much when they would ask me, in a wry, self-mocking tone, questions like "So, have any of us tried to convert you yet?" Typically, however, their efforts to broach the topic of my faith (or lack thereof) were respectful and tactful. No one insisted on subjecting me to a barrage of questions about my beliefs or my eternal fate, and most of the individuals who offered to share their personal testimonies with me did so in response to my willingness to listen.

Compared to a casual stranger, I was fortunate in this regard. Everyone knew that I was there for an extended period, and that I was attending church services and Bible studies and conducting interviews for more than a year. This allowed pastors and churchgoers the satisfaction of knowing that I was being regularly "fed" on the gospel in generous portions. They knew I would have ample opportunity to learn of God's grace, Christ's divinity, the urgency of repentance, and the sin of prideful disbelief. From their perspective, pressuring a visitor like me to make a faith decision by quick ultimatum was no guarantee that my born-again conversion would be genuine, and thus the purposes of evangelism would in no way be served. On the contrary, my presence as an ethnographer provided my interlocutors with an opportunity to share their faith holistically—through both word and deed—which they did by, among other things, encouraging and assisting me in my research. If converting me was a motive that influenced how evangelicals interacted with me, then it was certainly advantageous. It should also be pointed out that my desire to observe and analyze them as ethnographic subjects bore much the same significance.

There were, of course, individuals who took little interest in me or my work, regarded me as suspect, and avoided me altogether. Most of the people I approached, however, were accommodating and eager to invite me into their lives, for reasons of friendship as well as faith. I recall one night when I was invited to dinner at the home of Phil and Daisy Harkin, an elderly couple at Marble Valley Presbyterian. The Harkins were one of several families who made it their responsibility to make sure I got my fair share of home-cooked meals during my stay in Knoxville. The meal was standard Tennessee fare: grilled turkey steak wrapped in strips of bacon, served with baked potatoes, fruit salad, and sweet iced tea. Seated across from me was another dinner guest, a straight-talking, fifth-generation Knoxvillian named Charles who had been a close friend of the Harkins' for many years. He spent the first part of our meal asking pointed questions about my work, before announcing his conclusion that God had sent me to Knoxville for a reason. All I had to do, he said, was be open to learning what the reason might be.

As Phil and Daisy quietly looked on, Charles leaned across the table to me and asked, "Are we gonna try to convert you?" Before I had a chance to respond, he sat up and said: "I *am* gonna try to convert you! But do you know how? By *praying* for you. And you better believe I'll be doing that." Sensing a need to clarify what Charles meant, Phil explained that he and Daisy prayed for me every day, but not just for my salvation. They prayed that my work would go smoothly, that my car wouldn't break down (a much-needed intercession), and that my friends and family in New York would be comforted until my return home. The conversation then moved on to the topic of prayer, as Phil and Charles shared emotional stories about difficult times in their lives when the prayers of Christian friends helped them overcome sickness or despair. The attention had shifted away from me, but the stories were clearly meant for my consumption.

An interesting aspect of how evangelicals related to me was the extent to which they underscored the elements that confirmed my outsider status, rather than trying to suppress or ignore them. Two areas of my life were especially relevant in this regard: the first was my vocation as a scholar and ethnographer; the second was my Jewish ethnicity.

Instead of treating either of these components of my personal identity as relational obstacles, my interlocutors repeatedly drew attention to them as markers of cultural difference and recast them as sources of mutual affinity. For example, whereas some churchgoers were cautious or guarded in their willingness to participate in my research, others were enthusiastic and believed it would ultimately prove beneficial to them. They decided that the "objectivity" of my external scholarly outlook (a notion that my many caveats did little to dispel) offered a fresh perspective from which to analyze their behavior and gain new insight into their faith. They also believed that my research would inevitably bring me closer to God, the source of ultimate truth and understanding. Throughout my fieldwork I made an effort to assure people that I was not there to "dig up any dirt" on local churches and ministries—at least none other than that which normally graces the surface of everyday life—and I found that the more I stressed the inductive and participatory nature of ethnographic fieldwork, the more convinced they became that God had brought me to Knoxville for a reason, whether I knew it or not.

My Jewishness was a topic of endless commentary and novel fascination, almost to the point of distraction, a dynamic that was in many ways indicative of larger Christian themes regarding Jews and Judaism. On countless occasions I was asked to recite Hebrew blessings over meals, explain the meaning of Jewish ritual symbols and Yiddish catchphrases, or translate Hebrew words from the Bible and on jewelry that evangelicals brought home from Jerusalem tourist shops. Evangelicals claim to feel a profound spiritual connection with "God's chosen people," and tend to valorize Jewish traditions and customs that are seen as precursors of Christianity. They are staunch supporters of the state of Israel and strongly inclined to view modern Jews, including nonobservant secular Jews like me, as direct spiritual as well as ethnic descendents of the ancient Israelites. The belief that the Jewish people are marked by the fatal flaw of having rejected "Christ the Messiah" is mitigated—or perhaps exacerbated—by the belief that "God isn't finished with the Jews," and that many Jews will come to accept Jesus as their savior before Judgment Day.

Evangelical fascination with Jews is further enhanced by cultural stereotypes, including the assumption that Jews are inherently family- and community-oriented, possess a natural inclination toward religious piety, and have a God-given proclivity for intellectual pursuits. Early in my fieldwork I was given a tour of Eternal Vine Church by a staff member who asked me many questions that seemed motivated in part by a desire to corroborate these stereotypes. He was particularly interested to know what it was like growing up with a Jewish mother. I asked what he thought Jewish mothers were like. He assumed they must be great cooks, especially good at making chicken soup, and very nurturing mothers, perhaps more than most Gentiles. He stood quietly for a moment, then turned to me and said: "There is something about the Jewish family that supports closeness and loving care, I think. Maybe it's because the Jews are God's chosen race. I don't know. I'm definitely glad that I'm a Christian, that I came to know the saving grace of Jesus Christ. But sometimes I think, man, wouldn't it be great to be Jewish? Then I would really have it all!"

Flattery aside, sentimental expressions of affinity are complicated by anti-Jewish tenets in Christian tradition, including the belief that Christ's crucifixion abrogated Jewish law as the basis of God's covenant with the righteous, and that Jews will ultimately answer for their rejection of Christ and their adherence to archaic ritual codes. Ambivalence was seldom made explicit, but it was never entirely absent from my interactions. During my fieldwork I took part in a weekly men's Bible study where my Jewishness came up regularly in group discussions. At one point, the men took pleasure in nicknaming me "the Scribe." This was a lighthearted reference to the ancient Hebrew scribes who were responsible for the codification and generational transmission of sacred knowledge. The nickname for me was meant as a term of endearment, a somewhat tongue-in-cheek recognition that I, like the scribes of old, was inscribing religious truths for posterity. I was, after all, writing things down all the time. While I insisted that my knowledge of the finer points of Jewish ritual and theology was cursory at best, the men believed that my intellectual interest was an extension of my innate, presumably unconscious sense of religious commitment.

There was yet another more complicated layer to this affectionate nickname. The Hebrew scribes portrayed in the New Testament are among Christ's chief antagonists. In the Gospel of Matthew, Jesus angrily denounces them along with the Pharisees as "hypocrites," "blind men," and "vipers" who "lock people out of the kingdom of heaven." Clearly aware that I could potentially misconstrue my biblical moniker as an insult or provocation, the leader of the group (who coined the nickname originally) reassured me before long that no negative connotations were intended. As he was an extremely reliable contact and sympathetic friend, it was easy for me to take him at his word. All the same, I could not help noting that by identifying me directly with the persona of an ancient Hebrew scribe, he and others underscored the religious and cultural distance between us, hoping thereby to determine the relational conditions through which we might come to minimize those distances.

Another issue worth mentioning with regard to my positionality in the field—for a question like "Did they try to convert you?" concerns nothing if not issues of positionality—was my activity as a frequent volunteer for local charities, social outreach ministries, and faith-based service organizations. Many of the ministry workers and outreach coordinators I met struggled routinely with the problem of never having enough volunteers. The fact that I was doing a study that involved observing evangelical outreach activities meant that I always made myself available, and on several occasions I ended up being one of relatively few people to do so. This had the effect of intensifying some ethical concerns that already weighed on my mind. For instance, to what extent was I complicit in furthering the religious agenda of my fellow volunteers? Did I compromise that agenda in any way? Were my actions as a volunteer—such as serving hot meals to homeless people, delivering donated furniture to shut-ins, and repairing a screen door at a domestic violence shelter—actions that meant something more than what I might have personally intended because of the fact that at those precise moments I was basically an evangelical representative?

It was apparent to me that I could not fully account for the symbolic import of my presence in the eyes of other volunteers, social workers, welfare clients, and recipients of charitable aid, and that it was not the purview of my project to attempt to do so. I decided that it was counterproductive to avoid volunteering out of such concerns, and that the benefits for my research outweighed, in most cases, the conceivable drawbacks. I also felt that whether or not I was personally invested in the religious motivations of evangelical volunteers, I helped them provide useful assistance and vital services for needy and distressed people and underfunded welfare agencies. Although there were times when I was reminded of just how different the attitudes and intentions of conservative evangelical ministry workers and volunteers were from my own, I was often deeply moved by the sincere compassion and dedication of their efforts.

I was equally moved by the gradual and usually subtle shifts in attitude that I observed among socially engaged evangelicals as they deepened their involvement. Some of those who worked with the urban poor began to see indigence as a consequence of life-dominating circumstances and not simply the result of irresponsible individuals making bad decisions. Evangelicals who reached out to people with AIDS realized that the ministry required tolerance, open-mindedness, and a willingness to suppress the urge to vigorously proselytize. Such shifts were not the norm, nor did they entail full-scale conversions from conservative to progressive ways of thinking, as some churchgoers may have feared. Yet they were indications of how flexible social consciousness can be even among people from religious groups that appear steadfastly resistant to certain kinds of change. I do not think I had much of a role in changing the minds of any conservative evangelicals, but I must admit that on some level I probably looked forward to their possible conversions as eagerly as they hoped and prayed for mine.

CHAPTER 2

Awaking Sleeping Giants

Whether you are a newcomer or seasoned churchgoer, one of the serious challenges of attending a worship service at a suburban megachurch on Sunday morning is finding a decent parking spot. A novice in every sense, I learned quickly that to get a good space in the sprawling parking lots of either Eternal Vine Church or Marble Valley Presbyterian—the two evangelical megachurches where I attended services on an alternating basis—I would need to set out early and beat the rush. For most commuting churchgoers in Knoxville, getting to church on time means waking up early, feeding and dressing the kids, and loading everyone in the car for a drive of anywhere from five to thirty minutes (or more) along the congested interstate. With no children of my own and only a twenty-minute drive to church, I still somehow managed to arrive late. I would race through alternate routes, a cup of hot coffee in one hand, steering wheel in the other, only to end up idling behind a caravan of SUVs, minivans, pickup trucks, and shiny sedans waiting to enter an unforgiving maze of parked cars glistening under the steamy Tennessee sun.

Like all megachurches, Eternal Vine and Marble Valley Presbyterian hold multiple worship services to accommodate the size and growth of their congregations. At the time of my fieldwork, both congregations held two morning services—9:00 A.M. and 11:15 A.M.—in addition to early evening services usually catering to young adults (separate chapel services were held in the morning for children and teenagers).

On most Sundays I attended a morning service at one megachurch, and then would either stay there and sit in on an adult Sunday school class or ministry meeting or drive ten minutes to the other megachurch in time for its second morning service. In sanctuaries big enough to hold close to two thousand people it was not hard to be inconspicuous if I wanted to be, which was only the case on days when I chose to sit near the back and take notes. More often, especially once I became a "regular" at church, I sat with friends and informants who would in turn introduce me to their friends and family. Some people enjoyed giving me useful tidbits of information during services. When I sat next to Phil Harkin at Marble Valley Presbyterian, he would whisper things like: "That's Ron over there, with his wife Sue. He coordinates our Habitat for Humanity building teams. I'll introduce you to him later." After services we might all go to a restaurant for lunch, or meet up at someone's home for barbecue and iced tea.

Making contacts through other people on Sunday was crucial, especially in the beginning when it was difficult to come across adequate leads for my research simply by paying attention. I was eager to learn about outreach ministries and volunteer opportunities that were being organized, but they were almost as hard to come by as a good parking spot. This is apparently common among megachurches, which "rarely feature their social ministry involvements prominently in their advertisements and promotion. ... [M]inistries to the poor are not so visible or well known among church attendees" (Thumma and Travis 2007: 84). As I started to meet pastors and churchgoers who comprised the small minority of outreach coordinators and mobilizers at Eternal Vine and Marble Valley Presbyterian, I became aware that such ministries tended to be rather marginal and modest in scope compared to "in-house" ministries serving the needs of members. I also sensed the frustration of those I met, many of whom felt that the megachurches of Knoxville, including their own, failed to live up to their potential in terms of large-scale community impact. The prevailing sentiment among socially engaged pastors and churchgoers was that for all their wealth and prestige, the megachurches remained "sleeping giants" in need of awakening. Their sense of urgency had a decidedly revivalist ring to it, and it built on combined feelings of optimism and self-doubt with regard to the potential for evangelical megachurches to advance the work of evangelism and the cause of Christianization by methods that would be both culturally relevant and theologically coherent.

Although the social outreach activities of the megachurches were not advertised prominently when I arrived—few mentions if any in church bulletins, brochures, and Web sites—both congregations were in the process of accommodating a growing interest among churchgoers in addressing the welfare of the wider local community. Drawing implicitly on the increased attention to "faith-based initiatives" in the mass media, socially engaged evangelicals stepped up their efforts to schedule outreach workshops and events, create new social ministries, and integrate church-based small groups into various outreach initiatives. The fact that this occurred simultaneously at Eternal Vine and Marble Valley Presbyterian is one of several reasons why I treat them in this ethnography as complementary rather than contrasting field sites, despite their many differences. Both congregations are illustrative of religious and cultural trends coming into focus at a particular historical moment and in response to the same regional context. In addition, both congregations reached their megachurch status by demonstrating their potential for expansion and innovation, and by appealing directly to a "market niche" of well-to-do suburbanites and aspiring professionals (although Marble Valley Presbyterian is the older of the two, both historically and demographically).

They are not the only megachurches in Knoxville, but Eternal Vine and Marble Valley Presbyterian share the distinction of being among the best known. Their sanctuary buildings are visible from major commuter arteries, and the congregations are often featured in news stories by local media outlets. It comes as no surprise to many that the two megachurches are also linked to each other historically. When Eternal Vine was founded in the late 1980s, several founding members were former members of Marble Valley Presbyterian who wanted to start a church with a lively atmosphere and "contemporary" aesthetics, in contrast to the classical liturgical style of the latter. Over time, it was not uncommon for members of both congregations to move back and forth between them, settling for a period on one or the other to suit evolving personal and spiritual needs or new social circles. Although individuals I spoke to recognized that certain doctrinal nuances distinguish the two megachurches from each other, members tended to downplay those distinctions, preferring to highlight stylistic differences. In short, the megachurches are seen to present separate but essentially complementary versions of the same elemental Christianity. Eternal Vine is often described as the laid-back "come as you are" church, where people are likely to go when they need, as one member put it, "a place to heal emotional wounds." Marble Valley Presbyterian is known for its liturgi-cal formalism, classical music, and strong emphasis on Bible teaching and global missions. Yet an important element common to both is the diversity and innovativeness of their ministries. Aside from counseling, Sunday school, and other pastoral services, the megachurches support a variety of recreational, educational, and therapeutic programs, such as sports leagues, career services, financial seminars, activities for youths and single adults, arts ministries, and post-abortion "recovery" groups.

Another significant point of commonality is that both megachurches are affiliated with conservative Protestant denominations, and this is reflected in their theology. Eternal Vine is a member of the Evangeli-cal Free Church of America; Marble Valley Presbyterian is affiliated with the Evangelical Presbyterian Church (after previously belonging to the Presbyterian Church of America). From the pulpit to the everyday ministries, heavy emphasis is placed on reading and studying the Bible as a literal, authoritative text, upholding religious piety and traditional morality, and practicing evangelism. Furthermore, the social and politi-cal views expressed by pastors and prominent churchgoers are rarely extremist but lean decisively to the right. Throughout the United States, such congregations are known to have a strong appeal among white middle-class conservatives living in the suburbs, many of whom yearn to feel a sense of community reinforced by an uncompromising moral fabric. These are relevant factors for understanding the difficulties that socially engaged evangelicals regularly encounter in their efforts to promote new levels of social engagement on the part of megachurch congregations.

With all these points in mind, the aim of this chapter is to describe the institutional context of the two megachurches where a significant portion of my fieldwork was based, situate it in relation to the larger cultural context of the church-growth movement as a whole, including its general characteristics and controversies, and develop a sense of how the views and opinions that churchgoers in Knoxville held about what it means to belong to a megachurch influenced the moral ambitions and mobilization discourse of socially engaged evangelicals.

MARBLE VALLEY PRESBYTERIAN CHURCH

One of the oldest and most venerated churches in Knoxville, Marble Valley Presbyterian Church has been in existence for more than two hundred years and continues to thrive. A brochure for newcomers proudly states, "We are a congregation as old as the state of Tennessee, and as new as the babies who fill our nurseries to overflowing." The church is traditionalist in most respects, epitomizing "high church" liturgical Protestantism and maintaining strong emphases on biblical instruction, pastoral leadership, and missionization. In response to an impressive influx of new members in recent decades, church leaders set out to diversify their ministries and experimented with novel approaches to worship, corporate organization, and local outreach. As a result, the megachurch today is host to a wide and, to some degree, unexpected range of organizational and stylistic elements, accommodating the diverging tastes of its membership without forgoing standards of conservative Protestant orthodoxy.

The period of major growth for Marble Valley Presbyterian began in the 1960s, as the church's once rural surroundings turned into suburban strip malls and residential subdivisions. By the 1990s, the rate of congregational growth increased considerably as service-sector industries spread throughout Knox County. Between 1990 and 1999, the average number of people attending Sunday services more than doubled from fourteen hundred to three thousand. In 2002, the church's official number of registered members was listed at 3,648. This number does not include nonmembers, newcomers, and sporadic visitors, who make up a significant portion of weekly attendees. At the time of my research, I estimated that there were roughly five thousand people attending weekly worship services (including three Sunday services plus midweek vespers) and taking advantage of in-house ministries and programs. Churchgoers were predominantly white, likely to reside in affluent neighborhoods, and typically worked in white-collar professions such as law, medicine, corporate finance, real-estate development, and higher education. Several members owned small businesses, and some ran large corporations. The congregation included newcomers to the region as well as multigenerational families with deep roots in East Tennessee. Despite notable changes in the congregation's makeup over the years, Marble Valley Presbyterian's reputation as something of an aristocratic institution remains unchanged. Among the church's high-profile members are people with strong ties to Knoxville's economic and political establishment, including major corporate executives, elected officials and civic leaders, and a handful of local media celebrities.

The physical complex of the megachurch is located near a busy intersection on the edge of the county. It features a central facility composed of two adjoining red-brick buildings with white church spires and neoclassical facades. The main sanctuary is located in the east wing, which was constructed in 1973 and expanded in 1992 to make room for additional seating. The west wing is the older of the two buildings and contains a chapel (previously the main sanctuary) and administrative offices. The structure that connects the two wings functions as an education annex with several classrooms used for children's ministries, adult Sunday school classes, and small group meetings. The facility is surrounded by an expansive parking lot, an athletic field, some residence houses designated for visiting missionaries, and an additional building for educational and recreational programs, which take place almost every day of the week. Most of the complex was constructed in the late 1980s and early 1990s, after the megachurch purchased a number of private properties in the surrounding neighborhood.

Services in the main sanctuary are typically solemn and dignified, but not without frequent lighthearted moments and occasions for celebration. Congregants in conservative suits and dresses follow a formalized liturgy and sing from hymnals while seated in rows of cushioned wooden pews. The altar is a velvet-carpeted stage adorned with decorative flowers and chairs, a wooden lectern, and a baptismal font. At the back of the stage sits the church choir, dressed in black robes, singing classical hymns accompanied by a massive pipe organ, along with a band of hired musicians playing wind, percussion, and string instruments, including electric guitar and bass. The presence of modern instruments and trained audiovisual technicians is a conspicuous reminder of the megachurch's deliberate incorporation of contemporary elements into its worship services, including the expansion of the musical repertoire to include folk-influenced "praise choruses" thought to be popular among younger churchgoers. The self-conscious fusing of modern and traditional elements at Marble Valley Presbyterian is a common feature among North American megachurches. It is intended to satisfy diverse tastes and expectations but it can also become a source of discontent among members. Most churchgoers I spoke to said they appreciated the mix of stylistic elements at Marble Valley Presbyterian because it enriched their worship experience. Others expressed concerns about the use of contemporary music in the sanctuary and all the expensive technical equipment that it requires. By and large, churchgoers were prepared to tolerate modern adaptations as long as they felt that core values were never compromised. Traditionalists complained about new innovations but mostly accepted them with minimal resistance. To avoid offending their somber sensibilities, those with a preference for contemporary worship tacitly agreed to limit their ritual enthusiasm, which usually meant refraining from clapping their hands, swaying their bodies, or lifting their arms to the sky.

Like the worship aesthetic, the organizational structure at Marble Valley Presbyterian also reflects a mix of traditional and modern influences. In accordance with standard Presbyterian order, the highest ecclesial authority in the congregation is the senior pastor—Pastor Jerry—followed by a committee of male elders, known as the Session, which oversees the governance of the church and its ministries. At a secondary tier, male deacons perform administrative functions, along with paid staff members and ministry directors who may be male or female. In the late 1990s, Marble Valley Presbyterian expanded this structure to include an array of pastoral and administrative "teams" composed jointly of clergy, staff, and laypeople. The need to implement staff-intensive organizational strategies of this kind, which are found among megachurches worldwide, is brought on by the bureaucratic demands of managing multifaceted programs and services. In addition, the corporate team-based structure facilitates innovation and flexibility by decentralizing day-to-day operations and providing active churchgoers with opportunities to increase their commitment and participation in church affairs.[1]

Pastor Jerry is a self-possessed leader with a sympathetic demeanor and a passion for scholarship and theological discourse. His pastoral style is at once authoritative and diplomatic. His sermons are often meditative and erudite, rarely reaching the exuberant heights of the stereotypical southern preacher but no less stern on matters of core doctrine. New members often cited Pastor Jerry's homiletic skills as one of the main attractions of the megachurch. His ability to convey intellectual curiosity and doctrinal integrity in the same breath holds significant appeal for the congregation's educated, upwardly mobile demographic. When I first met him one Sunday morning after a worship service, he was surrounded by churchgoers waiting to speak to him or wish him well. Recognizing that I was an unfamiliar face, he immediately shook my hand and took me aside to answer whatever questions I had. We sat for more than an hour in the empty sanctuary, discussing topics ranging from the history of Knoxville to the lives of rural Appalachians to the effects of secular culture on evangelicalism. Pastor Jerry was intrigued by my academic work as an anthropologist and, perhaps in direct response, took the opportunity to describe his "intentionally postmodern" approach to Christian ministry. He talked about how he enjoys testing the boundaries of convention and explained his interest in "multiperspectivalism," by which he meant a commitment to understand the supreme truths of the Bible from a plurality of cultural perspectives. Although a staunch proponent of the belief that the Bible is the infallible Word of God, Pastor Jerry noted that "objectivity is the fallacy of modernity." He explained that the inability of Western Christians to see beyond their own interpretative traditions has produced limited understandings of the nature of God and weakened the capacity of the church to spread the gospel effectively on a global scale.

Pastor Jerry's intellectual and theological commitment to the idea of biblical orthodoxy as a multicultural project is reflected in Marble Valley Presbyterian's strong emphasis on global missions. Around the time of my research, 14 percent of the megachurch's five-million-dollar general budget (plus an additional two million dollars in targeted donations) was allocated to support more than one hundred international missionaries, Christian NGOs, and parachurch organizations that specialize in Bible translation and distribution in remote and underdeveloped parts of the world. In cooperation with missionary agencies, the megachurch "adopted" several indigenous societies, mostly in Asia and Africa, described by missionaries as "unreached people groups" that are assumed to have never been exposed to the gospel. Being a member of Marble Valley Presbyterian, one is constantly reminded of the importance of these and other endeavors through sermons, Sunday school classes, missions conferences, and community events that ritually reinforce the congregation's dedication to world evangelization. In addition to donating money for missionary causes, members (especially teenagers and young adults) are encouraged to gain firsthand experience by going on short-term group mission trips organized by the megachurch. The significance of cross-cultural evangelism—of converting not only individuals but whole *cultures* to Christ—looms large in Marble Valley Presbyterian's image of itself as a church with a missionary agenda. This very orientation is part of the congregational ethos that socially engaged members invoke in their efforts to develop substantive cross-cultural engagements with local communities in Knoxville.

In addition to foreign missionaries, Marble Valley Presbyterian supports "home missionaries" and parachurches working in North America, including a number of faith-based ministries in the greater Knoxville area. Historically social outreach was not a high priority for the congregation, generally limited to the informal efforts of individual volunteers, mostly elderly women, and always secondary to global missions in terms of program development and fundraising. In recent years the megachurch's outreach ministries have become more formalized, spurred on by socially engaged evangelicals looking to increase the congregation's involvement with local charities, social service agencies, and urban community organizations in predominately black neighborhoods. Not long before I arrived in Knoxville, the leadership hired a full-time staff member to coordinate outreach projects, or "compassion ministries." The person they hired, Margie McKenzie (who is featured among the ethnographic profiles in chapter 4), faced numerous obstacles from the start, including resistance among skeptical churchgoers and the absence of a bureaucratic infrastructure specifically suited to outreach mobilization. Nonetheless, from a perspective of social engagement the fact that such a position was created in the first place represented a significant move forward for the conservative and otherwise mission-minded megachurch.

In the 1990s, with pastors and churchgoers increasingly attuned to issues of social welfare, Marble Valley Presbyterian became a prominent player in social and philanthropic initiatives of various kinds. Pastor Jerry, for example, was one of only a handful of religious figures invited to participate in a brain trust of political, nonprofit, and business leaders working to develop comprehensive plans to revitalize the region's economy and civic culture. In addition, the megachurch formed several high-profile collaborative partnerships with nonprofit organizations such as Habitat for Humanity and an organization that sponsors the local "Principle for a Day" program, which puts members of the community in direct contact with area schools. One of Marble Valley Presbyterian's most celebrated undertakings was a partnership with a struggling black church in the inner city. The church received financial support in order to build a new facility and launch an ambitious community development project with help from commercial and nonprofit organizations with direct links to the megachurch. Pastors and churchgoers were motivated to pursue this partnership in part out of a desire to promote citywide "racial reconciliation," an aspiration that came with its own set of difficulties, as I later demonstrate (see chapter 7). All the same, such intentions were indicative of the extent to which a certain segment of white conservative evangelicals at the time were becoming interested in the Christianizing potential of social engagement. Whether their interest is attributable to the effects of church growth, changes in local attitudes about poverty, race, and urban-suburban reintegration, or a bourgeois concern for social respectability, there is little doubt that leaders and prominent members of Marble Valley Presbyterian were looking forward to raising the megachurch's public profile, not only as a religious institution but also as a vital contributor to the region's social and spiritual renewal.

ETERNAL VINE CHURCH

Unlike Marble Valley Presbyterian, where stylistic and organizational innovations take place but do not diminish the aura of ecclesial tradition, Eternal Vine Church is a congregation where members take great stock in freedom from tradition. In many ways Eternal Vine is a quintessential "seeker church," a church that excels at recruiting spiritually curious people who may be previously unchurched or disenchanted. Such churches typically embrace "an unconventional approach to Christianity, explicitly reshaping the presentation of the Gospel message to correspond to a suburban and exurban post-Christian baby boomer cultural style" while "reaching younger generations of religious seekers as well" (Thumma and Travis 2007: 39–40). From its inception, the church was fashioned as "a new way of doing church" in Knoxville, and its founding members (including former members of Marble Valley Presbyterian) implemented corporate growth and marketing principles pioneered by nationally known, trendsetting megachurches such as Bill Hybel's Willow Creek Community Church and Rick Warren's Saddleback Church. In particular, the founders used market research techniques to identify a target population of restless, overwhelmed, and upwardly mobile suburbanites and determine how best to attract the "spiritual seekers" among them who felt alienated by institutional Christianity but still yearned for "authentic" Christian spirituality and a sense of community. Their strategies worked. Eternal Vine grew from a small congregation to a megachurch by catering its ministries, programs, and worship services to the peculiar consumer fixation—that tireless pursuit of meaning and self-actualization through limitless choice—perceived as dominant among middle-class baby boomers and members of the so-called Generation X.

One of the obvious characteristics of Eternal Vine Church is the casual "come as you are" atmosphere, an informal, laid-back "vibe" that one notices immediately upon entering the building. On Sunday mornings, as churchgoers mingle freely in the large, brightly lit lobby before services, you will see men in golf shirts and khaki pants (sometimes shorts), and women in playful floral-print dresses or blouses and skirts (sometimes jeans). A worshipper wearing a suit and tie is conspicuous, and even children are dressed down. Entering the fifteen-hundred-seat "worship center," one senses an air of anticipation you might expect from an audience before a live concert. Indeed, worship services at Eternal Vine are highly performative, and churchgoers are repeatedly invited to take part in the collective energy. It is no accident that many churchgoers, particularly newcomers, describe the worship as being totally unlike what they imagine to be the typical Sunday church service. The ritual aesthetics at Eternal Vine are precisely intended to produce emotional investment and feelings of spiritual communion without appearing to rely on conventional or familiar trappings of "churchiness." The same principle applies to the megachurch's physical appearance. Apart from a sign at the entrance to the parking lot (stating the megachurch's name but not its denominational affiliation) and a simple cross engraved on an outside wall of the main building, there are virtually no markers explicitly indicating that it is a place of worship. Driving past Eternal Vine, it is easy to mistake it for one of the other fixtures that dot the suburban landscape, including office parks, shopping malls, college campuses, country clubs, and Barnes & Noble superstores. But few passersby make this mistake. Eternal Vine is very well known among Knoxvillians and has earned a reputation as the "hip" congregation where pop culture meets the Bible Belt.

Eternal Vine Church was founded in the late 1980s by a group of like-minded friends, with support from the Evangelical Free Church of America (EFCA). The founding members wanted to build a church that would be primarily devoted to developing relational spirituality and teaching the "bare essentials" of Christian theology, including core doctrines such as the inerrancy of the Bible, the Holy Trinity, salvation by faith alone, and the importance of converting others to the faith. With its minimalist yet no less absolutist approach to doctrine, energetic worship services, and attractive ministries, Eternal Vine was a quick success story, bringing in more than a thousand worshippers in a few short years. Within less than a decade, the congregation purchased sixteen acres of prime real estate close to a major thruway and constructed a six-million-dollar campus, financed mostly through internal fundraising. The main building complex features a large worship center, fully equipped with multimedia equipment (including two twenty-five-foot video screens) and comfortable auditorium seating. One staff member told me that the architectural design of the worship center was such that one of the outer walls of the building can be resituated to accommodate a 60 percent expansion if necessary, and that the ground beneath the parking lot was already fitted to accommodate structural foundations and utility pipes that would be needed for such a renovation. The rest of the facility includes meeting rooms and classrooms of various sizes, an expansive children's wing where separate youth-oriented services take place, and a suite of administrative offices where dozens of staff manage programs and ministries supported by the megachurch's multimillion-dollar annual budget.

Eternal Vine's official membership tally in 2000 was listed as 750, but on average the total number of people attending weekly services and ministry-related events was likely four to five times that. In addition to its ability to draw in young suburban professionals and families, Eternal Vine has been successful in attracting local college students, including frequent visitors from the University of Tennessee. Whether first-time visitors are committed Christians looking for a new church, spiritual seekers looking for a new source of inspiration, or curious and cynical hipsters just checking to see what all the buzz is about, Eternal Vine has caught the attention of thousands of locals who recognize the megachurch—either with admiration or scorn—as a spiritual "place to be" in Knoxville.

Newcomers to Eternal Vine are welcomed in the "hospitality room," a reception center staffed by volunteers from the "hospitality team," who greet visitors, answer questions, and offer free cups of coffee along with tape-recordings of recent sermons and brochures describing various church ministries, classes, and support groups. Popular devotional books and CDs are available for purchase, including studio recordings of the megachurch's worship band performing its repertoire of contemporary praise songs. When I first visited the reception center I was greeted by a cheerful elderly woman of unblinking composure, who patiently explained to me virtually every aspect of the congregation's mission and values. Aware that my interests were academic, she dutifully listed factual tidbits she thought would be of use to me before concluding that, all facts aside, nothing at Eternal Vine was more important than the mission to help people become true disciples of Christ through "authentic spirituality." "The people who come here come because they are tired of just being Sunday morning Christians. Our church has grown over the years because we have a vision that drives us, just as you have a vision that drives you in your studies. But for us, that vision is Jesus Christ. Without Jesus Christ, there is nothing." I was impressed by how effortlessly she managed to answer my questions while incorporating proselytic statements specifically catered to my career identity.

When newcomers express an interest in learning more or becoming active members, hospitality volunteers will ask substantive questions to determine areas of ministry that might best suit their needs (e.g., Bible studies, therapeutic support groups, family-oriented ministries, recreational activities, career seminars, etc.). They may also consult administrative or pastoral staff to find appropriate small groups for newcomers to join. As I mentioned in the introduction, monitored networks of small groups serve multiple functions at megachurches like Eternal Vine. They provide intimate venues for ritualized study and fellowship among churchgoers and help to reinforce moral and interpretive standards that are expected to remain relatively uniform in congregations committed to religious orthodoxy. Yet another function of small groups is that they offer an effective mechanism for assimilating newcomers who might otherwise fall through the cracks or simply remain anonymous and disengaged. This is just one of several ways that the value of "redemptive relationships" is repeatedly emphasized not only in the ritual and theological discourse of Eternal Vine but also in the very structure of some of the megachurch's most basic operations.

Worship services at Eternal Vine are self-consciously "contemporary" in form and content, with little in the way of formal liturgy. Many churchgoers, especially younger ones, told me that they liked attending services there because they were not too "churchy" and were never boring. The front of the main sanctuary is an auditorium stage, sparsely decorated with a few potted plants and a dimly lit wooden cross suspended overhead. A typical service includes about forty-five minutes of music and singing, led by a full worship band that performs popular praise choruses with sentimental refrains like "Open the eyes of my heart, Lord, I want to see you," and "I'm coming back to the heart of worship, and it's all about you, Jesus," as congregants sing and sometimes dance along. Audiovisual technicians at the back of the auditorium unobtrusively cue synchronized sound and lighting effects that add to the evocative power of the performance. Performers and pastors on stage encourage the members of the congregation to feel uninhibited—without losing all their inhibitions (it is church after all)—and open themselves up to an emotional and sensory encounter with God through worship and prayer. One of the interesting dynamics I observed during the worship services at Eternal Vine was a constant self-conscious effort, mostly on the part of church leaders, to find a perfect balance between ritual exuberance and restraint, as though the aim were to experience all the best aspects of religious enthusiasm without compromising the image of middle-class respectability that worshippers carefully maintain.[2]

The "worship and praise" portion of the Sunday service is followed by a half-hour sermon, usually given by the senior pastor but sometimes by other staff pastors or invited guests. Sermons at Eternal Vine are typically reflective and colloquial, full of anecdotes and references to popular film and literature (including secular as well as Christian media) that add insight to the main task of interpreting select Bible passages. Accompanied by PowerPoint slides, and sometimes video presentations or movie clips, the sermons are meant to make knowledge of the Bible and basic evangelical theology practical and immediately relevant to the personal, emotional, and professional lives of congregants. Topics often focus on abstract issues of faith such as the importance of prayer and humility, submission to God's will, showing love and mercy, struggling with doubt, and maintaining one's moral and spiritual accountability. The finer points of Christian doctrine are boiled down to a practical theology that is easily internalized by lay people and focused largely around existential questions and crises that are assumed to pervade the lives of believers as they seek to attain personal fulfillment. In the many sermons I heard, the topic of sin was recurrent and the challenges of resisting "the evil one" came up now and again, but most often the sermons revolved around a core message that Christians must reform their lives and social relationships by becoming radically recommitted to Christ and reoriented to God's will. To find the happiness you so desperately seek, they seemed to say, give up your need for control, let Jesus into your heart, and let the Spirit guide you in your thoughts, actions, and relationships.

The senior pastor of Eternal Vine during my fieldwork was Pastor Tim, who came to Knoxville from the West Coast specifically to assume leadership of the congregation when it was created. Pastor Tim is a soft-spoken yet charismatic preacher, whose relatively noncombative and often self-effacing style of Bible-based expository preaching represents a studied departure from the angry and exhortative preachers of old-school Christian fundamentalism. His pastoral demeanor, not unlike Pastor Jerry's, is that of a spiritual leader who seeks to come across as personable and accessible rather than indignant or intimidating. His religious authority derives not only from seminary training and theological pedigree but also an ability to demonstrate that he is essentially no different from other churchgoers: susceptible to the same insecurities, tormented by the same desires, and driven by the same aspirations. Listening to Pastor Tim's sermons and how churchgoers reacted to them, I realized that much of his success in reaching his audience depended on his use of empathy and his ability to express (or perhaps dictate) the conscience of the congregation. His participation in the discourse of outreach mobilization at Eternal Vine, as I describe later, was suggestive of the uses of pastoral influence for the promotion of evangelical social engagement, as well as its limitations.

Like Marble Valley Presbyterian, Eternal Vine supports missionary projects, but on a more modest scale. In 2001, a small percentage of the megachurch's annual budget was designated for international mission-ary work. Most of it was to support the training of foreign nationals in countries where new churches were being formed. The megachurch also sponsors short-term mission trips for members, usually in connection with church-planting efforts and humanitarian work, and has hosted missions conferences as well as conferences devoted to the Persecuted Church movement, an international activist network dedicated to com-bating anti-Christian persecution (see Castelli 2005). Such programs are meant to bolster and expand the megachurch's commitment to global Christian awareness and fellowship. Otherwise, Eternal Vine's evan-gelistic programs were mainly directed at the greater Knoxville area, particularly students and young professionals, and the megachurch took pains to reinforce its image as a vibrant center of religious and com-munity life for the region as a whole.

At the time of my fieldwork, Eternal Vine's social outreach ministries were not very extensive, but this began to change through the efforts of a number of socially engaged evangelicals, including Pastor Tim, several elders and staff, and active outreach volunteers. For the first time in the young congregation's history, a staff position was created for someone to develop and oversee new outreach initiatives. Pastor Tim preached more frequently on the subjects of compassion and care for the poor, and the megachurch offered study seminars focused on these topics as well (though they initially failed to attract much interest). Eternal Vine also established partnerships with local nonprofits and charity organiza-tions. Among the organizations that received institutional support from the megachurch, in the form of financial assistance and other practical resources like meeting space, was Paul Genero's newly formed faith-based organization the Samaritans of Knoxville. Relationships were cultivated with local religious and cultural organizations that represent minority communities, including immigrant churches and agencies that work with foreign refugees. Churchgoers at Eternal Vine were pleased with such developments, seeing them as positive trends away from the problem of white suburban apathy. Some complained, however, that the efforts did not go far enough and that the congregation risked becoming complacent about sending checks and holding periodic outreach events rather than committing to sustained social engagement.

As much as there was a desire to reach out to cultural strangers and contribute to the social welfare of the community at large, counter-vailing inclinations—including the social and theological conservatism of many evangelical churchgoers and the tendency for churches like Eternal Vine to function almost as suburban enclaves—made the task of outreach mobilization particularly daunting for the socially engaged evangelicals I got to know. Compounding their sense of frustration was the fact that most resources, ministries, and administrative energies at the megachurch were dedicated to the needs of existing members and the demands of rapid congregational growth. Such concerns can be felt acutely in megachurches like Eternal Vine, where even though people are drawn to the amenities of belonging to a megachurch they also worry about the drawbacks, including the perception (voiced by many critics) that megachurches represent little more than a corporate capitalist ethos masked as religiosity. The very mechanisms of church growth that allow megachurches to succeed are seen by some as com-promising the integrity of the gospel, and seen by others as effectively limiting social outreach to recruitment (often self-selecting) rather than organized benevolence or broad attempts at cultural transformation. Concerns and criticisms like these came up repeatedly during my field-work, voiced by members of Eternal Vine and Marble Valley Presbyte-rian as well as other local observers. They are not unique to Knoxville; they reflect trends, characteristics, and debates that surround the hugely influential church-growth movement as a whole, to which I now turn.

SPIRITUAL SPRAWL-MART?

The proliferation of megachurches in recent decades is a worldwide cultural phenomenon remarkable in the scope of its influence and the breadth of criticism and controversy surrounding it. Fueled by a veri-table church-growth industry (see, for example, Schaller 2000; Vaughan 1993), megachurches epitomize the enterprising and adaptive character of global Christianity in its newest and most dramatic forms. While church-growth consultants and megachurch pioneers have fashioned novel strategies for "increasing the flock" through the application of corporate business practices, marketing techniques, and pop-culture aesthetics, they have faced condemnation from religious purists and ultraconservatives convinced that such strategies undermine the sanctity and solemnity of Christian faith. The majority of megachurches are theologically conservative, but this has not stopped religious and secular critics alike from accusing them of diluting "true" Christianity, promoting cults of personality around celebrity pastors, fetishizing wealth and prosperity, and wasting valuable resources on flashy luxuries like Learjets and Jumbotrons. Such accusations reveal less about how megachurches actually function than they do about competing moral assumptions regarding what counts as "true" or genuine Christianity and what doesn't. They are indicative of ethical dilemmas that modern evangelicals have confronted for generations, especially concerning the ideal role of the Church in a world increasingly defined by consumerism, corporatization, and media sensationalism.

Evangelicals who attend megachurches are obviously inclined favorably toward them, but not without measures of ambivalence. Churchgoers at Eternal Vine and Marble Valley Presbyterian regarded them very positively in general but expressed certain fears as well, most notably the fear of falling prey to a "consumer mentality" that some believe is unwittingly reinforced by consumer-oriented approaches to ministry and discipleship. There was also a great deal of consternation over the possibility that by having so many of their personal needs fulfilled at a megachurch, white suburbanites intensify their social isolation and thereby actually limit their spiritual growth (see chapter 5). These unequivocally class-based insecurities are reflexive responses, in large part, to the upward social mobility that conservative evangelicals have experienced over the past half century (Shibley 1996). They are also rooted in the suspicion that megachurches, for all their visibility and power, remain essentially self-serving and ineffectual with regard to the imperatives of evangelism and the cause of Christianization.

The term *megachurch* is commonly used to refer to a Protestant congregation that averages more than two thousand attendees at weekend worship services. Although some of the world's largest megachurches are found in Asian, African, and Latin American countries, my focus in this chapter is on the characteristics and debates associated with evangelical megachurches in the U.S. context. According to research conducted by Scott Thumma of the Hartford Institute for Religion Research in collaboration with the Leadership Network (a Christian consulting agency), there are approximately thirteen hundred megachurches in the United States today, a number that reflects an exponential rate of increase in the last twenty to thirty years (see Thumma and Travis 2007: 84). Megachurches are found throughout the United States, but they are especially common in large metropolitan areas—especially in suburban and exurban regions—in Sunbelt states extending from the Southeast to Southern California. They are often situated near major roads and highways, on plots of prime real estate suited for the construction of modern church buildings and sanctuaries, educational and recreational facilities, and, of course, parking lots.

The best-known megachurches are truly massive, drawing upward of twenty thousand to forty thousand weekly worshippers to high-tech sanctuaries and stadiums, where services may even be broadcast to local and national cable television stations. Noteworthy examples include Joel Osteen's Lakewood Church in Houston, Bill Hybel's Willow Creek Community Church near Chicago, T. D. Jakes's Potter's House based in Dallas, and Robert Schuller's famed Crystal Cathedral and Rick Warren's Saddleback Church, both based in Orange County, California. Some of these—for instance, Willow Creek—expand their influence and resource base by creating satellite congregations and nonprofit organizations, so they begin to function almost as denominations in their own right (Sargeant 2000). The majority of megachurches, however, are comparatively modest in size, averaging an estimated 3,585 attendees per week, based on data from 2005 (Thumma and Travis 2007: 8). Regardless of their size, megachurches typically generate wide spheres of influence by virtue of the institutional fields and networks with which they tend to be affiliated, including media industries, schools and universities, nonprofit organizations, social movements, and community action groups.

Megachurches are often associated with organizational and stylistic innovations, features that make them consistent with what Donald Miller (1997) has called the "new paradigm church" in American Protestantism. Gaining prominence in the wake of the economic prosperity of the postwar era and the Christian counterculture movements of the 1960s–1970s (such as the so-called Jesus Freaks), new paradigm churches promote a "postmodern" religiosity defined by therapeutic, individualistic, and antiestablishment sensibilities, as well as an emphasis on variety, experimentation, and choice (1997: 20–22). New paradigm churches also promote doctrinal minimalism (1997: 121), reinforcing a popular belief that the core tenets of Christian orthodoxy can be reduced to a few straightforward, elemental truths from which other "nonessential" doctrines are derived.[3] In these and other respects, megachurches revisit long-standing populist traditions in evangelical revivalism, repackaged for an age when spirituality has become a valued target of consumer participation, and religious piety has become one of many viable avenues of self-expression and cultural identification. At the same time, and despite the fact that roughly a third of mega-churches are nondenominational, theological orientation remains extremely significant. Most U.S. megachurches self-identify as evan-gelical (a smaller segment as charismatic or Pentecostal), and the vast majority affirm conservative Protestant teachings on morality and biblical orthodoxy. Although megachurch leaders and representatives are keen to avoid the cultural stigma of fundamentalism, megachurches achieve much of their success precisely because they combine an atmosphere of growth and adaptability with a commitment to high moral standards and the appearance of uncompromising religious pedagogy.[4]

Aspiring congregations are known to use niche-marketing techniques adapted from the corporate for-profit sector and applied to the needs of church growth (Trueheart 1996). The business axiom "know your customer" is a mantra of sorts among church pastors and consultants who seek to emulate the strengths of corporate branding, specifically the ability to identify target populations, assess their wants and needs, and convince them of the viability of a particular product (or lifestyle) as a pathway to satisfaction and fulfillment. In perfecting their adaptations, church-growth specialists rely on the ideas of renowned management gurus such as Peter Drucker and Kenneth Blanchard, and the help of Christian consulting agencies such as the Barna Research Group, Lead-ership Network, and Willow Creek Association. The church-growth movement has thus cohered around a set of corporate strategies or "best practices" for recruiting and retaining new members, as well as reproducing effective bureaucratic structures, leadership training, and program development. Some megachurches have gone so far as to experiment with their own commercial enterprises, including on-site cafés, shopping centers, and fast-food franchises, or even more ambi-tious ventures such as real-estate development, investment funds, and credit unions.[5]

With all these innovations, cultural accommodations, and corporate capitalist adaptations, it is hardly surprising that megachurches would become targets of vehement critiques and cautionary warnings from Christian commentators (Guinness 1993; Hart 2000; Horton 2000; Pritchard 1996). Magazines such as *Christianity Today* and *Modern Reformation* have devoted entire issues to theological and ethical debates surrounding the church-growth movement. The most elaborated critiques focus on the idea that by relying so heavily on mass-media technologies and corporate management philosophies, megachurches become vulnerable to the corrupt moral value systems of secular society. They warn of the risk that contemporary churchgoers, in their eagerness to achieve personal satisfaction as defined by the media and the marketplace, will become ignorant of the rigorous, ascetic demands of Christian faith. While acknowledging the ability of enterprising megachurches to attract the attention óf the unchurched and disenchanted masses, evangelical critics argue that they distort the gospel message by emphasizing "fulfillment" over "faithfulness," and by ritualizing media spectacle to such a degree that churchgoers succumb to the "temptation of the image" (Pritchard 1996). Others, like the evangelical author D. G. Hart, have complained that megachurch pastors are so focused on the pragmatics of customer satisfaction that they overlook the "fundamentally organic and mysterious" nature of the church as a community of faith (2000: 22). Hart goes on to argue that there are fundamental differences between being a church pastor and being the manager of a Wal-Mart store, and that this distinction comes dangerously close to being confused when Christians promote corporate business models as strategies of church growth (2000: 24).

However one interprets these critiques, the sense of unease they convey with regard to the influence of commercialism and corporatization is undeniable. This is only to be expected, not only because megachurches are often compared to corporate shopping centers but also because the range of ministry offerings they provide is modeled, in some cases explicitly, on the one-stop-shop experience of the suburban mall (Schaller 1992; Thumma 1996). What critical observers seem to find particularly unsettling about megachurches is their seemingly limitless ability to convey religious idealism, predicated on detachment from crass commercialism and commodity forms, and simultaneously reproduce a rational pragmatism informed by the logics of late capitalism. Megachurches illustrate with alarming clarity the hegemonic resonance between religious voluntarism as a spiritual objective (i.e., the value of consciously choosing one's church—indeed, one's faith—rather than simply following tradition) and the terms of individual subjectivity prescribed by neoliberal market ideologies, although they are by no means the first religious institutions in U.S. history to highlight such affinities (Moore 1994).

Yet, despite these observations, it is worth noting that hegemonic resonances do not always find simple, uncontested expression in the everyday lives of religious people, or in the culture of local congregations, including megachurches. Evangelicals who attend megachurches are possessed of no small degree of self-consciousness about the choices they make, even to the extent of recognizing that their choices are not always as "free" and unmediated as one might assume. Notwithstanding theological debates about the role of free will versus predestination, conservative evangelical churchgoers are perfectly aware that their religious lives are characterized, at least in part, by habits and tastes determined less by inspiration than by mundane facts of social existence, such as class, ethnicity, and cultural upbringing. The paradox of being "in but not of the world" is an existential predicament that evangelicals wrestle with, anxiously at times, and not merely a paradigm they take for granted. While conservative evangelical churchgoers, like everyone else, may not always recognize the formative influence of structural and hegemonic forces in their lives, their inclination toward personal and social reflexivity (however limited, at times, by religious dogma) is such that they can hardly be accused of ignoring the theological and cultural implications of belonging to a suburban megachurch.

Churchgoers at Eternal Vine and Marble Valley Presbyterian rarely complained openly about the reliance on corporate management principles or new media technologies, and they rejected the criticism that the gospel was compromised or "watered down" for easy consumption. They lauded their pastors as great teachers and interpreters of the Word of God, and viewed their congregations as authentic and profoundly Christ-centered communities of worship and faith, models for society as a whole. What did bother them, however, was the insularity and cultural homogeneity of their congregations, and the fear of being overtaken by a "consumer mentality." Some were even reluctant to embrace the term *megachurch*, or framed it in scare quotes, perhaps to avoid associating themselves with controversial or negative connotations. Many individuals I spoke to expressed the concern that megachurches appear to outsiders like suburban country clubs: elitist, self-selecting, and extravagant. This concern was exacerbated by a widespread belief among churchgoers that such perceptions might in some ways be accurate.

Evangelical misgivings about the social priorities of megachurches correspond with individual spiritual concerns but also pertain to nagging questions about the larger implications of white suburban withdrawal, especially the intensification of social boundaries defined by race and class. Socially engaged pastors and churchgoers echoed these questions repeatedly, arguing in favor of social outreach ministries as means of redefining the boundaries that megachurches unwittingly reproduce. Still, they encountered resistance that reflected in part the very nature of the megachurch as an institutional form. Despite the claims of those who insisted that the needs of the larger community should be central to a congregation's mission, the priority of accommodating the needs of actual church members was regarded as more immediate. As the congregations of Eternal Vine and Marble Valley Presbyterian grew by leaps and bounds, substantial energy and resources were devoted to member services and congregational administration. Churchgoers responded to this practical reality with marked ambivalence, and at times churchgoers openly disagreed about whether it was an appropriate state of affairs.

When I attended a few meetings of Eternal Vine's ministry group for young adults (mostly individuals in their early twenties), I sensed an undercurrent of tension between prominent members over the question of what the group's main priorities should be. I later had an opportunity to speak privately with an informed member, a recent college graduate named Greg, who explained that a minor power struggle was going on and one of the issues of contention was a disagreement between those who felt the group should be more committed to social outreach and others who felt the group's resources were best spent on things like Bible study, workshops for enhancing spiritual growth, and fellowship-building activities such as hiking and kayak trips. The group already had a social outreach component that involved monthly visits to soup kitchens and community centers for inner-city youths, but some members, including Greg, felt that "we need to be more intentional about serving the community and less like a social club." When I asked Greg how those who took the other position justified their approach, he explained: "I talked to one guy who said that maybe the young adults ministry is just supposed to be about believers coming together and encouraging one another, and that community ministry is supposed to happen individually in each person's life, like in their jobs and everyday experiences. I guess there is something to that argument, but I still think we're altogether too much into being a little subculture at this church." Greg added that regardless of what happens, he had decided to volunteer as a tutor for international students at the University of Tennessee, where he felt he could be a better witness for Christ than at his day job as a retail clerk. He credited his peers at church for helping him make that decision: "God speaks through my friends, and because of their encouragement I know God wants me to tutor international students."

The inward-oriented proclivities of church ministries and small groups can limit outreach initiatives, but they also provide the necessary impetus and peer reinforcement for outreach initiatives to get off the ground. Kyle Anderson, Eternal Vine's first full-time outreach coordinator, saw the potential for church-based groups to stimulate outreach mobilization. He directed his initial efforts at small groups rather than individuals, encouraging them to get involved in outreach ministries or "adopt" specific areas of need that they could commit to and deal with as a group. Early on in his tenure, I asked Kyle whether he had already encountered obstacles to mobilization: "Of course! That comes with the territory. People always tend to see their own church and their own needs as the be-all, end-all, rather than seeing all this as a part of a larger picture. Here at Eternal Vine, we're trying to undo ten years of history, because this church hasn't been very big on outreach and now we have to convince people in the congregation to think of outreach as something more than just the flavor of the month."

For Kyle, as an outreach coordinator and mobilizer, promoting social outreach was all about effecting a paradigm shift in the culture of evangelical churches, how they conceive of their mission and engage their social environment. During our interview, he went on to argue that suburban megachurches and other affluent congregations fall prey too easily to the false conviction that the Christian lifestyle is one of withdrawal and introspection. For Kyle this constitutes a spiritual problem because of unseen, nefarious influences that cause people to focus on selfish things and put their own wants and desires ahead of the needs of people gripped by devastating or life-dominating circumstances:

> Satan deceives church people into believing that they are in need, and this keeps us from seeing that we are the ones with resources to give.... Just like how society makes us buy into certain standards of success or beauty—how much money you should have saved in your retirement fund, or how skinny you should be if you're a woman—and we measure ourselves against those standards, and that makes us feel needy. The devil uses images of false reality to keep us from using our abundance to help the truly needy.

Churchgoers generally agreed with Kyle's basic premise that, being part of a consumer culture, people are easily deceived by the devil and distracted from what is "truly" important from a Christian point of view. Disagreements would arise over questions about what counts as "true need," who among the needy are the most deserving, and what the best methods are to serve their needs effectively and righteously. In megachurches the range of diverging opinions can be wide, and finding enough consensus to institute large-scale programmatic shifts can be next to impossible. This does not mean that social outreach does not take place. Megachurches in the United States on average support a broad array of outreach ministries. Survey data from 2005 indicate that 99 percent of megachurches support programs targeting needy youths, 91 percent are involved in prison ministries, 85 percent sponsor substance abuse programs, and 78 percent support relief shelters and thrift stores (Thumma and Travis 2007: 81). The same survey found that megachurches are strongly inclined to partner with other churches and parachurch organizations on community service projects, with the megachurch often assuming a prominent role "because it has the staff and financial resources to drive the efforts" (2007: 80). In conservative megachurches, approaches to organized benevolence that emphasize personalized charity and spiritual guidance are likely to be favored over those that appear more activist in scope and tone. Nonetheless, social outreach ministries are among the key enterprises by which mega-churches of all kinds strategically raise their public profile and expand their existing networks of action and influence.

The moral urgency conveyed in the discourse of outreach mobiliza-tion among socially engaged evangelicals at Eternal Vine and Marble Valley Presbyterian was proportional to the tremendous potential that both congregations were believed to have, based on their sheer size and affluence. As the megachurches sought to develop their social outreach ministries, the efforts were spearheaded by a select and motivated few— small in number relative to their congregations—who drew attention to the tensions, paradoxes, and institutional dynamics of the megachurch as a corporate entity in order to combat the perceived impediments to outreach mobilization. In so doing, they added weight to regnant con-cerns and aspirations that resided in the hearts and minds of pastors and churchgoers who were already intent on making the most of the megachurch mystique rather than reinforcing its apparent shortcom-ings. At times, the urgency of the moral ambitions pertaining to these issues had an air of millennialist anticipation, fueled by the belief that the very existence of megachurches in Knoxville—that is, the fact that a few churches were growing and expanding at unprecedented rates—heralded a new period of religious awakening in the region. The prospect of such a transformation was predicated on an imperative to make sure that megachurches become more than just middle-class enclaves, or havens for self-absorbed suburbanites to count their blessings and heal their emotional wounds. As I discuss in the next chapter, this anticipation was further intensified by conflicted sentiments concerning the history and regional culture of Knoxville, including questions among evangelicals about whether the region is really the bastion of Christian religion that believers and nonbelievers alike imagine it to be.

CHAPTER 3

A Region in Spite of Itself

You are the light of the world. A city on a hill cannot
be hidden.
—Matthew 5:14

If I can't make fun of Knoxville, I don't want to live here.
—Matthew T. Everett, local journalist

Here in the Bible Belt, going to church doesn't make you a
Christian any more than going to McDonald's makes you
a hamburger.
—Staff Member at Eternal Vine Church

"*Why Knoxville?*" It seemed as though every other day someone would
ask why I chose Knoxville as the site for my research. Even local evangelicals, who might be expected to ask whether I was a Christian
before anything else, were initially perplexed and amused that I chose
to conduct my study in their city instead of another, presumably more
obvious location. The underlying assumption appeared to be that Knoxville, a "big town/small city" nestled in the Appalachian hills of East
Tennessee, lacks the cultural magnitude to which researchers like me
naturally gravitate. Knoxvillians certainly do not view their surroundings as insignificant, but many wondered if the place was perhaps too
peculiar or obscure to be representative of mainstream issues or trends.
This may well be a common response among people who find themselves the subjects of ethnographic research, undoubtedly a counterintuitive experience for most. Yet it is revealing that this question came
up as frequently as it did. A great deal of social discourse in and about
Knoxville is fixated on the enduring paradoxes of the city's history and

culture, which have had the effect of producing a regional consciousness in which regionality itself is more of an open question than a solid fact.

The local historian and author Jack Neely once wrote: "Knoxville is an unknown—and, forever, a paradox.... Crippled by its own confusions, confounded by its distinctive paradoxes, [Knoxville is] haunted by the fact that no one will ever tell us who we are" (1995: 154). I encountered this theme repeatedly in informal conversations with native residents, including journalists, activists, and educators. Even in the media, or at public events and civic forums, one senses little in the way of consensus regarding the character of the city or its regional and national significance as a place. This enduring predicament is particularly troublesome for activists, politicians, and urban planners who have spent years searching for new strategies to put Knoxville back on the map, as it were, and to construct a coherent sense of metropolitan identity that remains elusive.

From my perspective, the question "Why study Knoxville?" was the perfect reason to study Knoxville. If local residents regard their cherished city as lacking in qualities of self-evidence associated with places like Chicago, New York, Dallas, or Atlanta (places where, presumably, a question like that never needs to be asked), then to what extent do such assumptions influence civic and religious activities that try to make up for this? For socially engaged evangelicals who were drawn to the idea of developing outreach ministries focused on the region's urban core, the impulse to imagine the city as a valid mission field was partly driven by visions of urban revitalization that were similar in some ways to those held by other residents. The impulse was complicated, however, by the need to determine how to define the city as a cultural entity, and how to envision its future in tangible, programmatic terms, both especially challenging tasks, given that most of the region's population growth has been in the suburbs and a large portion of suburbanites are not Knoxville natives. Many of the evangelicals I met had moved to the region from other places and had relatively little knowledge of local politics and issues within the city limits, adding to the distance they had to overcome in the process of becoming socially engaged.

Evangelical pastors and churchgoers took pleasure, nonetheless, in insisting that a major transformation was about to take place in their fair city. "God is at work in this city," they would say, "*Something* is happening in Knoxville!" Auspicious trends in the evangelical community—for example, the vitality of the megachurches, collegiality among Christians from different ethnic groups and denominations—were taken as signs of spiritual and cultural changes already under way. It was imagined that as soon as evangelical churches and institutions in Knoxville started really coming together, achieving maximum capacities collectively, the city and surrounding region would experience a massive impact—a certain "something," extraordinary and indefinable. I was never entirely clear, nor was it ever clarified, what that "something" was understood to be. It was a figure of speech that perhaps was left intentionally vague, a verbal meditation on the mystery of divine providence. (Who, after all, would presume to know the details of God's plan?) What was clear to me was that anticipatory claims about "what God has planned for Knoxville" reflected a strong desire among evangelicals to take part in an unfolding drama of urban renewal and religious revival. They were poetic, performative statements that refashioned Knoxville as "eulogized space" (Bachelard 1964), and contributed to a cultural construction of "transcendent locality" (Howell 2008), linking a situated Christian identity to global and cosmic planes. However, as part of a revivalist discourse, such sentiments carried negative connotations as well. When evangelicals imagine a revival about to take place—that is, for waves of religious fervor to become *emplaced*—it means that spiritual awakenings and divine interventions are conceived as not only possible but utterly necessary.

This chapter explores aspects of local history and perceptions of regional character that contribute to an indeterminate sense of place that defines how many residents of Knoxville, including socially engaged evangelicals, think about where they live and its need for urban renewal and (for evangelicals) spiritual revitalization. My discussion is grounded in a theoretical understanding of locality and regionality as contested and unstable categories, constructed in a dialectical tension between local ideologies and historical and structural circumstances that influence the complex social ordering of regional and national cultures (Lomnitz-Adler 1992). I begin by describing Knoxville's peculiar culture of local pride, a mostly defensive posture that reflects feelings of inferiority and the city's ambiguous location in relation to popular regionalist paradigms, and I briefly link this back to a discussion of the benefits and drawbacks of regionalist thinking for studying the U.S. South. I then provide an outline of noteworthy events and trends in the history of Knoxville to which the indeterminate sense of place that exists today may be partly attributed, including the decline of the city's urban core and the contradiction between a prevailing ethic of "rugged individualism" and the region's longtime reliance on government-owned industries to ensure growth and sustainability. In the last section I extend these considerations into a discussion of evangelical attitudes about the validity of the so-called Bible Belt as a regional-cultural concept. The concept, as it is commonly used, underscores Christianity's hegemonic force in much of the South, but evangelicals in Knoxville question whether the institutionally fragmented, socially divisive, and (in their view) ineffectual nature of southern Christianity indeed merits such a name. It may be true that evangelicals in other contexts are similarly inclined to dismiss or diminish characterizations that treat cultural Christianization as a given fact rather than something that true believers continually strive for. Nonetheless, I want to emphasize the presence of interesting parallels between how evangelicals in Knoxville problematize the idea of a Bible Belt and how Knoxvillians overall wrestle with the slippery terms of regional identity in their hometown. The parallels are neither accidental nor arbitrary. The main differences, however, stem from the fact that evangelicals invoke revivalist ideals and aspirations in order to create the possibility of cultural transformation. For evangelical pastors and churchgoers in Knoxville, the city and surrounding region are not unlike sinners ripe for conversion. Yet much as the work of evangelism faces persistent obstacles, efforts toward revitalization—including the mobilization and bridge-building efforts of socially engaged evangelicals—face difficulties resulting from social and historical circumstances similar to those that Knoxvillians believe hinder their beloved city's progress into the brave new world of twenty-first-century urbanism.

INDETERMINACY AND DEFENSIVE PRIDE

Located in the center of East Tennessee, the Knoxville metropolitan area (a six-county statistical region) runs along both sides of the Tennessee River in a valley between the Great Smoky Mountains to the east and the Cumberland Mountains to the west. There is, however, an intriguing sense of cultural indeterminacy about Knoxville, the kind that might be expected from a city that was once described as "neurotically insecure about itself" (Neely 1995: 155). Contradictory historical trends in the city and surrounding region, including ambivalent attitudes toward outsiders and outside influences, have left many residents with an ambiguous and slightly confused sense of exactly *where* Knoxville actually is, culturally speaking. A passage from a theatrical review in a local paper reveals the extent to which Knoxvillians internalize, for better or worse, their indeterminate sense of place: "Knoxville isn't exactly Appalachian, but it isn't exactly Southern, either. Cotton doesn't grow well here. The land's too hilly, and, before the arrival of TVA [the Tennessee Valley Authority], was prone to flood. If you're not from Knoxville, you probably think the city is Southern, and if you're from Knoxville, you'll probably insist that it isn't."[1]

As the passage suggests, indeterminacy is as much a source of local pride as it is a cause for defensiveness. The need to "insist" on how Knoxville should or should not be classified is a resistance to the impositions of outsiders, a recurring theme in the region's history, and also a recognition that in some ways its indefinability is a problem that should be confronted and resolved. This recognition has plagued Knoxvillians as they have struggled for decades to revitalize the local economy, politics, and culture, without the benefit of definitive regional characteristics and consistently marketable qualities that are assumed to be necessary for revitalization to take place. The city's history is full of discord among seemingly incompatible interests competing for the loudest political voice: rural agriculturalists caught in cycles of mutual antagonism with urban commercial elites; socially progressive movements and activists fighting against a political establishment entrenched in a culture of provincialism; religious rivalries and racial tensions simmering beneath facades of southern gentility. The strains of political and cultural contention have made it difficult for consensus to emerge on issues of urban growth and sustainability. Despite the fact that locals pride themselves on their "rugged individualism"—an ethic of self-reliance and independence from governmental or corporate stewardship—some of the region's historic economic and social developments have been dictated by forces outside local control.

If Knoxvillians appear to be afflicted with a persistent inferiority complex, or what one observer has called a "defeatist self-image" (Wheeler 2005: 169), disparaging portrayals by outsiders have not helped the situation. Many Knoxville natives, young and old alike, readily recall the name of John Gunther, who famously described Knoxville as "the ugliest city I ever saw in America" in his popular travel book *Inside U.S.A.* (1947). Years later, when the city hosted the 1982 World's Fair, the *Wall Street Journal* ran a preview, ominously titled "What If You Gave a World's Fair and No One Came?" In the article, the author referred to Knoxville as "a scruffy little city on the Tennessee River," a tag that still circulates among locals in sarcastic but no less self-effacing tones. Knoxville has even been the butt of jokes on *The*

Simpsons. Taking such representations to heart, die-hard Knoxvillians nonetheless remain proud of and defend their city. In the words of Jack Neely, "we're not likely to fit anybody's schedule of theories. We're our own damn self. We and our prides and problems, our virtues and vices, are distinct from every other city in the country. Our facelessness is false. It's only a mask for our insecurity about the fact that we have so many faces" (1995: 157). For residents, the city's peculiar appeal is tied to its self-image as a perennial underdog. A local minister once wrote: "As unattractive as the inner area of Knoxville is, I prefer it to all other cities in which I have lived with an unreasonable love like that which a mother showers on her ugly duckling.... I feel possessive toward this city.... It is my city; I want to be proud of it" (Proudfoot 1990: 135). This is a common sentiment among Knoxvillians, which I came across in various iterations in casual conversations, public speeches, and comments posted to an online discussion group with more than seven hundred subscribers dedicated entirely to the topic of downtown redevelopment. Residents embrace the big town/small city dualism with gusto even as they lament the frustrations of the recent past.

Knoxvillians are justifiably proud of the city's rich cultural heritage, especially the important role it has played in the history of southern folk, country, and bluegrass music. In addition, Knoxville claims numerous literary notables among its past residents, including Alex Haley, Cormac McCarthy, and James Agee, who wrote about growing up there in his novel *A Death in the Family.* But for hometown pride, it is hard to find a more unifying symbol than the city's celebrated college football team, the University of Tennessee Volunteers. It is impossible to overstate the enthusiasm that locals feel for "the Vols" (and, to a slightly lesser extent, the accomplished "Lady Vols" basketball team). Every autumn the city is saturated in orange and white, the team colors, and every Saturday is a game day, a virtual holiday when other activities come to a complete stop and fans by the tens of thousands flock to Neyland Stadium. Whether or not they are sports fans in other respects, Knoxvillians know the names of key players, can discuss key plays from crucial games (especially from the team's 1998 championship year), and readily sing a verse or two of "Rocky Top," the university's Appalachian-themed fight song. More than once it was suggested to me, only half-jokingly, that college football is the *"real* religion" of East Tennessee.

Still, Knoxville's culture of local pride is tinged with ambivalence, an odd mixture of romanticism and shame. Residents relish the idea of living in a peculiar pocket of the Tennessee River valley, but they regret the city's provincial reputation and resent the fact that Knoxville, unlike neighboring cities such as Nashville, Chattanooga, and Atlanta, has been unable to reap many of the benefits of the New South renaissance. Of course, Knoxville is not entirely unique in terms of the ambiguities attending regional character and identity in the U.S. South, as other ethnographies have demonstrated (e.g., Eiesland 2000; Stack 1996; Stewart 1996). Southern communities have long struggled with questions of local identity and heritage, especially in metropolitan regions that have undergone periods of economic and social upheaval (Goldfield 1997; Schulman 1991), a fact that should complicate the all-too-common view of the South as a uniform and distinctive culture. Generalized descriptions of the "Solid South" as a region categorically defined by nativism, violence, and religious fervor (Reed 1972) have been part of the national narrative since the Civil War (Grantham 1994). Such stereotypes are reinforced in popular media as a way of either valorizing rural or blue-collar characteristics typically associated with white southerners or denigrating them (Hartigan 2005; Kirby 1978). The largely rural mountain region known as Appalachia has been subjected to endless unjust characterizations among urban elites, many of them resulting from outsiders' biased perceptions and the consequences of misguided federal policies and exploitative corporate practices (Batteau 1990; Lewis, Johnson, and Askins 1978; Shapiro 1977; Whisnant 1994).[2] Stereotypes about the supposed moral failings and degenerative traits of Appalachian "hillbillies" obscure the actual historical and political-economic circumstances that forced rural communities into an impoverished and defensive way of life in the first place. Popular misconceptions intensify discrepancies between imposed cultural categories and lived experience, while also perpetuating the marginalization of southern populations that may be excluded from mainstream regionalist narratives, such as racial and ethnic minorities (Beaver and Lewis 1998; Harrison 1998).

At the same time, regionalism can be useful as an analytical framework if it allows us to think about life in the South in systemic terms, as social researchers and activists have done through the years.[3] It is illuminating when it accounts for the diversity and fluidity of resident populations, interactions between structures of local and translocal governance, and the impact of commercial industries, new ones as well as those in decline (Hill 1998). Instead of thinking of regions as having fixed characteristics ingrained in distinct group behaviors, we do well to follow Claudio Lomnitz-Adler in defining a regional culture as an "internally differentiated and segmented culture produced by human interaction within a regional political economy" (1992: 22). Insofar as they figure into the construction of the nation as a diversely inhabited social space, regional cultures are produced in a dialectic tension between local ideologies and larger structural forces. The discomforting ease with which Knoxvillians deconstruct the monolithic edifices of local and regional identity—Are we southerners? Are we Appalachians? Is there really such thing as the Bible Belt?—suggests that when evaluating the significance of place in the United States it is insufficient merely to identify and delineate cultural features that distinguish one region from another. Rather, we should be asking, "to what are variations attributable, and how deep do they go?" (Spindler and Spindler 1983: 66). To that end, I turn now to a discussion of the history of Knoxville and the factors that have shaped the city and surrounding region as they are experienced and perceived by contemporary residents.

THE CITY IN THE MIDDLE

Established by Euro-American settlers in the late eighteenth century, the city of Knoxville stood out for many years as a focal point of regional commerce, but a fairly isolated one as well. Although the city's location along the Tennessee River made it a hub for economic activity, especially in periods of frontier expansion, its influence did not extend very far beyond East Tennessee due in large part to the surrounding mountain terrain. "The region and its chief city would have to live to themselves for generations, try though they might to break the natural barriers to transportation" (MacArthur 1978: 13). The local economy was initially based on rural farming, not the plantation system that was predominant elsewhere in the South. As the city's economy and political influence grew—including a brief period as the capital of Tennessee—Knoxville became a vibrant center for merchandising and manufacturing (mostly textiles) and a popular way station for traders and travelers.

In the second half of the nineteenth century, as today, the majority of residents in Knox County were staunch Republicans, particularly in mountainous rural areas. This left them at odds with much of the rest of the South, where states were politically aligned with the Democratic Party and dominated by plantation-owning aristocracies. At the start of the Civil War, the state of Tennessee voted to secede from the Union and joined the Confederacy, but Knox County residents were sharply divided on the issue. Whereas rural farming communities voted heavily against secession, having little stake in preserving the slave-based economy of the Deep South, Knoxville's urban elite voted in favor of secession in order to maintain economic and political ties with Confederate states. Once military conflict was under way, Knoxville became a strategic front in the war because it was one of the major railway hubs in the South. In 1863, after a series of skirmishes, the city was eventually captured and fortified by the Union Army, with the help of loyalists spread throughout East Tennessee. It remained under Union control until the end of the war.

Many Knoxvillians still believe that disagreement between rural agriculturalists and urban elites over the question of secession and the Civil War set in motion a cycle of antagonism that has lasted for generations. As the region became more economically developed, increased integration of rural and urban populations only served to intensify their mutual hostility and distrust. As in other areas of the postbellum South, Reconstruction brought about profound changes in social and economic life in East Tennessee. Rural white farmers and former black slaves flooded into the cities looking for new economic opportunities, sparking accelerated urbanization. In the early twentieth century, Knoxville was a fairly progressive city, with civic development and industrial growth consistent with other booming southern cities, but the steady influx of laborers from agrarian communities had distinctive cultural effects. As rural Appalachians were absorbed into the urban population, they brought Appalachian mores with them, including "their suspicion of government and authority at all levels, their rough-and-tumble democratic politics, their belief in the superfluity of education, their fundamentalist religions, [and] their hatred of those who possessed more than they did" (Wheeler 2005: 27). These entrenched attitudes clashed with the progressive ambitions of local politicians and urban planners, thereby contributing to a cultural climate characterized by ambiguity and conflict over the prospects of urban industrial growth and modernization. In time, as job security and wages became unstable, the city was plagued by labor unrest and racial tensions, including race riots fueled by white working-class support for the Ku Klux Klan.

In the tumultuous years leading up to the Great Depression, Knoxville was a city beset by problems of cultural fragmentation and political divisiveness, which limited much of the prosperity that other industrializing cities came to expect (Wheeler 2005: 55). It has been suggested that Knoxville's urban boosters were far too ambitious in promoting plans for development that exceeded the city's capacities. According to this view, the city was doomed to lag behind in the modern era because it had simply been oversold (MacArthur 1978: 49). In the 1920s, in an attempt to regain economic footing, Knoxville's city government adopted a model of municipal administration that effectively handed considerable governing power over to local business managers. The plan, similar versions of which were implemented elsewhere in the South, lasted for a relatively brief period but solidified a trend that would continue in Knoxville for decades to come: the indomitable influence of "outstanding business and professional leaders" in the political and cultural life of the city (1978: 55). Overall, the outcomes were less than stellar. In the middle of the century, the political establishment in Knoxville appeared "narrow, parochial, and visionless" and was beleaguered by strife among civic leaders and businessmen (Wheeler 2005: 83). In the atmosphere of political malaise, Knoxville's leadership generally "bowed to the fearful and dispirited voters' wishes for low taxes and limited change" (2005: 83). Economic decline, coupled with population decline, exacerbated the nagging sense of urban stagnation all the way through the postwar era.

There were, however, three developments over the course of the century that shaped the culture, economy, and regional significance of the Knoxville metropolitan area in generally more positive ways: (1) the creation of the Tennessee Valley Authority (TVA) as part of the New Deal; (2) the establishment of the Oak Ridge National Laboratory (ORNL) during World War II; and (3) the postwar expansion of the University of Tennessee (UT). These institutions played pivotal roles in creating jobs, stimulating growth in a variety of economic sectors, and modernizing the region's urban-suburban infrastructure. To this day, many of East Tennessee's key decision makers and power brokers are executives, administrators, and trustees of these institutions. The fact that all three institutions came about through public initiatives managed by federal and state governments is noteworthy, given that the whole notion of an "Appalachian mentality" (as locals call it) rests so heavily on radical populism. As suggested by the region's unofficial motto "We can do it ourselves, thank you very much," East Tennesseans tend to be suspicious of and even hostile toward state interventionism or, for that matter, any historical impositions that they feel unable to resist or control. Aside from its celebration of rugged individualism and mountaineer gumption, this attitude is informed by decades of real experiences of community disempowerment and corporate exploitation (particularly at the hands of the coal and timber industries). The arrival of TVA and ORNL and the expansion of the university were projects built on promises of regional revitalization, many of which came to fruition—but others that did not, with dire consequences.

Some discussion of each of these developments will help to highlight their contemporary relevance and consequences. TVA was formed by the federal government in 1933 as a cornerstone of Roosevelt's New Deal in response to the Great Depression. The city of Knoxville was chosen as the organization's headquarters. The initial purpose of TVA was to oversee the construction of dams along the Tennessee River that would generate electricity for towns and farming communities throughout the South. TVA soon became one of the largest employers in the region. Its importance was accentuated by the promise of major social and economic improvements, heralding a new era of industrial progress, modernization, and urban boosterism. TVA's control of floodwaters brought a flood of new residents to Knoxville, stimulating local commerce and the establishment of new cultural institutions such as the East Tennessee Historical Society and the Knoxville Symphony, but also inspiring discontent among longtime locals who harbored "a deep and abiding resentment in many quarters against the outsiders who came with TVA and against all they seemed to stand for" (MacArthur 1978: 62).

From a developmental perspective, TVA is widely seen to have fallen far short of expectations. The construction of the dams involved the displacement of thousands of people and the flooding of entire communities, leading to social and environmental hardships that tarnished the corporation's reputation, despite its technological advances. By the 1970s, TVA's fledgling social programs were compromised by the company's need to accommodate the nation's heavy energy needs at the time. Turning its focus primarily to large-scale energy production, TVA invested in strip mining and nuclear power. Negative environmental effects were felt throughout southern Appalachia, and the company's limited credibility weakened further (Whisnant 1994: 64). The effects have taken a long-term toll on Knoxville, which for these and other reasons is consistently listed among the U.S. cities with the worst air pollution. In the 1980s, corporate mismanagement and revenue loss forced TVA to implement massive layoffs, causing high unemployment and a mass exodus of people and businesses away from Knoxville's urban core. The city's previously bustling business district became a virtual ghost town. Office buildings and warehouses fell silent in the shadow of the TVA's twin office towers, visible from almost anywhere in the decimated downtown.

Similar benefits and drawbacks came about as a result of the establishment of ORNL, located in the once "secret city" of Oak Ridge about twenty-five miles outside Knoxville. At the height of World War II, scientists on the Manhattan Project were looking for a secure location to produce enriched uranium for the atomic bomb. The site had to be remote but close to water sources, highways, and electricity. The federal government purchased all the land in what is now Oak Ridge, displaced hundreds of families, and secretly built a military-scientific complex and a small residential town in which to house scientists, engineers, and technicians who worked at the plant. After the war, ORNL expanded its nuclear research and maintained its air of secrecy until the 1950s (the city of Oak Ridge was incorporated in 1959). The plant's activities gradually diversified beyond strictly military purposes, and today it is a center for biomedical and energy research. While continuing to attract scientists and skilled professionals from all over the world, ORNL has also lured new industries to the region. However, the strength and longevity of economic growth in Oak Ridge was for many years dependent on the plant and the results were often less than what many had hoped for, contributing to the region's instabilities in periods of population decline and fluctuating employment.

The postwar expansion of the University of Tennessee–Knoxville was arguably one of the more celebrated government-sponsored initiatives in East Tennessee. The flagship campus of the statewide UT system has thrived for the most part, helping to boost the city's economy and culture. Bolstered by the efforts of the state and federal governments to improve higher education, UT benefited from public and private funding for research facilities and academic initiatives, especially in the fields of science and engineering. With the student population growing to thirty thousand by the 1970s, the expansion of UT also attracted diverse scholars and researchers from around the world, many of whom had high levels of education and brought progressive attitudes that reinvigorated the intellectual and cultural life of the city. In a state with no income tax, public education in Tennessee is perpetually disadvantaged and UT has faced numerous severe budget crises. However, the presence of the university has consistently been a boon for Knoxville's long-term growth and viability, especially in the period after the 1960s when manufacturing jobs began to disappear and middle-class residents retreated ever farther into the suburbs.

Apart from these government-led programs, Knoxville has had its share of homegrown initiatives, such as hosting the 1982 World's Fair. With a vast infusion of public and private investments, the fair was an aggressive effort to attract new businesses and tourism to the region. The theme of the exposition, "Energy Turns the World," played on the confluence of energy-related industries and the rich natural landscape of East Tennessee. More than eleven million visitors and representatives from twenty-two countries participated in the World's Fair, which took place in a redeveloped rail yard close to downtown Knoxville. Despite the fair's success, reviewers from the national press were unimpressed and continued to describe the city in unflattering and condescending tones.[4] The day after the fair ended, an investigation was launched into the financial dealings of one of its chief organizers, who was eventually convicted of bank fraud and sent to prison. The scandal overshadowed people's memories of the event, as did the fact that commercial and cultural life in downtown Knoxville started to wane in its aftermath. The park constructed specifically for the fair remained lifeless for the better part of twenty years, and the abandoned site became a source of embarrassment, as well as an object of derision. In a 1996 episode of *The Simpsons,* Bart Simpson and his friends venture on an ill-advised road trip to Knoxville, eager to see the 266-foot-tall Sunsphere monument at the World's Fair Park as advertised in an outdated AAA travel guide. Reaching the park, the boys find it empty and dilapidated, and discover that the fabled Sunsphere has been converted into a retail warehouse for wigs—a cruel but effective bit of satire that spoke directly to local insecurities while playing on a stereotypical image of white southerners as purveyors of lowbrow commodities and tourist kitsch.

The World's Fair Park was renovated and reopened along with a new ninety-three-million-dollar convention center in 2002. The convention center was the centerpiece of a comprehensive but ill-fated downtown redevelopment plan named "Renaissance Knoxville," which was the subject of political wrangling and public debate for several years. The plan was ultimately undermined by a combination of factors, including political infighting between city and county officials, negative reactions to what residents felt was a lack of openness to public input, and competition over property development in the central business district. Interestingly, problems of urban self-definition figured into the mix as well. Debates about redevelopment were frequently caught up in questions about exactly how to package the city for tourist consumption, questions that highlighted the indeterminate sense of place I described earlier. Despite Knoxville's opportune location at the crossroads of two interstate highways (I-40 and I-75), the city has generally been less of a tourist destination in its own right than a stopping point for amusement parks and other attractions in the nearby towns of Gatlinburg, Sevierville, and Pigeon Forge (home of Dollywood). Even Knoxville's marketing tag as the "Gateway to the Smokies" is a reminder of the city's mostly supportive role in the regional tourism industry. Efforts to improve the city's cultural image continue to walk a fine line between, on the one hand, emphasizing progress and metropolitanism and, on the other hand, honoring the character and folk traditions of the region's Appalachian heritage.[5]

In recent years a wave of new residents, artisans, and commercial businesses has helped bring new life to downtown Knoxville, sparking a grassroots movement of "city center revitalization" (Wheeler 2005: 194) alongside conventions, music festivals, and riverfront development. Yet Knoxville remains for many residents a place of untapped potential, an enigma waiting to discover itself. Some locals blame this on the limitations of the "Appalachian mentality"; others blame the traditional business-political elite and their penchant for "risk aversion." Whatever the reasons, much of the region's demographic and economic growth has occurred not in the city limits but rather in the sprawling northern and western suburbs. Although Knoxville lagged behind other Sunbelt cities in attracting new high-tech industries, the metropolitan region experienced overall job growth of 60 percent between 1978 and 1997, outpacing population growth.[6] Much of this job growth was in the service-sector industries, notably government, consumer retail, health services, and news and entertainment media.[7] As the service sector expanded, the hot spots of business and real-estate development relocated to outlying rural communities, now peppered with busy highways, strip malls, office parks, and residential subdivisions. The swift tides of suburbanization, signified in all its inevitability with the opening of West Town Mall in 1971, coincided with the arrival of an educated, uprooted, and upwardly mobile middle class. Skilled and white-collar professionals were (and continue to be) drawn to the region for reasons that include the relatively low costs of homeownership, seasonable weather conditions, proximity to nature getaways and tourist attractions, and one of the lowest tax burdens in the country.

With the growth of the suburban population, downtown commercial and residential development stalled and Knoxville's urban core suffered considerable decline. Inner-city residents "increasingly tended to be elderly, black, and poor," as the mostly white middle class in the suburbs no longer worked and shopped downtown and retail businesses were lured "away from the city and into the malls" (Wheeler 2005: 154). The consequences were devastating for inner-city communities left to cope with poorly funded schools, substandard housing, high crime rates, and an inadequate public transportation system. With concentrations of wealth and social prestige far removed from the spaces of urban decay, the general public outside the city limits no longer had the means or incentive to remain fully informed about problems affecting the inner city. As is true elsewhere in the New South, "Poverty is not thought to exist or is not considered a problem because it is unseen by the white collar army that advances and retreats from home and workplace in hermetic safety, with many no longer needing to venture into the city at all, either for work or for shopping" (Goldfield 1997: 263). As if to drive the point home, one teenager in the suburbs of Knoxville told me that she had no memory of ever being closer to downtown than the West Town Mall (almost ten miles away by interstate), and although she knew about inner-city poverty in other cities she visited with her church youth group, she "didn't know that Knoxville even *has* an inner city."

The process of suburbanization exacerbated the problem of racial alienation in Knoxville. Although racial tensions have always been present in the region, they were never as prominent as in other parts of the South. This may be partly because the African American population is relatively small in Knox County, representing less than 9 percent of the total population in 2000. However, African Americans make up nearly 17 percent of the population within the city limits, and remain concentrated in deeply impoverished sections of East Knoxville. Since the region's socioeconomic disparities fall along lines of geography as well as race, affluent whites in the suburbs rarely have much direct or sustained contact with poor and working-class blacks, but they tend to assume nonetheless that race relations in Knoxville are basically civil and unproblematic. Such willful ignorance, as some see it, provides a convenient smokescreen, "an excuse for not doing any of the things which good race relations would seem to make mandatory" (Proudfoot 1990: 176). During the civil rights era, desegregation was slow to take root because civic and religious leaders (whites and blacks alike) were "hesitant, confused, and timid" about dealing directly with race issues that had been left unacknowledged for so long (1990: 10). In the years since, moderate progress has been made as business leaders, philanthropists, and urban boosters worked to improve the region's racial politics and make the city more attractive to prospective investors. But underlying racial disparities and structural alienation remain strong, and efforts to address them have tended to be short-lived and situation-specific (usually in response to public controversies of one kind or another).

Urban poverty relief and the need to combat racial alienation became a more central part of the regional development agenda in the 1990s, a time when suburban expansion appeared to be reaching its territorial limits. After a period in which the city government stepped up its attempts to annex revenue-generating property in the suburbs, the idea of forming a more sustainable equilibrium between the city and surrounding county became attractive to politicians and residents in both locations. In 2000, a deal was brokered between the city council and the county commission to limit the permissible urban growth boundaries for the coming decade. In exchange the county would provide financial contributions for community development initiatives within the city's federally designated Empowerment Zone. As part of the Empowerment Zone program, administered by the Department of Housing and Urban Development, the city of Knoxville received a ten-year one-hundred-million-dollar grant to improve housing and generate jobs in several inner-city neighborhoods. Suburban businesses and organizations, including evangelical churches, now recognized opportunities and incentives to participate in projects of urban renewal, including the development of mixed-income communities in place of public housing projects. A number of the socially engaged evangelicals I met were actively involved in such initiatives, and they acted on their commitments by mobilizing support for grassroots organizations and institutional partnerships and, in a handful of instances, moving with their families from the suburbs to live in the inner city.

Whatever the long-term impact of such efforts may be, they reflected the sense of optimism at the time of my fieldwork, when politicians, community organizers, and other civic and religious leaders in Knoxville felt inspired to address the city's problems comprehensively and systematically, taking into account the oft-ignored symbiotic nature of the urban-suburban divide. Different groups rallied around the prospect of devising an auspicious future for Knoxville by creating a unified vision among its diverse and dispersed populations.[8] Evangelical pastors and churchgoers at the megachurches I attended pointed to the upsurge in collaborative urban renewal projects as proof of social transformations on the horizon, and hinted at their greater spiritual significance by reasserting their faith that God was clearly up to "something" in Knoxville. Their anticipation hinged on more than just issues of development, sustainability, and civic participation. When they approached questions of regional culture they did so on the basis of religious imperatives rather than strictly social or economic concerns. They believed that only a revival of true Christian faith would produce the kind of far-reaching changes that were presupposed by urban revitalization. Yet when it came to the prospects of revivalism, evangelicals in Knoxville were as cautious as they were optimistic.

UNBUCKLING THE BIBLE BELT

The Bible Belt—a term that evokes the ubiquity and fervor of southern Christian revivalism—is hardly the uniform cultural entity it is assumed to be. Historically, Protestant revivals have flourished in the South, and the region remains a bastion of evangelical religiosity, particularly among churches in the Baptist, Wesleyan-Methodist, and Reformed traditions. However, the prevalence of evangelical Protestantism should not distract us from the fact that the history of Christianity in the South is marked by diversity and conflict among rival churches and denominations vying for dominance in public life (Heyrman 1997; Mathews 1997; Ownby 1990). In other words, from an early stage southern Christianity was a subject of cultural contestation rather than a given fact. Institutional frictions, denominational and doctrinal schisms, and sharp divisions along lines of race and class continue to be the norm rather than the exception. Yet at the same time, anyone passing through certain parts of the South can see why it came to be known as the Bible Belt. From the church steeples that pierce the sky at virtually every corner to the highway billboards and bumper stickers reminding passersby to get right with God, the landscape is saturated with Christian symbolism.

Revivalist influences have, of course, played a key role in creating the perception of the South as a unified religious culture. The extraordinary revivals of the eighteenth and nineteenth centuries, and the violent upheavals of the Civil War and Reconstruction era, gave rise to a lay orthodoxy preoccupied with repentance, sacrifice, and salvation, enduringly salient notions in the historical consciousness of much of the population (Wilson 1980). A religious revival is often understood to be a specific event, such as a special church gathering or camp meeting, characterized by high levels of religious enthusiasm. The word *revival* may also be used to describe an extended period or era during which enthusiasm and innovation occur in multiple locations, linked together by ritual expressions and conversion narratives that produce a sense of temporal and spiritual confluence. According to the historian Frank Lambert, Christian revivalism typically flourishes in contexts where there is: (1) a *culture* that "expects a periodic showering of God's grace," (2) a perceived *need* for revival, "when the state of religion is thought to have sunk to a low point," and (3) the practical *means* for ministers and laypeople "to prepare men and women for a special outpouring of divine grace" (1999: 22). The city of Knoxville shares these characteristics in spades, but I am particularly interested in the second criterion: the perception of a dire need for revival. Of the various sentiments that animated the moral ambitions of evangelical pastors and churchgoers who wanted to help bring about large-scale changes in Knoxville, one of the most palpable was the sense that a great transformation was not only possible but desperately needed, not in spite of the region's entrenched religiosity but in some ways because of it.

A college professor in Knoxville told me that trying to describe Christianity in East Tennessee was "like asking someone to describe air." Many residents would agree. Conservative Protestant morality, symbolism, and ritual (especially prayer) pervade many of the essential venues of daily life, including college campuses, restaurants, civic ceremonies, and athletic events. There are a number of well-known Christian colleges in the region, as well as institutions of higher learning that are either sectarian in origin or denominationally affiliated. The most active charities and social service organizations in Knoxville are either faith-based organizations, such as the Salvation Army, or secular agencies that rely heavily on the support of local churches. Politicians and leaders in the business community are often professing Christians, and rarely does any public event begin without someone reciting a prayer that ends with "and we pray these things in the name of our lord, Jesus Christ. Amen." Far from being smug or self-satisfied about such hegemonic displays, conservative evangelicals I spoke to in Knoxville seemed to regard them as having potential drawbacks as well. They were pleased that their civil religion was, in essence, a Christian one; but they harbored deep concerns that such religiosity was easily taken for granted. They worried, in other words, that the Bible Belt was maybe a bit too "religious" to be authentically Christian.

A staff member at Eternal Vine once said to me that one of the hazards of living in the Bible Belt was that "religion can become a cultural thing." Clearly invoking a negative connotation of "culture" as something routine and predictable, the speaker was arguing that religiosity risks becoming superficial when it is merely ascribed by tradition or performed for the sake of conformity and custom, rather than being derived from unique, spontaneous, and unmediated spiritual experiences. In a confessional tradition that stresses deep sincerity as a path to redemption, rote religion raises troubling questions. In the process of embodying the dictates of faith, evangelicals are ever cautious to avoid complacency. They are wary of false confidence, and insistent that superficial markers of religious adherence do not amount to much if, in the final analysis, Christians are simply "going through the motions." In the words of another megachurch staffer, "Here in the Bible Belt, going to church doesn't make you a Christian any more than going to McDonald's makes you a hamburger."

To substantiate their claims that Bible Belt Christianity comes dangerously close to reproducing shallow "cultural" predictability, evangelicals in Knoxville pointed to the persistence of problems such as competition and disunity among local churches, racial alienation, socioeconomic disparity, and prominent Christians succumbing to moral vices such as indifference, cynicism, or worse. They insisted that the role of Christian churches should be to inspire unity, fellowship, and moral fortitude among all those who adhere to true Christian principles, across social and denominational boundaries, and in turn to revitalize the rest of society through their example and guidance. Anything short of this, they reasoned, stifled the collectivized Body of Christ and hindered the aims of evangelism. Socially engaged evangelicals were prone to challenge the common assumption that Knoxville was already a Christianized place because they were convinced that local evangelical churches remained stubbornly ineffective when it came to addressing the social welfare needs of the urban community. Jim Elroy is an outspoken evangelical in Knoxville and an unapologetic proponent of this critical viewpoint. During my fieldwork he was the director of a homeless shelter and an active member of Marble Valley Presbyterian. In response to a question I had asked him about the religious character of the city, Jim speculated that Knoxville had a reputation for "having religious fervor but being spiritually void," especially when it comes to the influence of

Christian principles in community affairs and public policies. With a wistful laugh, he added:

> I think there certainly is a great deal of religion that goes on here, and some-times I wonder how much influence—not just in Knoxville ultimately—how much influence that really has in the decisions that are made on a day-to-day basis, and policies that are made. I think if we were more Christian, there are some things that are happening in Knoxville that wouldn't happen.... If Knoxville rose up we could do something about all of the people who are homeless and chronically mentally ill.... Let me say all this another way: *I think there would be more vision.* I think there would be more risk taking. We wouldn't struggle with the issue that we're struggling with now, as a city, of downtown redevelopment. If we were more of a faith community there would be a willingness to jump out and take some risk and stretch for the good of the whole community.

Jim Elroy's comments convey a prophetic critique that the strength of a population's adherence to Christian principles is reflected in the degree to which local communities, including churches, deal with issues of social welfare and care for the poor. In the force of his critique Jim tended to go much further than other conservative evangelicals I interviewed, to the point of advocating views that were at times remarkably progressive in their political implications. In other ways, however, his argument and sentiments would ring true and familiar to the majority of conservative churchgoers. By suggesting that "if we were more Christian" the churches and city of Knoxville would be better at handling social problems and implementing visions for a better future, Jim echoed the concerns of many evangelicals both about the lack (or marginality) of authentic religiosity in public life and the inability of local churches to properly motivate churchgoers to exercise their faith in purposeful and impacting ways. Interestingly, he also echoed common opinions among secular and nonevangelical observers who routinely criticize Knoxville's political and civic elite for lacking enough vision and courage to produce a viable strategy for developing the city's central business district.

Religious leaders in the evangelical community in Knoxville were particularly concerned about problems of Christian disunity and racial alienation, prompting a number of them to participate in collaborative projects that were designed to bring together pastors and church leaders from across various denominations and backgrounds. One of these projects was what came to be known as the Pastors' Prayer Network, a coordinated network of prayer cells organized by two unaffiliated preachers who received financial support from participating churches, including substantial funding from Eternal Vine and Marble Valley Presbyterian. The idea behind the endeavor was to have local pastors—mostly Protestant and evangelical, but not exclusively—meet on a regular basis in groups of as many as twenty to a cell, usually on weekday mornings, for approximately an hour of unstructured group prayer. The rationale, as expressed by one of the active participants, was that "unity in prayer releases spiritual power," and that collective prayer would help pastors who cared about bringing the Kingdom of God to Knoxville fight off feelings of spiritual "impotency." Pastors that were involved used these sessions as opportunities to share news from their congregations, express their admiration for one another, confess personal failings, and occasionally air personal grievances. Once or twice a year the different prayer cells came together for a full-fledged "regional prayer summit," a carefully moderated retreat for several days during which pastors prayed together on designated themes and topics. The summits promoted an image of regional fellowship, what one participant described as "Christians coming together like puzzle pieces." A chief organizer explained to me that the summits offer one of the best possible visualizations of what he and others boldly described as "the Church of Knoxville."

Prayer networks and summits are part of a long-standing tradition in North American evangelicalism, in which the deliberative and performative aspects of public prayer serve both to reinforce religious discipline and to create feelings of Christian unity across social boundaries. They help to strengthen bonds of affinity and bridge cultural gaps while also contributing to greater strategic efforts by evangelical groups and institutions to establish what Charles Hirschkind (2006) has called a religious "counterpublic," a space of moral action conceived in contrast to the dominant ethical modalities of secular society. These efforts carry tremendous weight and appeal in this postdenominational era, as a growing number of churches and denominations have come to realize with unprecedented clarity that they stand to gain more by reaching out across traditional lines than by keeping historical and institutional barriers rigidly intact. In Knoxville, citywide prayer networks were understood to provide viable contexts for communication among churches and communities that previously were unable or unwilling to have much to do with one another, let alone imagine themselves as constituting a "city church" broadly conceived. Accordingly, their prayer sessions often focused on issues such as the tensions that prevented churches from cooperating with one another both historically and in the present, the problem of spiritual complacency that many felt had taken hold of the entire region, and the foreseeable prospects for regional revitalization in relation to the very fellowship they sought to create through prayer.

For all the credibility and momentum that the Pastors' Prayer Network had gained, it faced challenges as well, many of which stemmed from lingering disagreements and tensions among church leaders. Pastors diverged on issues of ritual style, some preferring a solemn, contemplative form of spoken prayer while others, including pastors from charismatic and Pentecostal churches, tended to pray more exuberantly, speak in tongues, and emphasize demonological notions of "spiritual warfare." Doctrinal disagreements surfaced periodically in debates about the workings of the Holy Spirit, the nature of the Trinity, and biblical inerrancy. Debates arose whenever someone questioned the participation of another member who was seen as representing an unorthodox or heretical tradition, which raised the question of whether it was possible (or desirable) to accommodate diverse perspectives and still maintain essential unity. Friction between white pastors and black pastors became evident at times, especially in situations when issues of racial and social justice were raised, as black pastors asserted liberal views that did not always sit well with conservative white evangelicals. Last but not least, a few pastors from small or underresourced congregations worried that their participation in the "big tent" of the prayer network meant that they were acquiescing to the influence of prominent megachurch pastors who supported the movement and were seen to have an interest in determining its course, such as Eternal Vine's Pastor Tim, who for a period was one of the network's more public figures. Such perceptions fueled resentment and competitive instincts that were stoked by the fact that churches were losing members to the megachurches and facing a decline in their institutional stature.

The problems that came up in the prayer network in Knoxville existed because of doctrinal differences and lasting antipathies among divergent church communities, but for evangelical participants those factors were epiphenomenal to what they considered to be the underlying spiritual dimensions. The persistence of disunity among Christians in Knoxville confirmed their fear that Christianity in the Bible Belt is "a mile wide and an inch thick," as one preacher put it, meaning that it is culturally ubiquitous but spiritually shallow. Their concerns fed on an enduring revivalist rhetoric fixated on the conditions that breed division and indifference, and the human failings that prevent people from seeing how seriously in need of revival they really are, even in a region so closely identified with revivalism in the first place.

I observed strong expressions of this revivalist rhetoric after the September 11 terrorist attacks. Within a few days of the attacks, as happened throughout the United States, a massive prayer gathering was organized at the Civic Coliseum and broadcast live on local television. The "Prayer for America" event featured twelve area pastors; ten of them were white, two were black, and all of them were Protestant. In a predetermined order, the pastors took turns performing evocative and rousing prayers on behalf of the families of victims, police and firefighters in New York City, the president, the military, and so forth (a prayer was even offered on behalf of the suicide bombers themselves). The final prayer, led by an energetic black preacher from an AME Zion church in the inner city, focused on the theme of "spiritual renewal." Falling to his knees, the preacher instructed the audience of roughly five thousand people to hold one another's hands. Then, in tones of unhinged desperation, he prayed aloud for a spirit of revival to take hold of "our hearts, homes, and churches" and spread out to the entire country. He called on the city to come together in unity and faith, drawing implicit links between the spiritual vitality of Knoxville and the prospects of revival elsewhere, as though the tragedy of September 11 were an opportunity for local pastors and churchgoers to take stock of their religious commitments not only for themselves but for the sake of the nation. A couple of weeks later, Knoxville's annual March for Jesus concluded with a prayer rally near UT's Neyland Stadium. A Baptist preacher took the microphone and offered similar appeals, making even more explicit references to what he and others portrayed as the all-too-casual superficiality of Christianity in Knoxville: "It's not the world that needs change today, it's the church! We're called to be the light to the world but we hide that light under a bushel! [Addressing God:] You tell us to pray, but we don't! *We scream and yell and get excited at football games, but we become as stiff as wood when we go to church!*" Like most exhortations of this kind, however, the prayer ended on a hopeful note as the preacher took it upon himself to announce the city's contrition before God, a crucial performative step in the process of regeneration.

Such rhetoric is hardly novel or unique to evangelicalism in Knoxville, but its inflections in this context correspond interestingly with the general tendency among Knoxvillians to give expression to the problems and ambiguities that define—or make indefinable—the place where they live. Although revivalist themes that dwell on the interplay between religious self-condemnation and anticipation are substantively different from the indeterminate sense of place and defensive culture of local pride described earlier, I would argue that the manner of their coexistence in Knoxville is not entirely coincidental. As the region's evangelical churches, including megachurches in the suburbs, take an interest in issues of urban development and community affairs, they bring to the civic table their own models of revitalization while reinforcing elements of a geographically situated historical consciousness in which paradox and ambivalence feature prominently.

Many of the evangelical pastors and churchgoers I observed were actively trying to carve out a place for engaged orthodoxy in the realm of urban revitalization, and for some this meant partaking in the cultural work of fashioning a coherent sense of place, or at least the sense of a place's immanent potential, out of a more complex and inchoate set of experiences and characteristics. Their moral ambitions, in other words, were not detached from considerations of locality and regionality. Much as they participated in a collective effort to destabilize the notion of a Bible Belt, not for the purpose of discarding it but for bringing it to actual fruition, they made moves to confront issues of social disunity, indifference, and alienation that they feared prevented Knoxville from becoming the place God intended. They were eager to inspire hope in the possibility that places—like people—are not foregone conclusions but conversion narratives in the making. They exposed the limitations of their cultural environment in order to create the context for surpassing those limitations, just as they dedicated themselves and tried to encourage others to overcome the limitations that prevented suburban middle-class Christians from fully enacting religious virtues in their own lives.

CHAPTER 4

The Names of Action

The socially engaged evangelicals described in this book are not social
or political activists in any conventional sense. They do not adhere to
a particular social movement or activist identity; they do not organize
rallies, protests, or other forms of direct action meant to sway public
opinion or impress and intimidate public figures. At least these were
not primary concerns of those I knew, who may participate in mass
actions organized under the auspices of the Christian Right but invest
their personal commitments otherwise. The efforts I observed were
mainly concerned with promoting organized benevolence on a relatively
modest scale, figuring out what it takes to raise conservative evangelical
churches to a higher level of social engagement, and creating new opportunities for community evangelism. Nevertheless, I believe that these
efforts are demonstrative of an activist orientation. They are explicit in
their ideological content, call attention to altruistic deeds conceived as
vehicles of social and spiritual renewal, and respond, however implicitly,
to regnant political concerns and civic trends. Conservative yet socially
engaged evangelicals may not "take it to the streets" or "speak truth to
power" in the same ways that other activists do, but if we view them
on their own terms we must recognize that their actions are performed
with similar intentions and, as they see it, potentially more radical
consequences.

Writing about new forms of cultural activism among indigenous
peoples, Faye Ginsburg argues that "focusing on people who engage

themselves with new possibilities for their own collective self-production allows us to ask more general questions about the political possibilities inherent in self-conscious shifts in cultural practice" (1997: 122). Such questions address issues of human agency in relation to structural constraints and opportunities, and they uncover a lot about the expressive and moral norms that social actors bring to bear in the process of enacting new modes of public engagement. Self-conscious shifts in practice are conducive to what Ginsburg calls "transformative action" (1997: 122), which is to say they create templates for action that allow people—as individuals and as members of cultural groups—to embody technologies, talents, and virtues that increase their real and imagined capacity to effect personal and social change.

Ginsburg's analysis of transformative action among indigenous groups can be extended to other populations as well, including groups that already benefit from privileged access to cultural capital. Whether transformative actions are undertaken from positions of power or subaltern struggle, or in the name of religious or secular causes, they should not be measured solely with respect to what they may or may not achieve politically (Coutin 1993). They should be recognized also for the degree to which they reflect specific values and practices in a cultural community, promote those values and practices in areas of public life where they were previously excluded or restrained, and make it possible for community members to renew their investments in collective identity while revising key elements according to changing needs and aspirations. Evangelical attempts to capitalize on the currency of "faith-based initiatives" and the resources of suburban megachurches exemplify these characteristics in that they are driven by a desire to Christianize the welfare sphere through missionary intervention, as well as a desire to revitalize and even reform evangelicalism from within.

Socially engaged evangelicals have always tended to accentuate the transformative dimensions of their ministries, not only in terms of personal or social redemption in an abstract sense but also with regard to the paradigm-shifting influence of apostolic or missionary activity in the lives of people like themselves. From the reform movements of the antebellum era to the Social Gospel, prominent revivalists and reformers often invoked narratives of post-conversion "rebirth" to explain their uncommon commitment to social action and moral protest (Abzug 1994; Curtis 2001; Young 2006). This notion of a "second conversion"—a common trope among Christian missionaries, evangelists, and activists—is based on the idea that one's faith, established at the moment of initial conversion, will be bolstered or regenerated when an individual is compelled, through a combination of circumstance, will, and spiritual guidance, to embrace righteous social and religious causes. My informants rarely described their decision to become socially engaged as a second conversion (at least not explicitly), but they implicitly drew on this idea when they explained that it was an expression of their maturing faith rather than something that happened immediately upon being born again. Typically, it was sometime *after* they became professing Christians that they were convinced of the theological imperative to serve the poor and needy, and decided to convince others to do likewise. Although not conversion testimonies, their reflections on the revelation process were often testimonial in tone, especially insofar as they would claim to have found the true meaning of God's grace only when they stopped focusing on themselves and learned to adopt a compassionate disposition toward others. Realizing the need to mobilize their fellow churchgoers was akin to a "calling" in the vocational sense. As a by-product of the second conversion, the work of outreach mobilization is not unlike the work of a preacher who calls on sinners to repent, or a pastor who steers his congregational flock away from apathy, not only by instruction but by using his own spiritual journey as a point of comparison.

In this chapter I offer ethnographic profiles of four individuals who personify the activist orientation of evangelical social engagement, and embody the virtues, struggles, and moral ambitions that go along with it. The profiles are not based on interview data alone, nor are they the product of life histories articulated by the subjects themselves. They are narratives of my own construction, based on the sum total of my extensive observations and interactions with these individuals in a variety of contexts, including homes, churches, and sites of ministry activity. I have chosen to categorize the profiles thematically according to four biblical archetypes: the Apostle, the Teacher, the Prophet, and the Missionary. I use this literary device to convey the models of idealized Christian personhood that the individuals in question evoked in my imagination and, in some cases, among their admiring peers. I do not mean to suggest that the individuals would necessarily boast of such designations for themselves (it is, after all, unseemly for a polite churchgoing Tennessean to boast of any such thing), but these archetypes are relevant for understanding the kinds of cultural roles that active figures play or are perceived as playing in evangelical communities. In this sense, these profiles are truly ethnographic in that they reveal culturally significant group dynamics as much as they portray the characteristics of specific individuals.

My appropriation of Christian categories of personification is meant as a reminder that the terms of evangelical subjectivity are defined by biblical archetypes and stories, that being evangelical means locating oneself "on a narrative landscape which simultaneously speaks biblical and contemporaneous dialects" (Harding 2000: 186). The names of action that populate this narrative landscape are signifiers—signposts, as it were—indexing distinct modalities of comportment and intentionality, and representing what are understood as unique and indispensable gifts possessed by every believer, which are destined to be put to the service of God's kingdom. In conservative evangelical churches and communities, where active social engagement is rarely a preferred norm, the relative paucity of immediate role models to guide socially engaged evangelicals in their pursuits makes every intimation of a biblical archetype that much more pertinent and necessary.

THE APOSTLE: PAUL GENERO

For Paul Genero, the path to becoming one of Knoxville's prominent outreach mobilizers was marked by a series of epiphanies, a process of learning to recognize signs from God indicating what he was meant to do and where. Paul was born in the Midwest and raised by a single mother in what he described as a "blue-collar" community. He often cited his working-class background as having a strong impact on his character as a Christian, including his commitment to "hands-on" types of ministry, and his concern to help suburban churchgoers get more involved in the lives of people in poor and working-class communities. "I've always had a heart for the underdog," he once said to me.

Paul first moved to Tennessee to attend college, where his primary interests were chemistry and basketball. As a student he got involved in a Christian ministry on campus, and it was there that he met his future wife, Melanie. Shortly after college he enrolled in an evangelical seminary, where he received theological and pastoral training and was eventually ordained. During his time at seminary he took classes on urban ministry and global church planting, classes that raised his awareness of social problems around the world and fed his desire to become a missionary abroad. He was particularly moved by missionary reports about the devastating conditions of urban slums of Southeast

Asia, where he hoped to someday bring his family and serve as a full-time missionary himself. Except for a few short-term mission trips, however, his plan never came to fruition. Nonetheless, Paul's experiences on those trips and at seminary intensified his passion to serve the physical and spiritual needs of suffering people, a passion that would define the course of his professional life.

Paul and Melanie eventually moved to Knoxville and joined Eternal Vine Church, where they were active members for several years. When Eternal Vine planted a satellite church in a nearby suburb in the late 1990s, they joined a critical mass of young families who built the new church from the ground up with support from the megachurch. Paul became a staff pastor at the congregation, and it was in this capacity that he started to become aware of the low priority given to social outreach ministries in middle-class suburban churches. It was also at this time that Paul felt God placing a "burden" in his heart for the city of Knoxville. Acting on the same impulses that once sent him overseas, Paul decided to become better informed about the city and its social environment, especially the conditions of poverty and decay that plagued the inner city only a few miles from his West Knoxville home. Eager to raise a similar awareness among churchgoers, he launched a research project to collect data and information about social problems and the state of existing social services in the greater Knoxville area. The results of his research, conducted with help from church volunteers, faith-based organizations, and private donors, were published and disseminated among several local churches. Paul hoped that once churches and churchgoers gained a comprehensive perspective, they would become more enthusiastic about ministering to people in need, assisting local welfare agencies and charity organizations, and addressing the root causes of social problems in Knoxville.

Paul Genero founded the Samaritans of Knoxville as a coalition of pastors, ministry professionals, and laypeople committed to outreach mobilization, training, and collaboration. Modeled on faith-based organizations in other cities, the Samaritans of Knoxville was meant to serve an intermediary role in the Christian community, facilitating networks of cooperation among affluent churches, social service agencies, and underprivileged populations. The largely volunteer-driven organization was also meant to stimulate social concern among white suburban evangelical churches with resources that could be channeled into the charitable nonprofit sector, where vital resources were typically scant. "The screaming need," he said at an organizational planning meeting, "is for those of us involved in outreach ministry to go back and *infect* our congregations with our passion and expertise."

Within a few years of its founding, the Samaritans of Knoxville claimed an unofficial membership composed of representatives from at least 120 local churches and more than a dozen separate Christian (mainly Protestant) denominations. During the initial stages of mobilization, however, the effort relied on a core group of a few dozen friends and supporters, including pastors, church staff, and faith-based social workers, a number of whom were affiliated with Eternal Vine and Marble Valley Presbyterian. Several participants were laypeople— slightly more women than men—who were frustrated and galvanized by the lack of overall commitment to social outreach in their respective churches. With his charisma and infectious enthusiasm, Paul was well suited to mobilize the loosely united group around an organizational mission. He did so in part by routinely extolling the virtues of "active compassion," a notion that carried added symbolic weight at a time when the political rhetoric of "compassionate conservatism" held the national spotlight. Paul resigned from his role as a church pastor and began planning training workshops and volunteer-based outreach events, and working to create partnerships with community organizers and agencies throughout the nonprofit sector. Although some participants were not always comfortable with Paul's leadership style or his insistence on strategic planning at every level, he was recognized as a principal figure in a local movement of evangelicals seeking to achieve what he once described as a "radical paradigm shift" in the religious and civic culture of the city, and especially the suburbs.

In the inaugural stage of the organization, Paul planned a series of special events for evangelical volunteers to get better acquainted with the idea of social outreach. Borrowing the language of Steve Sjogren, a Cincinnati-based evangelical pastor and author, Paul described the events as "low risk/high grace" opportunities for church groups to get in the habit of "servant evangelism."[1] The first such event I attended took place on a frigid evening one late December. Paul gathered a crowd of volunteers at an apartment complex in a remote neighborhood in North Knoxville that many of them had never seen or heard of. They were gathered for the purpose of singing Christmas carols and delivering fruit baskets to the dozens of foreign refugees who lived there, especially families with young children. The families represented a small segment of the more than two thousand foreign refugees, including Iraqi Kurds, Bosnians, Vietnamese, and Sudanese, who had arrived in

East Tennessee during the previous decade. Most of those who came to Knox County were settled in this apartment complex by state agencies, effectively ghettoized and unable to communicate with English-speaking neighbors, let alone one another.

Two local organizations responsible for assisting refugees at the time—one public, the other an ecumenical nonprofit—actively encouraged churches to sponsor refugee families, usually with little success. Refugee sponsorships are considered essential for the welfare and assimilation of refugees, many of whom find it difficult to achieve self-sufficiency and develop viable social networks. As one social worker explained, "there is no choice but to get the churches involved," given the weak financial support that refugee services receive from the state. However, few area congregations were willing to make strong commitments, and those that did often ran into administrative problems or, in some cases, issues stemming from an unwillingness to follow the refugee agencies' guidelines for how refugees should be treated. Knoxville's conservative evangelical churches were open to refugee sponsorships in theory, but according to representatives from refugee agencies to whom I spoke there was a lot of ambivalence from this constituency. Some churches were reluctant to sponsor certain kinds of refugees, especially those who came from African and Muslim countries (other churches, it should be noted, were eager to sponsor these groups). More often, pastors and churchgoers who had reservations about working with refugees cited past negative experiences related either to the difficulty of convincing refugees to adapt to new cultural norms, or the frustration of being told by social workers that they could not proselytize under any circumstances. Although there were a number of celebrated success stories, partnerships between conservative evangelical churches and local refugee agencies were generally strained and less rewarding than members of both parties would have liked.[2]

Paul decided to make refugee sponsorships one of the issues around which to mobilize volunteers and generate interest in the Samaritans of Knoxville. He reached out to local churches as well as representatives of refugee agencies, to whom he gave assurances that his organization was all about sharing God's love, but not through aggressive proselytization. The night of Christmas caroling was intended as a "coming out" of sorts, a chance to put evangelical refugee ministry on public display, at least in the limited space of the apartment complex. When I arrived at the location I was alone at first, standing in a cold, dark parking lot and wondering if I had come to the right place. Within minutes my fears were allayed with the arrival of a caravan: two cars, two vans (one of which belonged to Eternal Vine), and a pickup truck filled with crates and baskets of fruit. There were roughly twenty-five volunteers, including ten enthusiastic children and a man dressed as Santa Claus (driving the pickup). After unloading the fruit, the group huddled in a circle as Paul's co-organizer, Sally Travis, handed out song sheets and candles in Styrofoam cups. Sally was a member of Paul's church who had ministered to refugees on her own for a few years. She personally knew most of the refugee families in the apartment complex and volunteered to help them manage their finances, medical needs, and employment issues. She explained to the gathered crowd that most of the families were open and friendly and had been informed ahead of time about the caroling. She introduced a representative of the public refugee agency in town who was in charge of refugee resettlement. The representative accompanied us through the buildings, sang along with the carols, and repeatedly expressed her appreciation to Paul and Sally for their efforts.

Over the next two hours, the band of brightly dressed carolers went from household to household, assembling in narrow hallways and stairwells outside each apartment as Santa Claus greeted refugee families at their doors. Baskets of fruit were distributed, children were given toys, and pictures were taken with Santa. One person, usually Paul or Sally, took each family aside to ask if they had any pressing concerns or problems that needed attention. They were then brought out before the entire group and introduced by name. Those who spoke English were invited to say a few words if they wished, which only a handful did. Some talked about hardships they endured and the pain of being displaced from their homeland, but mainly they expressed gratitude. For each household, the group then sang two or three Christmas carols as the families—most but not all of whom were Christian—smiled and listened politely, albeit awkwardly. Some of the families asked volunteers to pray for them; others granted permission to volunteers who asked if they could pray for them. The carolers prayed aloud on the spot for each family before moving on to a different household. They did not, however, pray aloud in front of refugees who were known to be Muslim, so as to avoid offending them.

At one point Paul introduced a Sudanese family and took the opportunity to make a short speech about the value and personal benefits of refugee sponsorship. "My wife and I have adopted this family right here," he announced, "and it has changed our lives. We love them like they are our own, and they love our children and love us. We've received far more than we ever have given them." He described the apartment complex as "the most fascinating geographical spot in the whole city, because you've got more diversity here than any other concentrated spot." He concluded with a direct plea: "If you want to further your experience with refugees, please contact us after the holidays, because we want to get you more involved in refugee ministry. It will change your life."

As the event drew to a close, the carolers reconvened in the parking lot and gathered in a circle. Paul invited a male member of the group to lead them in a final prayer. "Father, it's a wonderful thing to honor you by singing the story of your incarnation.... And we would ask blessings upon these families that have recently become part of our country and have joined our community. And we ask, Father, that they would learn to know you more fully and walk with you." At the end of the prayer, Paul, perhaps sensing a missed opportunity and eager to make up for it, jumped in to offer additional words (still in the idiom of prayer) emphasizing the value of refugee ministry as an act of Christian devotion: "Let me pray one more thing. Lord, would you show us how to serve better here? We want to get better at being servants. How do we love refugees? Show us all practical ways, help us to free up time, to *give away* time, to give away our love more, to become active in lives around us like this. Please, Lord, life by life by life, show us how to embrace people. Thank you, Lord."

By emphasizing the personal, one-on-one (or "life by life") nature of this form of social outreach, Paul signaled that the Samaritans of Knoxville was committed to traditional conservative evangelical notions of social ministry. His comments also hinted at an active agenda to inspire individuals to make willing sacrifices of their time—to "give away" what middle-class suburbanites cherish most—and to convince the church community as a whole to accept the importance of ministering to refugees all year round, not just during the holidays. Yet despite such appeals, one of the biggest challenges he faced in the early stages of mobilization was simply getting enough people consistently involved.

I experienced this firsthand one weekend when Paul invited me to join him and other volunteers as they renovated a dilapidated shelter housing victims of domestic violence in East Knoxville. Aside from offering a kind gesture to the shelter's staff and clients (mostly battered wives and women with small children), Paul hoped to bring church volunteers into direct contact with people at the shelter so that strong interpersonal bonds could develop and evolve into ongoing relationships. On a date prior to the renovations, Paul organized an informal get-together at the shelter for families from his church to socialize with women and children staying there. The group of churchgoers was small in number, and they were nervous beforehand. They expected to be intimidated in the presence of bitter and wounded women consumed by hatred for men, but as Paul later recalled, the affair was lighthearted and rewarding for everybody involved, which was precisely what he was aiming for. "We did crazy things at the battered women shelter. We got all the battered women playing charades and stuff, and we were just cracking up with them. It's all about just getting our people out in hurting places across the city so they can see that these are normal people. They're just normal people that need a *friend,* you know, and you need them too."

Hoping to build on the momentum, Paul organized a full-scale interior renovation of the shelter's three-story building. He called on volunteers he knew from different churches who donated time and materials over the course of five weekends, after which he wanted the shelter to "look like a bed and breakfast." As he explained, "We repainted every room, and then each group redid the furniture, tore out old quilts and put in new quilts, new shades. We painted the walls whatever color the staff wanted, put up new pictures, new light fixtures, and just totally redid it.... Our people really got into that, it was a physical thing they could do." The work was not fully completed, however, and the weekend I was invited to join was supposed to be the time that everything got finished. Paul sensed that the excitement was dying down but he was eager to see the job through and hoped that enough people would show up to finish it in two days. It rained continuously that weekend and only a small handful of volunteers showed up. As I walked into the shelter and noticed the conditions of the rooms that still needed work—including two offices in total disarray and a foyer that had not been cleaned in years—I wondered if we would actually get it done. Other than Paul and me, only one other volunteer came on the first day (luckily for us, she was highly skilled in advanced home repair), and then four other volunteers on the second day—a young couple and two older men. Before getting to work each day, Paul gathered everyone together and prayed aloud, asking God to bless our work and bless the shelter, concluding each prayer with: "And we do it in the name of your son, Jesus."

It was a long, grueling weekend of sweeping, scraping, and painting, and no one worked harder or more energetically than Paul. He was determined to leave the shelter in a state of marked improvement, in both appearance and functionality. In addition to cleaning and painting and adding new decorative wallpaper, we were tasked with reorganizing office spaces to make life easier for the shelter's overburdened staff. Paul consulted with staff members as we worked, asking them where furniture should be placed or which paint colors they preferred. He reminded church volunteers repeatedly not to develop a false sense of ownership of the project. He wanted everyone, including the staff, to understand that they were there to serve the needs of the shelter and its clients. When one of the staff members complimented Paul by saying, "Your walls look great," he was quick to remind her that the walls were hers in fact.

Late on the first day, I was crouched under a dusty wooden desk, clumsily applying primer to the molding of a wall. Paul peered down at me, laughing, and said: "You probably didn't expect to be doing this much work!" I knew what he was thinking. Neither he nor I had expected there to be so few volunteers. Yet Paul made a concerted effort to keep spirits high while we worked, and to appear undaunted by the low volunteer turnout. He played upbeat Christian pop CDs from a boom box and joked around with the staff. We talked about our lives and backgrounds, and compared stories from our college years. Paul seemed particularly surprised, and somewhat bemused, to learn that I had attended a liberal arts college with co-ed bathrooms. The hours passed and by the end of the second day, to my amazement, the rooms we had worked on were fully painted and looked almost new.

None of us had much direct interaction with the women or children staying at the shelter, mainly because the area where we worked was separate from the lodging area. Occasionally residents walked by and quietly smiled, and I wondered what they made of our presence. At one point, while I swept the front porch, a police car arrived, delivering a young mother with two small children, accompanied by a social worker who admitted them to the shelter. As I stood with my broom and imagined the ordeal they must have endured, I felt irrelevant and inconsequential in light of their pain. I thought of how the horrors of domestic violence are too real to be easily glossed over with a coat of paint. At the same time, I felt a deep sympathy for the new arrivals and a sense of personal satisfaction at having done something, however minor, for their benefit. I realized that I was experiencing just the kind of moment that Paul hoped his volunteers would experience. Though it was a fleeting instant, it is a vivid memory I have kept from that weekend.

There were awkward moments as well, as Paul occasionally allowed his frustrations to break through his cheerful demeanor. For example, I could see that he was bothered by the clutter and disorganization of the shelter's administrative offices. On the second day he noticed a full-length mirror leaning precariously in the corner of an office where it seemed to have little use but to take up space. He picked it up and asked a staff member, "Do people really need to look at themselves in a mirror while they are working?" She replied that it was always there and should probably stay. With an incredulous shrug of his shoulders, Paul acquiesced and put the mirror back on the floor. Later when he and I were working alone in another room he vented some of his frustration over the state of affairs at the shelter, though he was careful to avoid blaming the staff directly because he knew they simply lacked resources. In such moments, his desire to be generous and nonjudgmental conflicted with his ideas of efficiency and professionalism, ideas that he wanted to impart to others. Like other socially engaged evangelicals, Paul remained constantly aware of the risk of offending or alienating the people he needed to work with in order accomplish his aims, and so he tried to avoid being overly assertive or dogmatic in such situations, though he was rarely able to suppress his instincts completely.

By Sunday evening the other volunteers had gone and, with a couple of hours left to work, Paul decided that he and I should go to the large storage space behind the shelter where various donated items were piled in precarious heaps. As we sorted through boxes of used clothing, furniture, and toys, Paul spoke frankly about the difficulties of outreach mobilization. Despite drawing a fair number of evangelical churchgoers to outreach events and workshops, he felt that as of yet he had "failed" to achieve his goal of facilitating programs that result in "life-on-life relationships" between churchgoers and people in need. Ideally, he explained, activities like this were meant to foster interconnectivity. He wanted volunteers to really get to know victims of domestic violence, for example, on a deeper and more personal level, perhaps even to the point of becoming positive influences in their lives and inviting them to church. Earlier in the fall, he had offered a thirteen-week course at his church that "explored different subjects relating to compassion ministry that we felt were weaknesses we needed to work on." He urged those who took the course to speak out and encourage others to get involved as well, but the results fell short of his expectations. As he often did, Paul attributed the lackluster interest of suburban churchgoers to an insufficient emphasis on social outreach in the evangelical community as a whole. He also acknowledged that on a pragmatic level there was the additional problem that suburban churchgoers were simply unable to find time for outreach in their busy schedules. Yet the need to redefine the basic priorities of evangelical pastors and churchgoers was precisely the problem that shaped Paul's moral ambitions and became the target of his apostolic verve.

As we finished up in the storage space, Paul received two calls on his cell phone that caught my attention. The first was from a volunteer letting him know that she would no longer be participating in social outreach ministries. From overhearing Paul's end of the conversation I got the impression that she felt exhausted and overworked and needed to take time off from volunteering. Paul's response was sympathetic, to a point. He reassured her that he understood her personal needs but also expressed his disappointment, especially at the fact that she had simply announced her withdrawal rather than discussing the matter with him before making a decision. He encouraged her to get involved again when she felt ready but emphasized that she should come prepared with a clearer sense of the contribution and commitment she was ready to make. Paul was emotionally drained after the long phone conversation. He sat on the edge of a wooden crate and talked to me about the challenge of setting high standards for volunteer participation without making people feel guilty in the process. From a theological standpoint, a guilty conscience is the worst reason for an evangelical to get involved in social outreach. Evangelicals believe that one's motives should be based in faith and inspired by pure, unmitigated compassion stemming from faith. However, guilt inevitably figures into the rhetoric of moral suasion that mobilizers like Paul deploy as they try to recruit outreach volunteers, a reality that Paul ruefully acknowledged.

The second phone call was from Stacy Miggs, a member of Eternal Vine and one of the active laypeople associated with the Samaritans of Knoxville. It was immediately apparent from Paul's tone that she was upset. He offered moral support as she vented her anger about what she perceived as the megachurch's reluctance to take seriously the outreach initiatives for which she and others had been asking support. He reminded her of the importance of what she was doing and encouraged her to persevere. When the conversation was over, Paul became unusually quiet and pensive, stunned by the realization that even his most dedicated collaborators were struggling to maintain their enthusiasm in the face of obstacles. We discussed the matter no further, and turned our attention to a cluster of boxes and garbage bags full of old toys, rusty appliances, and shards of broken glass that needed to be thrown away. The rain outside started to fall heavily. Suddenly, an eager smile returned to Paul's face, as he seemed to regain his sense of purpose. "How about we load all this trash in the pickup and haul it out to the dumpsters!"

THE TEACHER: STACY MIGGS

I first met Stacy Miggs in the reception hall of Eternal Vine. She was advertising the annual Angel Tree program, in which churchgoers donate Christmas gifts for underprivileged children in and around Knoxville. This was one of many outreach projects that she was involved in at Eternal Vine, and because it coincided with the holiday season it was among the more successful. But for Stacy this was only the tip of the iceberg. What she really wanted was for the megachurch to adopt a wide array of social outreach ministries that would bring congregants into direct, sustained contact with people in need. Stacy had a generally cheerful, unobtrusive, and at times reticent way about her, but she exhibited great seriousness and resolve when it came to the things she cared about as a Christian. High on that list was her desire to convince the members of her church—teach them, if necessary—that helping the poor and distressed should be a top priority for those who wish to follow the will of God.

A Knoxville native and a lifelong churchgoer, Stacy was raised by an uneducated working-class father and a "stay-at-home mother." Like Paul Genero, she described her upbringing as "blue-collar." After graduating from the University of Tennessee with a degree in business, she married a physician and had a career marketing educational software. After the birth of her second child, she decided to give up her business and become a homeschooler so that she could devote more time to her children. The decision was a difficult one, but she believed it was necessary for the benefit of her family. "Financially it was a sacrifice," she explained to me, "but I think when you make a decision to have children you have to commit your life to their upbringing. I want to be the one deciding what goes into my children.... Family life has broken down a lot in this country, and I'm just not gonna go there. If your children are gonna have a strong connection with you and the values that you want to impart on them—biblically, morally, ethically—then you have to spend time with them."

Stacy lived in an affluent suburban neighborhood with her husband and four children. Several households in their neighborhood were also families from Eternal Vine, which Stacy admitted was no mere coincidence. Some of her neighbors became members because of her influence; others moved into the neighborhood because they were part of her social network at church. Stacy and her husband first joined Eternal Vine after several years of trying different churches, most of which she described as "too legalistic" and "spiritually dead." The Miggses were eventually drawn to Eternal Vine because they felt it was a place where people were willing to try new things and "think outside the box" while upholding moral and biblical standards. The only thing that disturbed Stacy about the megachurch was the number of dual-income families. She explained to me that too many Christian women fall victim to the strain of balancing family responsibilities and professional ambitions: "I see women in this church dying—spiritually, physically, emotionally—because they are taking care of their family and are also in the workforce. It's too much, too much for someone to do. I don't think women are trained anymore that you can do the home thing and it be held up as an esteemed thing."

Stacy's worldview and lifestyle affirm a conservative gender ideology that primarily assigns women roles as wives, mothers, and domestic caregivers, removed from the masculinized public sphere. Nonetheless, her dedicated work as an outreach volunteer and coordinator allowed her to carve out an alternative space of religious and civic engagement well beyond the confines of the private sphere. Withdrawing from the professional workforce never meant for Stacy a complete withdrawal from activities that required time and personal investment away from home. On the contrary, her decision to do "the home thing" presupposed, perhaps paradoxically, that she would remain heavily involved (indeed, become even more so) in the social enterprise of organized benevolence. She managed this balance by incorporating social outreach into the homeschool curriculum she developed for her children. Between math, history, and art lessons, Stacy and the kids volunteered at local charities and visited the sick and elderly.

Stacy knew from an early age that she had what evangelicals call the "gift of mercy." Following scripture (notably Paul's letter to the Romans), evangelicals describe mercy as a gift because, like other talents and traits that mark the life of the believer, it is understood to come from God. The faithful, in other words, are endowed with qualities that originate from a divine rather than human source. Although not a prerequisite for practicing acts of loving kindness in the name of Jesus Christ, the gift of mercy is believed to be an essential ingredient in effective charity work and ministry. To be possessed of this gift, whether one knows it or not, is to be uniquely suited to the task of serving as a vessel of divine compassion. Sitting with Stacy and her family in their living room, after being thoroughly entertained by an impressive display of her children's musical and artistic talents, I asked how she came to know with such certainty that she had this spiritual gift. She answered:

> Probably by watching other people and realizing in myself something that related to people who are hurting or are in stress.... I realized that I reacted to them differently than most people. As I watched other people respond to situations, I realized that mercy is not just a thing where you go and do something for somebody. It's a heart thing. The gift of mercy is not always just the fact of doing. It's about hurting for somebody and caring about somebody who is hurting and in need. And it's always been there, I've always been that kind of person.

Stacy described the gift of mercy as an almost visceral compulsion rather than a cognitive choice, a force that impels her to get involved in other people's lives. It made her want not only to improve their lives materially but also to inspire them and help them discover the means of achieving spiritual transformations. She admitted that pursuing such goals in real-life relationships is no easy task. Figuring out how to help the needy while openly sharing her faith has been a process of continual trial and error. "The key has been spiritually deciding in my own heart how to impart the love of Christ and how he is really the answer. That's been a learning experience. You know, this is not just about being kind to somebody. This is about what the Lord did for me overall, and how to impart that fact to nonbelievers and people that are struggling. How do you relate that fact? I can't say I'm there yet."

The difficulty of finding the perfect balance of mercy and evangelism—the kind of balance that would render them virtually indistinct—never deterred Stacy from trying, nor did it weaken her resolve to encourage others along the same path, including her own children. Her homeschool curriculum integrated activities for "learning to love people," including family trips to nursing homes, hospitals, crisis shelters, and urban community centers where the children interacted with people they would be unlikely to meet otherwise. Education, socialization, and indoctrination all came together as Stacy used these opportunities to impart biblical and moral lessons about the virtues of mercy, humility, obedience, and faith. She wanted to guard her children against self-centeredness and frivolous consumerism. By exposing them to the realities of suffering and deprivation in the world, Stacy hoped to teach her children the value of using money as a resource for doing God's work. This approach did not preclude, however, spending money on activities that were "character building," such as athletic sports, creative arts, and, in the case of her youngest daughter, horseback riding.

Mobilizing churchgoers at Eternal Vine was for Stacy an extension of her responsibilities as a mother and homeschool teacher, except with less control and more resistance. Despite a growing interest in social outreach, spurred on by occasional sermons in which Pastor Tim extolled its religious virtues, Stacy felt she received little in the way of direct support for the outreach initiatives she organized as an active member of the women's ministry. She complained about lackluster commitments from church elders and congregants. Her efforts to encourage would-be participants were met with statements like "I'm too busy," or "I'm not gifted in that area," which she attributed to misplaced priorities and faulty theology. Much as she loved her church, Stacy felt that one of the drawbacks of Eternal Vine was that members grew too easily accustomed to the idea that one could work on spiritual growth without necessarily leaving the comfort of one's church, and the idea that if outreach to the community was important, then someone else (i.e., someone like Stacy) was surely taking care of it. She also complained about the absence of a reliable administrative structure to make full use of those volunteers who were willing to commit. Like many others, Stacy's moral ambitions were fueled by a desire to see the megachurch utilize its strengths as an institution of Christian discipleship while maximizing its inherent potential as a force of Christianization in the larger community.

Stacy received permission from the leadership at Eternal Vine to teach an adult education class, an eight-week elective devoted to exploring the meaning of Matthew 22: 39: "Love your neighbor as yourself." According to the course description, the objective was to get churchgoers "to join other committed believers in a strategic, well-planned, and consistent effort to show compassion in our city." The course was offered under the auspices of the women's ministry and scheduled for Tuesday mornings at 9:30 A.M., when only stay-at-home moms like Stacy were likely to enroll. In addition to devotional books and Bible guides, the syllabus featured works by evangelical authors such as Ronald Sider,

Timothy Keller, and Bill Hybels, as well as essays by Christian researchers and policy analysts such as George Barna, Marvin Olasky, and Amy Sherman. Stacy invited Paul Genero to give a guest lecture about social outreach opportunities in Knoxville, and for the end of the course she planned field trips to community centers and shelters in the inner city.

When the course was over, I asked her how it had gone. She looked out her kitchen window and shrugged. "Not a helluva lot of response," she answered. Only four people had signed up, and there was no indication that Stacy would be expected or invited to teach it again. She wanted to try something like it again, except maybe as a series of workshops rather than an intensive course, and with the cooperation of a few selected small groups rather than open enrollment. But more than anything else, she was simply frustrated, exhausted by the "constant dead ends." She pointed out that even popular activities like the annual Angel Tree program, which attracted so much interest during Christmas, never generated enough momentum to keep going for the rest of the year, despite the fact that poor children remained poor after the holiday season was over.

Stacy's experiences coordinating social outreach at Eternal Vine were not always frustrating, however. She derived great pleasure, for example, from her role in facilitating a partnership between the women's ministry's and a Christian faith-based organization that operates as a pregnancy clinic. The clinic offers medical advice, religious instruction, and psychological counseling for women with "unplanned pregnancies," with the aim of convincing them to carry the fetus to term. The staff is trained to give classes in prenatal and neonatal care, and to help clients if they choose to give their babies up for adoption. In addition to contributions from private donors, the clinic receives support from churches and religious organizations, including substantial assistance from Eternal Vine, where the clinic's executive director happens to be an active member. On top of financial support, Eternal Vine periodically sponsors special events for the clinic, including mixers where churchgoers are invited to interact with clients, and luncheons prepared by church volunteers in honor of the staff. In an attempt to build on the sense of connection that churchgoers felt with the clinic, and to encourage their desire to reach out to its vulnerable female clients, Stacy started a program at Eternal Vine called the "Sewing Blitz." The program involves women in the megachurch coming together periodically to fashion homemade maternity jumpers from donated fabrics. The jumpers are then presented ceremonially as gifts to women who have decided to have their babies. Compared to other events that Stacy coordinated or worked on, this one usually got a big response in terms of donations and volunteer participation, and she relished it. In all likelihood, the success of this particular initiative may be attributed to the symbolic weight of abortion, one of the defining social and political issues for conservative evangelicals. Moreover, it is worth noting that the Sewing Blitz, unlike volunteering in poor neighborhoods and homeless shelters, was probably appealing to churchgoers precisely because it was periodic and required fairly little in the way of social interactions that might be regarded as potentially upsetting or unpredictable.

As for Stacy, the more invested she was in the lives of cultural strangers, and the more contact she had with people in difficult circumstances, including prostitutes, battered women, and the sick and elderly, the closer she felt to the role that God intended for her. Her experiences also reinforced grim assessments of the human condition that figure so centrally in evangelical thought. "I hate this world," she said in a soft, pitying voice. "The more I see, and the more you get in the down-and-out of what happens in our world, the truth is that heaven looks absolutely more precious every day." Yet individual lives in this world can always be improved, she would insist, through faith in God and redemptive relationships with other faithful Christians. In our conversations she repeatedly mentioned free will, underlining her belief that our circumstances in life reflect the decisions and moral choices we make. But she would also stress that Christian social ministries need to be collective and systemic, and not purely individualistic, in order for people to have opportunities to make the right decisions and benefit from them. I asked Stacy what Knoxville would look like if all the churches lived up to their collective potential. She replied:

> You mean, if we were doing what we're supposed to do? Just say it! If we were doing what we're supposed to do! [laughs] Oh my gosh, if we were living up to the potential we have, I can't imagine how every nook and cranny of the hurting world would not be touched. There would be a place for every AIDS patient to go, every patient that people don't even want to look at, there would be somewhere for them to be and somebody with them. There would be places for the homeless to stay. Shelters for battered women in Knoxville remain full. There would be healing there, where those women would go on with their lives and hopefully make new choices.

Stacy never predicted that sources of human suffering such as AIDS, homelessness, and domestic abuse would go away, but instead she reinforced a view of the Christian church as a beacon of hope and redemption in a fallen world. Although she recognized that uncontrollable circumstances and social structures may limit or complicate the choices people are able to make, she rarely pursued such notions very far, but rather emphasized issues of personal morality and responsibility. She resigned herself to the reality that there will always be homeless people, that some low-income women will never overcome difficult circumstances, and so on. From this position she maintained that the success of the church in terms of outreach should be measured by the extent to which true-believing Christians are sufficiently prepared to meet the needs of suffering people and provide them with moral and spiritual guidance to make the right decisions in their lives, particularly the decision to "accept the Lord." Unlike Paul Genero, Stacy did not talk about grand cultural transformations or paradigm shifts. Yet the intensity of her moral ambitions developed in response to the "constant dead ends" she encountered in the process of outreach mobilization and which she saw as endemic to the culture of evangelicalism (and society as a whole). Implicit in her efforts was the idea that, in order to overcome these dead ends, evangelical churches and communities need to address matters through comprehensive self-examination and education. Along with her responsibility to teach her children, and provide guidance to people in need, Stacy felt an obligation to use her gift of mercy in the service of a moral pedagogy; to teach churchgoers how to embody, not just tacitly accept, biblical virtues relegated for too long to the margins of Christian life.

THE PROPHET: JIM ELROY

Jim Elroy liked to describe himself as "a middle-aged suburban redneck." Bearded and broad-shouldered, he had a rhythmic southern drawl, a quick wit, and a special affinity for hunting and fishing. He attended Marble Valley Presbyterian and lived in the suburbs, where his children attended a private Christian school. Jim's professional life, however, led him right to the heart of downtown Knoxville, where he was the director of the Fuller Street Mission, one of the city's largest homeless shelters. With more than twenty years of experience in the field of urban ministry, he enjoyed a reputation as one of the community's most outspoken and provocative advocates for the urban poor. As a committed Christian with seminary training, his public calls for social and economic equality in Knoxville were framed in terms of what he called "biblical justice." He argued that followers of Christ are obligated by biblical mandates to oppose social structures that deny poor people equal access to economic and social opportunities. "There is a spiritual connection between our spiritual commitment to God and helping the poor," he explained. "I think that it is absolutely clear from scripture that one who is spiritually connected to God is going to have a heart for the poor."

The Fuller Street Mission provides food, shelter, emergency services, job training, and religious and psychological counseling to homeless and destitute people from all over the Knoxville area. The mission serves up to seven hundred meals a day and houses more than two hundred men, women, and children. The facility includes large dining halls, classrooms, communal sleeping quarters for men (many of whom are mentally ill), and housing units for families. There is also a chapel where volunteer preachers, teachers, and worship leaders offer sermons, lectures, and short worship services. Long-term residents are expected to participate in Bible classes and other religious activities considered essential to the mission's rehabilitative functions. The mission used to have a policy requiring homeless men who spent the night to attend evening services in the chapel, but the policy was abandoned when the shelter became inundated with clients in the wake of city and state budget cuts.

Jim was raised in a fundamentalist church and later received pastoral training at a conservative Baptist seminary, but he generally avoided identifying too closely with any one brand of Christianity. "One of the struggles in my life," he told me, "is that I don't fit very neatly into any of the categories." Despite his fundamentalist background, which leaned him toward strict principles of biblical orthodoxy, Jim saw value in other styles of Protestant practice, including the classical liturgies of mainline churches and the energetic worship of charismatic churches. Although his theological and political views were very conservative, especially on issues such as abortion, homosexuality, gun control, and U.S. foreign policy, his ideas about gender (particularly the treatment of women in the church) were surprisingly moderate, and his views on issues of social justice remarkably progressive. The ambiguities that characterize Jim's sense of religious identity are not completely idiosyncratic. They demonstrate deep-seated tensions within evangelicalism and highlight the plasticity of religious faith as an expression of complex individual tastes, aspirations, and cultural influences.

From early in his career in social ministry, Jim was focused on problems of urban life, working for charities on behalf of the urban poor but also advocating publicly for social reforms and calling on Christians to do likewise. As director of the mission he continued to advocate through various forums and media outlets, including newspaper editorials and weekly radio messages. He appeared frequently as a guest speaker for local churches, Sunday school classes, community associations, and faith-based organizations, including the Samaritans of Knoxville. Often when he spoke before churchgoing audiences he told stories from the lives of poor and homeless people in order to counteract negative stereotypes, such as the belief that they would rather be dependent on welfare than work for a living. He talked about specific individuals whose lives were improved when they received spiritual guidance *as well as* better access to vital social and economic resources. The implications were clear, as he explained to me: "What poor people need are the same opportunities that people with resources have to face life-dominating problems and to respond positively to the opportunities. People who have alcohol and drug-related problems who are poor need to be able to get alcohol and drug treatment. Same with mental health care, and education, and job training opportunities."

Like any preacher, Jim punctuated his case studies and moral arguments with verses from the Bible—Old and New Testaments—to reinforce his main point that God not only expects but commands his people to help the poor and repair the injustices that lead to poverty. His high public profile and credibility in the conservative evangelical community made his prophetic indignation and emphasis on social justice that much more interesting and provocative. By suggesting that evangelicals in Knoxville needed to become attentive to the systemic or structural roots of poverty, and insisting that to do so was an essential religious imperative for any Christian, he challenged basic assumptions among conservative churchgoers about the nature of poverty and the mission of the church. Against those who claimed that equal opportunities already existed and that destitution usually resulted from personal failures and moral vices, he portrayed Knoxville as a place of socioeconomic segregation, where equal opportunities in fact did not exist and underprivileged people faced great obstacles that kept them from improving their lives even if they knew how.

On the topic of welfare, Jim thought the scaling back of the welfare state was a good idea and saw much to be gained from federal faith-based initiatives intended to channel government funds to religious charity organizations and social services. He had serious doubts, however, about the consequences of the state withdrawing too far from

its once-central role in the welfare arena. As a social worker and director of the Fuller Street Mission, Jim experienced firsthand the effects
of budget cuts at the state and federal levels. Almost daily, the mission
fills beyond capacity as homeless people are turned away from state
mental hospitals and scores of poor families flock to shelters for lack
of basic necessities and opportunities that might otherwise be available
through state safety nets. At the same time, Jim was concerned that if
faith-based and community organizations became dependent on government funds, there would be less pressure on Christian churches and
donors to step up to the plate. "I worry that the church will respond
to the federal funding of faith-based organizations the way it responded
to Johnson's War on Poverty in the 1960s. The church will say, 'Oh
good, the government is going to take care of it. We don't have to
worry about it.' Christians will walk away from their responsibility.
That really concerns me. I think the poor will be hurt greatly if the
church walks away from them."

As I had done previously with Stacy Miggs, I asked Jim to describe
what Knoxville would look like if evangelical churches lived up to the
standard of social outreach that he envisioned. His response differed
from hers in that he more explicitly stressed reform and equal opportunity, coupled with the familiar evangelical theme of the importance
of "relationships":

> If this was God's community, I think it would be a just community. It
> would be a community where there was equal opportunity for all people—all
> people, no matter your race, no matter your sex, no matter your economic
> standing. There would be equal opportunity for everyone. And it would be
> a community that was driven by the value of relationships. It would be a
> community where we understood one another, but it's more than that; we
> would actually value relationships with other people, value relationships
> with people who aren't like us. But I think the primary issue is that it would
> be a just place. It would be a place where there were equal opportunities.

Whenever I observed Jim staging his prophetic interventions in front
of an audience of evangelicals, their responses were mixed but usually
amounted to one form of evasion or another. There were those pastors
and churchgoers who took his words to heart, affirming his criticisms
of modern churches and their deficiencies on questions of social impact
but rarely offering direct support for programmatic initiatives along
the lines of what he proposed. There were others who undermined the
specific progressive implications of his critique by simply ignoring them,
refusing to seriously consider thinking about social welfare and poverty

relief in broadly systemic terms. Finally, some pastors and churchgoers openly confronted Jim's argument with the counterargument that social and political reforms never make any real difference in people's lives, and that it is only through one-on-one relationships with righteous people of faith that poor people learn to become financially, morally, and spiritually accountable.

All of these responses were on display when Jim was invited to speak to an adult Sunday school class at Marble Valley Presbyterian. The group was composed of mostly middle-aged churchgoers and seniors, and Jim was offered two consecutive Sundays on which to discuss with them any topic of his choosing. I had been sitting in on this group periodically for several months, and I was particularly interested to see what would happen when Jim Elroy showed up to speak his mind. For one thing, Marble Valley Presbyterian was a major source of financial support for the Fuller Street Mission, so Jim appeared there not only as a member of the megachurch but also as a beneficiary. Several members of the mission's board of directors were also members of the congregation, and at least one of those board members was part of the Sunday school class. The class also included a church elder who was in charge of missionary allocations, which was relevant because the money that went to the Fuller Street Mission came out of the megachurch's missions budget. Given all these factors, and the fact that this particular class was known for debate and lively banter, I anticipated that Jim would provoke a revealing dialogue, one that he would have to navigate carefully and with some diplomacy.

Jim began the first lesson with a blunt generalization: "The church community never talks openly about its responsibilities regarding the poor." He spoke of how Christian bookstores were full of books on topics like marriage and self-improvement but very few dealing with urban poverty and decline. He cited this as an example of the fact that Christians have an unfortunate habit of regarding social ministry and care for the poor as marginal components of Christian faith. He then listed a string of Bible verses, mostly from prophetic scriptures in the Old Testament, and led the group in reading each verse aloud before discussing how they conveyed the will of God on the subjects of justice and compassion.

Shifting gears, Jim asked the class to imagine a life of poverty, to "think about what it feels like to always be dependent." He asked them to put themselves in the position of the working poor, earning extremely low wages, living without health insurance, and struggling to support families under harsh circumstances. He explained the conditions of an unstable workforce and the risks people face in losing public benefits (like housing or Medicaid) before reaching self-sufficiency. His disquisition came to a climax as he hammered the point home that poverty cannot be explained away simply by focusing on the individual merits or proclivities of poor people, and that it is a falsehood to believe, as many do, that the urban poor are all willfully lazy and dependent:

> I've never met anybody who felt good about living off the system, about being dependent. I have not found that we have to convince a person who is cut off from the mainstream of life and seen as worthless in society that they are sinners. I have never met an alcoholic who would argue that his or her excessive drinking was okay. They believe it's wrong to cope with their problems the way they do, but their pain is so great that they can justify anything to ease the pain.

After a brief conclusion about the need for local churches to step up their social awareness and advocacy, Jim opened the class up for discussion. Initial respondents echoed Jim's basic sentiments, repeating the refrain that local churches—especially middle-class suburban churches—have a regrettable tendency to focus on their own needs and priorities at the expense of others. A couple of individuals shared personal anecdotes about poor people that they had met or tried to help in some way. In more than one case, the speakers used their anecdotes to support familiar claims about the persistent failures of the welfare state. Although the discussion was lively, hardly anyone took up the structural dimensions of Jim's main argument. No one followed his lead in thinking about possible avenues for churches to approach social problems through larger frameworks of social action and reform. After a few minutes, Jim tried to steer the conversation back to this when he asked, "But what do we as a church need to do, *systematically?*" Whether the question fell on deaf or reluctant ears, the response was clearly less than he had hoped for. The discussion returned, as if by gravitational force, to the theme of relationships and the importance of showing God's love through direct personal influence in people's lives. Barely containing himself, Jim said, "See, now this is the typical evangelical response," explaining that evangelicals are so focused on "one-on-one ministry" that they consistently overlook key political and socioeconomic aspects. Evangelicals, he complained, are guilty of an egregious double standard: "When it comes to issues that affect our own community, we don't hesitate to contact our political representatives, we don't mind looking for political solutions. But we never consider such options when it comes to the poor!" The room was silent. "It's not that we are evil," Jim hastened to add, "it's just that we never think about it."

From the awkward silence that ensued, a voice of opposition chimed in from the back of the room: "Jim, what you call the 'typical evangelical response' is actually what the Bible tells us to do! One-on-one solutions to poverty can go a lot farther than the kinds of solutions you suggest, mostly because those social solutions too often ignore the one-on-one." The speaker was an elderly man named Bob, a member of Jim's board of directors at the Fuller Street Mission. Jim offered a quick reply:

> That's not the whole truth, Bob. The prophet Isaiah talks about defending the widows. What does it mean to "defend" the widows? Isaiah means more than just getting the woman a job, helping her out personally—although that's very important too. What he's saying is that the church should rise up and speak out on issues affecting women, the issues that make it hard for them to get by in society. After all, this is what we do with abortion today, isn't it? Why don't we think about poverty the way we think about abortion?

The men debated the issue and it became apparent that it was a well-rehearsed disagreement between them. I asked Jim later if this caused problems for him in running the mission, and he told me that it did not because they were good friends who enjoyed getting into heated debates. Nonetheless, the clash of opinion between Jim and Bob represented a serious bone of contention among conservative evangelicals when it comes to social engagement, one that showed no signs of resolution on this or any other occasion I observed. Aside from Bob's intervention challenging the notion that churches are mandated to promote structural reforms to combat poverty, there were very few members of the class who addressed Jim's main agenda at all, either positively or negatively. No one tried to answer his question about why religious conservatives get politically engaged about abortion but not about poverty. One outspoken woman expressed her opinion that "charity begins at home" and if evangelicals wanted to fix social problems they needed first to address problems in their own homes and churches such as the lack of respect for women. A young male graduate student came in from a different angle, arguing that there are "dangers" in catering to the interests of liberal politicians who claim to be compassionate but use public policy as a way to uphold "a reliable constituency of dependent people who will vote for them." On this point Jim conceded that Christians should indeed be wary of misguided policies that encourage welfare dependency, but he quickly moved toward one last attempt to make his case. He reminded the group that "Jesus authenticated himself as the Messiah through his ministry to the poor," and that, likewise, "our ministry to the poor is the sign of authentic faith."

Many of the same themes came up the following week as well, although that discussion revolved around how to define "the poor." "*Poor* is a relative term," said one churchgoer. "Some people are poor in spirit, others are poor in resources." "Yes, yes," Jim replied dismissively, indicating that he had heard this rationalization before. "But when the Bible talks about the poor it refers to people who are *really poor*, people who lack resources and finances. To say that someone who lives in a big house on Cherokee Boulevard [a wealthy section of Knoxville] could be as 'poor' as someone who sleeps at the mission is to miss the biblical point." A young woman, cradling a newborn baby in her arms, asked, "So can you define the poor for us then?" Jim placed both his hands on the wooden lectern at the front of the class, and answered: "Poor people are people who, because of a lack of resources, can't get the opportunities of people who do have resources. It's fundamentally about opportunities and resources."

"But even with equal opportunities," someone in the front row blurted out, "there are going to be people who fail." Jim agreed that equal opportunities do not automatically create an equal society but added that they are a big part of what makes a just society. By this point it seemed as though Jim had pushed the matter as far as it would go, so he reverted to a more familiar idiom. He talked about personal success stories from the mission and cited statistics on the number of born-again conversions that had taken place there in the previous year (326, by his count). He concluded his discussion with one final plea: "Biblical justice will only happen when we as a church allow information about the poor to filter into *how we think*.... If Christians want to have an impact on the world, the church needs to use its powerful voice to speak for the powerless, not just for evangelizing. After all, there is no condemnation in scripture for not evangelizing, but scripture does say that God strongly condemns injustice."

As a conservative evangelical and welfare activist, Jim Elroy has spent much of his career at the intersections of conflicting moral economies of altruism. He has had to walk a fine line between progressive notions of social justice, which he refuses to deny, and the prevailing conservative ethos of the evangelical subculture to which he belongs and on which the mission heavily relies. Jim saw this as an unfortunate and unbiblical discrepancy. One way that he dealt with the problem was to venture, now and again, outside of a strictly evangelical worldview; to augment his knowledge and expertise by studying books and research by secular as well as religious scholars and analysts. He had no compunction about opening himself up to a plurality of intellectual and ideological influences. In fact, it was stubborn resistance to outside influence that he felt caused so many evangelicals to remain essentially ignorant about the meaning of biblical justice. God's truth, he explained, sometimes comes in forms that people are unaccustomed to or are unwilling to accept. As I saw it, though, there were even stronger social and institutional forces at play. Public discussions like the ones described here are crucial for outreach mobilization, in that they represent key opportunities for socially engaged evangelicals to put their social concerns into circulation. But as we have seen, they are indicative of the extent to which progressive ideas are subverted, co-opted, or repressed in congregational settings where hegemonic norms seldom give up their ground.

THE MISSIONARY: MARGIE MCKENZIE

Margie McKenzie's office at Marble Valley Presbyterian was cluttered with dozens of small metal buckets, each filled with canned goods and other donated items. The buckets were stacked precariously in columns that looked ready to collapse with the slightest nudge. "They're AIDS buckets!" Margie exclaimed with a smile. Every year the megachurch sponsors a "gift bucket" program, collecting goods for local charities and service organizations that then distribute the buckets to needy clients. A different group or organization is selected each year, and at Margie's urging the buckets were designated that year for a local hospital program that works with people with HIV/AIDS. The choice was not uncontroversial. She initially faced resistance from a few church elders and a lot of fear and prejudice among churchgoers, including one who refused to touch the buckets upon finding out whom they were meant for. Eventually, Margie convinced the leadership that it was worthwhile to get involved in "AIDS ministry" and now the fruits of her effort filled her narrow office space from floor to ceiling. As she gingerly wove through the piles to her desk, she started laughing and said, "It's funny right? That in such a big church with so many rooms we still have to stack all these gift buckets in my tiny little office." I smiled and said that the same thought had just occurred to me too.

As a staff member at Marble Valley Presbyterian, Margie was charged with overseeing the megachurch's social outreach ministries, which meant coordinating charity drives, scheduling outreach events, and organizing workshops on outreach-related topics. The bulk of her work involved generating enthusiasm and soliciting volunteers for benevolence activities, such as delivering food to shut-ins, working in soup kitchens and food pantries, and itemizing donated goods such as clothing and furniture. For years Marble Valley Presbyterian maintained links to organizations such as Habitat for Humanity and the Salvation Army, but social outreach involving direct volunteer participation was otherwise limited to short-term projects and charity drives, rather than continuous long-term initiatives. Margie's job essentially was to boost this area of congregational life through program development and mobilization. However, much of the time she would have spent on strategic planning was actually spent doing the work of outreach herself because there was rarely a critical mass of volunteers available to get things done without her immediate involvement. At times it seemed almost as though she *was* the social outreach ministry, just waiting for others to follow her example and help her build momentum toward a sustainable program of social engagement, a passion she herself developed only recently.

Margie was born and raised in East Tennessee. Her father was a successful businessman and an abusive alcoholic. Her parents were not regular churchgoers and Margie described the limited exposure she did have to Christianity as "the angry, God-fearing variety." As an adult she followed her father's footsteps into the world of business and finance, and for several years she was "focused on nothing else but climbing the corporate ladder." It was during that period that she also fell into what she described as patterns of self-destruction, including alcohol abuse and other "improper" behavior. Her life kept on this way until one year when her teenage son became a Christian after having a born-again conversion experience. Margie was so inspired by this that she "suddenly realized I just had to have God in my life." On the advice of coworkers, she underwent Christian counseling and, along with her husband, Harrison, joined Marble Valley Presbyterian, where they soon became official members. Looking to finalize the transition from her old to new self, Margie left a high-paying corporate job to take an administrative staff position at the megachurch.

The next major turning point for Margie occurred when she was asked to be a chaperone for a church youth group on their biennial "spring break mission trip" to Washington, DC. The purpose of the trip was to provide evangelical teenagers an opportunity to gain first-hand experience doing humanitarian mission work in an urban setting (one relatively close to home). They spent most of the week in the poorest areas of DC, volunteering at homeless shelters, goodwill centers, and day-care programs, and attended Sunday services at a small black church in the inner city. The trip was meant to be a new and deeply moving experience for the teenagers but Margie may have been the most profoundly affected of all of them. She was particularly inspired when she discovered that ministering to the poor was integral to the teachings of Jesus.

> One night when we gathered round to talk about our day, we studied Matthew 25, the parable of the sheep and the goats,[3] and suddenly it just jumped out at me. I realized that the Lord was telling me that caring for others is not an option, and he was showing me the importance of sharing his love with others in a loving way, not a condemning way. I realized how important it is to serve the same people that Jesus served all the time: the prostitutes, the sick, the poor. This is how we can be Jesus' hands and feet.

She returned home to Knoxville with an eager desire to replicate her experience in DC on a regular basis. She became so involved in social outreach activities that the leadership decided to create a new staff position for her so she could devote more time to it. As part of her new role, Margie would serve as a liaison to the charities, social service agencies, and faith-based organizations that solicited support from the megachurch. She therefore immersed herself in the region's nonprofit sector, working to expand the megachurch's network of existing partnerships and gain credibility among social workers and community organizers. As an early supporter of the Samaritans of Knoxville, she was closely involved with the organization from its inception. Within a few short years, Margie and Harrison (who also left a career in business to work in philanthropy) sold their West Knoxville home and bought a refurbished Victorian house on the edge of an inner-city neighborhood known for high levels of poverty and violent crime. It was the site of a public housing project that was about to be demolished and "redeveloped" into a federally subsidized mixed-income community. With permission from church elders, she shifted her base of operations to her new home, performing double duty as a coordinator of church-based outreach initiatives and a promoter of social ministries "in the field." With her children fully grown and out of the house, Margie had for a long time considered the possibility of moving out of the suburbs and into the heart of the city. She wanted to pursue a "hands-on" approach to social outreach, and she felt that she could achieve this much more effectively by becoming embedded in the inner-city community, rather than ministering from a distance.

Margie took great comfort and pride in the transformation she had undergone from leading a life of sin and materialism to leading one guided by compassion, social awareness, and personal sacrifice. Like many evangelicals, she relied on biblical narratives and tropes to provide meaningful frames of reference for her life experience. "Do you know the story of the woman at the well?" she asked me. "Well, I was the woman at the well!" She referred to a story in the Gospel of John (John 4:1–42) in which Jesus is traveling with his disciples and meets a Samaritan woman along the way at a well once owned by the patriarch Jacob. To everyone's astonishment, Jesus speaks to the woman and asks her for water, blatantly transgressing ritual prohibitions against contact with Samaritans. He tells the woman about the "living water" of eternal redemption that he alone can provide and proves his divinity by revealing the woman's sins to her. Convinced that Jesus is the savior he claimed to be, the woman rushes to the city and persuades others by the sheer power of her testimony to come see the Messiah for themselves. Jesus' brazen violation of religious proscriptions is instructive for evangelicals because it is taken to represent, among other things, the virtues of "risky" compassion (see chapter 6) and the belief that crossing religious and cultural boundaries is what Christian ministry and missionary evangelism are all about. It also demonstrates the relationship between grace and repentance, a theological pairing that evangelicals hope to reproduce in all manner of human interactions, especially in the context of social outreach. The woman at the well confronts her sins brought to light by the very person who treated her with kindness despite her impurity, and in response she not only becomes a faithful follower of Christ but essentially a missionary as well. Margie McKenzie's identification with the character corresponds to her cultivated self-identity as a redeemed sinner, who has chosen to give witness to her newfound faith by going forth with her testimony to the city, quite literally.

From her home-office in the inner city, Margie maintained a busy schedule of meetings and visits. She worked with local ministries and organizations, spent time with families in the neighborhood, looked after people's children for them, and delivered home-cooked meals to sick and elderly residents. Before long she was known affectionately as "Miss Margie," recognized throughout the neighborhood for her help and hospitality. She was popular among a number of young children, who would show up occasionally at her door for milk and freshly baked cookies or to play videogames. She attended workshops and events held by local associations, ever on the lookout for worthwhile opportunities for her congregation and new insights to be gained from the experiences of others, particularly with regard to the more difficult emotional and ethical dimensions of urban ministry. Her goal was to absorb as much information as possible while giving as much as she could to the community, and her immersion expanded her own base of knowledge and experience considerably, even as it opened up new challenges and conundrums.

Not all of Margie's work focused on issues specific to the inner city. At a certain point Margie developed an interest in partnering with groups that were involved in providing aid and assistance to people with HIV/AIDS. One morning I accompanied her to an HIV/AIDS awareness workshop at a local hospital. The workshop, called "Demystifying HIV Disease," was intended to facilitate open discussions among health care professionals, patients, and church representatives about the realities of the disease and the qualities required of caregivers, including empathy and tolerance. The workshop was led by a specialist at the hospital and cosponsored by a Southern Baptist church with a nascent HIV/AIDS ministry of its own. Aside from me and Margie, other attendees included a Southern Baptist pastor, a member of Marble Valley Presbyterian with a background in medicine, a handful of people from other evangelical churches (including an elderly couple whose son had HIV), and four individuals—three gay white males and one black single mother—who were HIV positive and were there to provide first-person accounts of life with HIV.

The discussions that day were frank and quite moving. One of the gay men mentioned his shock upon learning that evangelical churches were interested in working with AIDS patients and willing to offer space in their church for support groups. He insisted, at the same time, that evangelical "well wishers" should learn to suppress their urge to "badger" people about homosexuality or tell them they have to go to church and stop drinking alcohol. The Southern Baptist pastor, a young and sympathetic man, spoke at length about the difficult questions that evangelicals wrestle with on this topic. He said that evangelicals will always uphold their belief that "the Christian answer is the best answer," but he acknowledged that "the power of language" can cause pain to people who are already hurting and admitted that Christians would probably be better at sharing their faith if they were willing to "just be there for you." He explained: "The primary goal of pastoral care is to make contact, then after that listen, and only after that to begin to minister, to offer words of hope." When asked by a nonevangelical hospital worker how he reconciled intolerant beliefs with the need to simply "be there" for AIDS patients, the pastor agreed that "there is a constant tension" but insisted that there is always room for "common ground" once people are open and truthful with one another.

For most of the workshop, Margie was still and contemplative. She no doubt thought about her congregation and the allies and foes she would deal with as she tried to establish an HIV/AIDS ministry at Marble Valley Presbyterian. By midafternoon, however, I noticed that her attention was drawn to the HIV-positive single mother seated next to her. The African American woman in her early twenties looked sheepish and withdrawn. She remained silent for much of the day, eyes cast downward, until a point in the afternoon when she was asked to talk about herself. She talked about her day-to-day health issues and the struggles of taking care of her children, making financial ends meet, and being dependent on her mother. Tears streamed down her face as her sadness welled up into quiet rage. Margie patted the young woman gently on the back and shifted her chair slightly to bring them closer together. For the rest of the day Margie consoled her and talked with her during session breaks. The woman seemed reluctant at first to open up to Margie but eventually became more responsive to her sympathetic demeanor. At day's end, they exchanged phone numbers and made tentative plans to meet again. A couple of weeks later I asked Margie if anything had developed after this initial encounter. She told me that they were in frequent contact and had developed a friendship. It was evident that as a struggling single mother of two, the woman just needed a friend and "a chance to get out of the house," so Margie took her out for a meal and a movie. When she needed dental work done but could not find an affordable dentist in Knoxville willing to treat people with HIV, Margie drove her to see a dentist in the town of Maryville, about an hour away. This was exactly the sort of relationship that she envisioned when she moved to the inner city. From Margie's perspective, regardless of whether or not the young mother needed spiritual guidance, the friendship served a "redemptive" purpose by enriching both of their lives with a relational spirituality constituted at its root by God's mercy and grace. Undoubtedly, Margie imagined all kinds of hopeful prospects for change in the woman's life, but she also wanted to experience the friendship as a concrete expression of Christian faith, and therefore an end unto itself. When I returned to Knoxville for a visit more than a year later, Margie cheerfully told me that the two remained in close touch.

In addition to forming this friendship, Margie's participation in the HIV/AIDS workshop led her on a path of self-education about HIV/AIDS as well as broader issues concerning health care and homosexuality (which for many conservative churchgoers remains synonymous with AIDS). She consulted mostly Christian resources but, like Jim Elroy, she did not confine herself to books and articles written exclusively from an evangelical perspective. Her desire to become better informed and more tolerant with regard to a controversial subject was reinforced by her expectation that she would have a hard time making the case for HIV/AIDS ministry to her fellow churchgoers, many of whom reacted to the idea with fear and revulsion. Mobilizing support at Marble Valley Presbyterian for controversial outreach initiatives required confidence as well as diplomacy, not to mention a firm grounding in the kind of theological reasoning that socially engaged evangelicals in Knoxville were forced to master and, to a certain degree, reinvent. When Margie first raised the idea to a group of church elders, one of them reprimanded her, insisting that "homosexuality is an abomination." She accepted this statement from a biblical perspective but tried to redirect the focus from condemnation to compassion. She told me that as she became more tolerant over time with people outside the faith, it was getting harder to tolerate the harsh, unforgiving reactions of people within the faith. As she saw it, the belief that homosexuality is worse than other sins not only hindered the work of outreach and evangelism but also stood on weak theological ground. "We are all equal at the foot of the cross," she explained. "People have to remember that one sin is no worse than any other. *Every* sin is an abomination, it's just that some of us hide ours better!"

The four ethnographic profiles presented in this chapter illustrate the range of emotions, tactics, and experiences associated with the efforts of socially engaged evangelicals to mobilize conservative churches and churchgoers and at the same time perform the actual work of serving social needs through volunteerism and organized benevolence. Although the religious virtues exemplified and promoted by these individuals were esteemed by others, they also represented areas of tension and uncertainty in conservative evangelical communities where ministry activities of this kind are less well established and subject to debate. As a result, their positions relative to the congregations they belonged to and sought to mobilize were complex and precarious, making the task of generating support and resources that much more of an uphill struggle. To argue as I do that their cultural roles presuppose an activist orientation is to highlight the aspirational and provocative nature of what they do, and to emphasize that they are intermediary figures working to bridge the divide between resourceful yet relatively disengaged communities of faith and the wider fields of public life where those same communities wish to exert their influence.

All of the socially engaged evangelicals portrayed in this chapter were inspired to create stronger alignments between their individual lives, personal convictions, and the religious and ideological commitments of conservative evangelicalism. They all aimed to become better Christians through social outreach, to make other churchgoers better Christians through outreach mobilization, and to spread the gospel by "sharing the love of Christ" with cultural strangers and disadvantaged people. In the process of pursuing these moral ambitions they contributed to the reformative evangelical project to Christianize the world, one relationship at a time, yet they also felt compelled to reform evangelicalism from within by expanding the terms of engaged orthodoxy to accommodate outreach ministries inspired by notions of active compassion, personal sacrifice, social justice, and moral tolerance. They did not openly refute dominant ideological paradigms so much as seek to recalibrate them according to what they came to see as more authentic, and therefore more potent, standards of biblical faith. Their activist orientations can thus be linked to transformative action of a kind that builds on an existing cultural repertoire, teasing out its inherent ambiguities along with its presumed strengths, in order to enhance its effectiveness as a vehicle for religious revitalization both individually and collectively.

The fact that their efforts more often than not produced frustration and discord does not negate the transformative dimension, but rather serves to remind us that significant discrepancies exist even in religious groups that may appear uniform or monolithic to outsiders. It also reminds us that while orthodox religiosity presupposes uniformity and absolutism, there are always social practices and reflexive discourses that bring to light those religious imperatives that may be internally contested. As the remaining chapters in this book demonstrate, conservative evangelicals are almost habitually reflexive. For socially engaged evangelicals affiliated with Knoxville's suburban megachurches, this propensity for reflexivity sometimes exacerbated the spiritual and emotional dilemmas they faced in their outreach efforts, but it also served as one of the most readily available strategies of moral suasion.

CHAPTER 5

The Spiritual Injuries of Class

No servant can serve two masters. Either he will hate the
one and love the other, or he will be devoted to the one and
despise the other. You cannot serve both God and Money.

—Luke 16:13

You can't follow God and the American Dream at the
same time.

—Member of Eternal Vine Church

There was a time, not so long ago, when conservative evangelicalism
was widely assumed to be a "religion of the dispossessed" (Niebuhr
1929), a rigid sectarian faith reserved for the poor and uneducated
masses who reject modernity and all that comes with it. On the contrary,
many North American evangelicals are educated, economically well off,
and well acquainted (perhaps to the point of unease) with the trappings of secular culture (Shibley 1996; Smith 1998; Warner 1988). With
increasing prominence, in fact, evangelicals occupy high positions of
political power and corporate influence, and are closely associated with
new media and cosmopolitan trends (Lindsay 2007). As issues of social
class have received renewed attention in the study of North American
religion (McCloud 2007), scholars have demonstrated the relevance of
class for analyzing the cultural politics of evangelical engagement with
the modern world (e.g., Griffith 2004; Hendershot 2004; Kintz 1997).
Somewhat less attention has been paid to the fact that evangelicals who
identify as "middle-class" wrestle self-consciously with the implications of class status in relation to religious faith. Reflexive critiques of
middle-class identity are pervasive in evangelical culture. Even as they
embrace the promises of upward social mobility, suburban evangelicals

are fixated on the moral pitfalls of consumerism, self-indulgence, and complacency that they fear go along with the so-called middle-class lifestyle.

In this chapter I examine the reflexive critique of class and the ways that it feeds into the discourse of outreach mobilization among socially engaged evangelicals. This critique is entirely distinct from and somewhat antithetical to the "prosperity gospel" notoriously associated with charismatic televangelists and preachers like Joel Osteen and Creflo Dollar. Rather than touting a gospel of wealth, the critique described here draws on a far more pervasive evangelical discourse of antimaterialism, which among other things provides suburban evangelicals with theological concepts, such as "incarnation" and "stewardship," with which to negotiate their conflicted sense of class awareness. Pastors and churchgoers concerned with social outreach talk continually about the need to convince suburban evangelicals to leave their "comfort zones" and transcend the culture of apathy and insularity that the materialistic impulses of a consumer society are seen to create. The reflexivity intrinsic to the critique is based on a felt need to confront what it means to be "middle-class"—a vague category associated with broadly discernible social attainments and privileges—and a desire to reconcile the apparent incongruities between class-based aspirations and Christian virtues of sacrifice, humility, and benevolence. Suburban evangelicals strive to embody a righteous and transcendent faith, yet they readily admit to feeling the pressures of status anxiety and the temptations of material comfort and prosperity. Not unlike the Protestant communities that Max Weber observed when he visited the United States (Weber 1946b), contemporary evangelicals regard entrepreneurial vitality and economic success as signs of moral fortitude and divine favor. But they remain troubled by their complicity in modern versions of the American Dream that seem far removed from the inner-worldly asceticism of ages past.

Although the evangelical discourse of antimaterialism is inflected by class awareness, it is not a straightforward critique of capitalism. The structure of social stratification under a capitalist economy is not typically treated as a problem in and of itself. Rather, the critique highlights cultural habits and privileges viewed as intrinsic to a generalized image of the middle-class lifestyle, including consumerism, upward mobility, frivolous "busyness," and family egoism. Suburban evangelicals are not so preoccupied with what Sennett and Cobb (1972) called "the hidden injuries of class" as they are with what we might call the *spiritual* injuries of class.[1] The social implications of the critique are limited in their ideological scope, focusing primarily on spiritual rather than political-economic forces, and moral rather than structural reforms. Yet the critique is reflexive in tone, and profoundly disconcerting for some. By engaging in this discourse, suburban evangelicals embrace what they regard as a counterintuitive or "radical" approach to both introspection and cultural criticism. They attempt to work through their existential anxieties using a framework of class reflexivity that is interpreted as a mark of authentic faith, both because of its theological import and its perceived benefits to Christian evangelism and social ministry.

There are gendered aspects of the evangelical discourse of antimaterialism that are worth taking into account. Implicitly, the critique can be read to suggest that women (specifically mothers) bear much of the burden to guard against the spiritual injuries of class in the Christian home. Although this was rarely made explicit during my fieldwork, the virtues of sacrifice, humility, and benevolence presupposed by the reflexive discourse surrounding class are conceptually similar to the virtues that evangelicals attach to idealized notions of female domestic responsibility. Such symbolic affinities encourage and facilitate women's participation in various forms of voluntary civic engagement mediated by church ministries.[2] In religious contexts where women are expected to perform distinct, separate, and generally submissive roles relative to men, these affinities may also have the effect of reinforcing the marginal status of social outreach compared to other ministries that receive the lion's share of congregational resources. However, this need not diminish the fact that evangelical antimaterialism, in principle, is otherwise neutral with regard to gender. The moral ambitions evoked by this discourse are meant, in earnest, to apply equally to men and women. It is, after all, a critique that hits remarkably close to home for the average suburban churchgoer, tapping into the most disconcerting aspects of the very comforts that upwardly mobile people work so hard to attain.

The key themes are particularly salient in affluent megachurches where pastors and churchgoers are likely to feel a need to justify their abundance according to the logic of Christian servitude rather than unmitigated prosperity. Socially engaged evangelicals at Eternal Vine and Marble Valley Presbyterian were especially keen to present social outreach as a necessary corrective and an avenue through which to promote selfless piety in the service of God's kingdom. Even catered to the rhetoric of outreach mobilization, however, the critique of materialism and class was always delicate business that needed to be handled with sensitivity and tact.

SINS OF OUR SOCCER MOMS

On May 3, 2001, Knoxville native Tina Wesson briefly became America's most famous soccer mom. That night she emerged victorious on the popular reality TV show *Survivor II,* having outlasted and outwitted her fellow contestants after forty-two days of competition under harsh "primitive" conditions in the Australian outback. In winning the one-million-dollar grand prize, Wesson—a forty-year-old mother of two—pulled a surprise victory that the media represented as a triumph of intuition and perseverance over the haughty pretensions of Generation Xers from the coasts. With her winning smile, soft southern drawl, and impressive knack for outdoor athletics, the former flight attendant and part-time nurse epitomized the image of the ambitious and active soccer mom, a paradigm of idealized femininity in the twenty-first century.

As it turned out, Tina Wesson was a member of Eternal Vine Church who openly identified as a born-again Christian. During the weeks when *Survivor II* was being aired I expected to hear her name come up periodically at church, and I figured that there would be some recognition by the pastoral leadership of the fact that one of their own members was in the national spotlight. To my surprise, the subject hardly ever came up in casual conversation, and up to the night of the final episode there was no official mention of it; no blurb in the church bulletin or announcements during Sunday services. Whatever private discussions took place about Wesson's participation on the show generally remained private. Not surprisingly, all this changed after her big victory.

On the Sunday following the end of the show, Pastor Tim began his morning sermon by offering warm, almost sheepish words of congratulation. Although Tina Wesson was not able to be present that morning, the congregation honored her spectacular success with energetic applause. Almost as soon as Pastor Tim mentioned her name the congregation erupted with enthusiasm for the hometown girl. There seemed to be a sense of relief, as though the sanction on a tabooed subject had finally been lifted. After all, the last time Pastor Tim had mentioned *Survivor* was several weeks earlier, before Wesson even appeared on the show, when he criticized its cutthroat, competitive spirit and insisted that a real Christian could never win such a thing.

Now referring back to those comments with charming humility, he admitted that not only did a Christian win but she happened to be a member of his own church. "Great things are happening in the Body of Christ!" he joked, much to the congregation's delight. He then shifted quickly to another topic, and preached on the importance of planting new churches at home and abroad.

I found it intriguing that, aside from that one morning, there was such a low-key overall response to the sudden celebrity of a fellow churchgoer. What could have been the reasons for this? Churchgoers obviously harbored mixed feelings about the *Survivor* series altogether. It did, after all, represent just the kind of "worldly" commercial media spectacle that conservative evangelicals regard as morally suspect. Furthermore, although Wesson did make her Christian faith known, she drew relatively little attention to it over the course of the show and made no obvious effort to share her faith testimony once the show was done. As a result, some evangelical churchgoers regarded her time in the limelight as far less of a momentous event than it would have been had she used the opportunity to give witness to the gospel before a national viewing audience. As she traveled the country on a post-*Survivor* publicity tour, friends and pastors at Eternal Vine prayed that she would find opportunities to profess her spirituality with confidence. Against the din of secular media entertainment, casual and noncommittal witnessing through minor sound bytes just didn't seem to offer much in the way of cultural impact.

However, there was another significant reason why churchgoers at Eternal Vine had such a subdued response to Tina Wesson's participation on the show, and it had little to do with the show itself or anything she said or did not say. Although she presented herself in a positive light that made members proud, the image of her success must have provoked a troubling self-consciousness on the part of churchgoers. As she skillfully manipulated temporal circumstances for material rewards, Tina Wesson represented the deep yearnings and anxieties of many suburban evangelicals. The ambivalence of her fellow churchgoers, in short, was meaningful because by and large they were just like her: young to middle-aged suburbanites making a living and multitasking their way to financial, emotional, and spiritual fulfillment. They were educated moms and dads, husbands and wives, professionals and homemakers, striving for perfection in a culture of competition and seeking transcendence in born-again religiosity. Watching Tina Wesson gain an advantage on the material side of that equation, along with an enviable fifteen minutes of fame, must have been like watching themselves in a dream that was both satisfying and angst ridden.

The desires of upward mobility and evangelical piety stand in awkward, contradictory tension with one another. There are positive connotations to wealth and prosperity, including the belief that they represent one of the ways that God blesses the truly faithful. Yet evangelical theology also places heavy emphasis on biblical principles that pose ethical dilemmas for evangelical churchgoers living fairly prosperous lives in affluent communities. From an evangelical perspective, to live in full accordance with the radical ideals of true faith, Christians must recognize that all wealth and material assets belong to God and must be acquired and spent in the service of God's kingdom. All earthly ambitions must be surrendered to the will of God and must be oriented toward the demands of serving God, especially through charitable and evangelistic acts that benefit the poor, needy, and unsaved. Evangelical pastors lash out against a culture of unbridled materialism where a true Christian lifestyle is hard to achieve, where people become attached to worldly goods and ambitions and thus even more alienated from God than they already were. Consequently, evangelical churchgoers struggle endlessly with a problem that has confounded Christians for centuries, the problem of "God versus Mammon,"[3] which has never been as simple a dichotomy as the faithful might like to believe.

As with other conundrums in their religious lives, churchgoers rely to a large extent on guidance from pastors, church elders, and literary theologians in working through the contradictions and guarding themselves against their susceptibility to materialist desires. At Eternal Vine and Marble Valley Presbyterian I observed such guidance communicated in the form a densely layered critique of materialism that is widespread, though not uncontroversial, in North American evangelicalism. There is a wide variety of opinions about the consequences of different kinds of economic activity, the extent to which affluent Christians should bemoan their wealth, the degree of compatibility between Christianity and capitalism, and the proper means of resolving tensions between theology and practice. These issues have been addressed from diverging standpoints in a large body of Christian literature in recent decades (e.g., Chilton 1981; Keller 1997; Schneider 2002; Sider 1977). Despite differing interpretations, however, opinions are united by their consistent ideological condemnation of unbridled materialism and its negative moral and spiritual consequences, all of which are believed to be especially rife in industrialized Western societies.

At the church level, especially in congregations that are conspicuously affluent, the discourse of antimaterialism and its accompanying religious and social commentaries are intensified by reflexivity about class. It is no wonder, then, that the conservative evangelicals I observed in the suburban megachurches of Knoxville internalized the critique so profoundly and revisited it repeatedly in their worship services, sermons, and small group discussions. The critique is a framework for problematizing upward mobility, and it is a spiritual discipline that must constantly be rehearsed and re-engaged. The concept of class is an explicit point of reference through which churchgoers imagine the forces of materialism acting on them, and through culturally refined notions of class they look for the moral fortitude to withstand the impact. This is no simple equation. As many suburban churchgoers struggle to make ends meet in times of financial uncertainty, the demands of evangelical piety collide with profane status anxieties, including the prevailing middle-class fear of social disorientation associated with loss of status and downward mobility (Newman 1988).

The meanings attached to class, and the anxieties surrounding social status, do not circulate apart from concrete objectification; they require symbolic mediations. As the example of Tina Wesson demonstrated, one of the symbols through which the spiritual injuries of class are subjected to the weight of contemplation is that of the all-American "soccer mom," a metonymic icon denoting popular conceptions of feminized middle-class domesticity, consumption, and family socialization. In her relentless dedication to the well-being of her children, the soccer mom appeals to conservative family values and gendered norms of caregiving. The soccer mom is a model of nurturance and productive consumerism, making personal sacrifices in order to provide her family with worldly amenities befitting a lifestyle of leisure and security that typically remains elusive (cf. Miller 1998). The image is suggestive of a precarious balance of work and home in a shifting economic landscape and represents, even more poignantly, "a community of women who are always on the verge of failure" (Rosenbaum 1999). For conservative evangelicals, the overburdened soccer mom is thus an ambiguous and worrisome icon to the extent that she exemplifies some of the core problems and pitfalls of modern society. The striving for comfort and self-actualization that she is seen to embody resonates with middle-class sensibilities that many suburban evangelicals recognize within themselves, but this is precisely what they fear most. The impulse to gravitate toward the familiar "comfort zones" of a suburban lifestyle is seen as a dangerous habit that lures the faithful away from their calling to reject frivolous things and attend selflessly to the needs of the larger community.

The phrase *comfort zone* ranks high among the everyday figures of speech that I encountered most often during my fieldwork. It was not always used in exactly the same way but generally referred to the areas of life where one feels safe from unfamiliar or unpleasant elements. The term appears to have secular origins in developmental psychology. Cognitive theorists and educators influenced by Lev S. Vygotsky contrast comfort zones with what Vygotsky called "zones of proximal development." A zone of proximal development is a situation in which a child's capacity to learn is optimized by an appropriate balance of instructional supervision and independent problem-solving, a state in which the child is given opportunities to achieve and be challenged in equal measure (Vygotsky 1978). A comfort zone, by contrast, is a situation in which a child's abilities are no longer tested by new challenges; the state is therefore static and unproductive. The concept has evolved in meaning with both positive and negative connotations as it has moved through a range of discursive fields including New Age spiritualism, therapeutic seminars, self-help literature, and real-estate marketing. The term is even used in business management as part of the linguistic toolkit with which corporate managers are trained to evaluate strategic initiatives, assess worker productivity, and conduct risk-benefit analyses. In all these contexts, it may be used to describe a space of emotional contentment and existential calm, tucked away from the neuroses of daily life, or it may alternatively be used to direct individuals away from cycles of passivity that limit human achievement, happiness, and (from a market perspective) financial gain.

The ambiguous connotations of the comfort zone carry over into evangelical parlance. Churchgoers sometimes use the term to describe healthy social or religious contexts where they feel safe and experience spiritual growth, such as their churches and small groups. But the flip side of this is to view one's comfort zone as a kind of moral quicksand, something to "get out of" rather than sink more deeply into. This usage is the more common of the two. Preaching on the subject of following one's "calling," Pastor Tim boldly told his congregation that "many of you are stuck in a middle-class whale gut" (referring to the story of Jonah and the whale). He admonished them to resist complacency and accept whatever challenges God calls them to, even if they involve risks and sacrifices. Pastor Tim understood full well the difficulties that churchgoers face in finding adequate opportunities to take morally and spiritually meaningful risks in their quotidian lives. As he casually remarked to me one day over coffee, "We all continue to struggle with what it means to really follow Christ in a comfortable culture where you can't get martyred anymore."

In evangelical churches, the need to escape one's comfort zone comes up often in relation to ministries that involve cross-cultural evangelism, when "getting out of your comfort zone means interacting with and, ideally, evangelizing persons with whom one would not normally relate" (Garces-Foley 2007: 132). This was a recurring theme in the discussions among socially engaged evangelicals in Knoxville, who spoke continually about the importance of broadening their cultural horizons and confronting fears and prejudices that prevent them from reaching out to people in unfamiliar social settings. In addition to emphasizing the benefits to evangelism, they described the spiritual growth one gains in the process as an effective antidote to the spiritual injuries of class. Pastor Tim again, from a different sermon on the topic of outreach: "When you get involved in the lives of the poor you experience the love of God in ways that you can never grasp in your West Knoxville soccer games and three-piece suits."

Direct references to recreational soccer, as quoted above and elsewhere in this chapter, seldom mentioned soccer *moms* explicitly, yet it would be a mistake to ignore the logical implication. The soccer mom is a ubiquitous cultural symbol in U.S. popular and commercial culture, synonymous with white heteronormative conceptions of middle-class life. She has gradually replaced the iconic "Stepford wife" of yore, a stereotype of feminine docility and sterile conformity (based on the 1975 cult classic *The Stepford Wives*) from which suburban evangelical women are keen to distance themselves. The soccer mom embodies the heroic hyperactivity of the contemporary suburban housewife and, by extension, the social aspirations of her whole family. It is reasonable then to suggest that any mention of soccer as a marker of class is likely to evoke gendered images and sentiments connected to the soccer mom, if only by insinuation. In the evangelical context, moreover, Pastor Tim's pairing of "soccer games and three-piece suits" reinforces a traditionalist gender ideology based on a division of labor in which men are breadwinners and household authority figures and women are consigned to child rearing and unpaid domestic labor (Wilcox 2004). The discourses of antimaterialism and outreach mobilization implicate lifestyle choices managed largely (but not entirely) within the parameters of the feminized domestic sphere, and this reinforces a worldview in which the responsibility to overcome the pitfalls of class rests primarily on the shoulders of individual consumers and homemakers. While commercial, political, and social activities associated with the male-dominant public sphere are not spared the arrows of reflexive critique, nor is the church as a corporate body, the more consistent themes revolve around issues of individual and family morality. This is particularly so with regard to the nuclear family household, which is idealized as a place of male headship but also recognized as a space inhabited and supervised by women, even in families where both parents work salaried jobs.[4]

When enthusiasm started to surface around outreach ministries at Eternal Vine and Marble Valley Presbyterian, several initiatives developed with the help of church-based women's groups. During my field-work, the volunteer force at both megachurches was composed mostly of women (as is generally the case with church voluntarism in the United States), though by no means exclusively. Male congregants, including pastoral staff, ministry professionals, laymen with flexible work schedules, and retirees, were often just as involved as the women in helping to conceive and implement new strategies of social outreach. As I indicated earlier, on the surface the rhetoric of outreach mobilization was indiscriminate with regard to gender. It was intended to increase volunteer participation among all churchgoers, and to enhance the public profile of the evangelical community as a whole through social engagement. However, the fact that the rhetoric built on existing cultural critiques with gendered overtones such as I have described may help to explain why mobilization efforts rarely achieved the level of publicity that socially engaged evangelicals hoped for.

The affinity between domestic family responsibilities and the care-giving virtues that characterize social ministry reproduced an intuitive sense among suburban churchgoers that social outreach was essentially a private matter, one that needed to be addressed by individual believers (presumably women) but not necessarily by the church polity as an organized whole. Ironically then, capitalizing on suburban evangelical preoccupations with the spiritual injuries of class may have produced some unintended drawbacks for socially engaged evangelicals in Knoxville, including the tendency for social outreach ministries to be treated as lesser priorities than other areas such as worship, spiritual growth, and missionary evangelism, which were more readily understood to require collective programmatic investment. At the same time, such reflexive critiques were clearly persuasive for churchgoers who did become involved as outreach volunteers, many of whom recognized the opportunity to refashion their religious and moral selfhood according to ideals that stood opposed to what they saw as the rampant materialism of the secular culture in which they lived. Social outreach became for them an avenue through which to navigate the tricky existential contours of class consciousness. This is certainly true among evangelical women, for whom class reflexivity and civic voluntarism may be especially salient, but it applies to the entire suburban evangelical community, where class is seen quite literally as a blessing and a curse.

CLASS ACTS

The resurgence of religious conservatism in the late twentieth century was aided by the growth of suburban communities across the Sunbelt that became havens of retreat and relative enclosure for middle-class professionals and families, including many who gravitated toward conservative values that were easily mobilized in support of right-wing causes (McGirr 2001). Conservative activists tapped into the aspirations, fears, and resentments of middle- and working-class whites facing uncertain prospects in an age of profound cultural change and economic neoliberalization, enabling waves of reactionary sentiment that bolstered antiliberal policies and xenophobic attitudes. Today white middle-class conservatives in suburban churches remain a core constituency in right-wing politics. But it must also be noted that the experience of class positionality can work in other ways, triggering forms of social awareness at the grassroots that are channeled into civic and charitable voluntarism.

According to research in congregational studies, large urban and suburban churches whose members typically have middle-class incomes and high levels of education display congregational norms favorable to the promotion of social outreach ministries, including churches that are ideologically and theologically conservative (Ammerman 2005; Chaves 2004; Cnaan et al. 2002). We can posit several reasons for this, including bourgeois notions of noblesse oblige or ethics of social responsibility internalized by white-collar professionals seeking opportunities to demonstrate their capacities for benevolence, social entrepreneurialism, and upstanding citizenship. Feelings of guilt and frustration can be factors as well, as people in affluent congregations become conscious of class privileges that reflect socioeconomic disparities and may be associated with certain ethical failings but also provide the very means of implementing an array of social interventions (see Coutin 1993). Socially engaged pastors and churchgoers at Eternal Vine and Marble Valley Presbyterian were extremely sympathetic to the fact that even though many of their fellow churchgoers were preoccupied with the pressures of upward mobility, or simply maintaining a respectable standard of living, they were also eager to make a difference in the world as Christians, as agents of domesticated wealth, and as arbiters of public morality. The search for meaning through purposeful and compassionate action was a recurring theme among evangelicals focused on outreach mobilization, who advocated for social outreach on the grounds that it represented one of the best methods for suburban evangelicals to venture out of their comfort zones and overcome the hazards of materialism and complacency. Take, for example, the following statement by Paul Genero, which was made during an interview but was consistent with the type of rhetoric he used when addressing any crowd of potential donors and volunteers:

> If you start to actually get your church involved, it's like feeding the fire because people start to get really into it, and God begins to use them in ways they've never been used before. They feel it, they feel somehow significant again, or maybe for the first time. They sense God's spirit reaching out through them to touch somebody else's life, and they're changed. People are changed, and it's so radically different than their kind of comfortable, cozy West Knoxville home, with their nice little soccer practice and college education all planned. It's not *safe* anymore. It's out of the bounds. It's risky. It's, you know, uncomfortable. But yet because of those things it's very rewarding.

Paul's references to "nice little soccer practice" and "comfortable, cozy" suburban family life address cultural tendencies that he and others hoped to counteract. The idea that stressed-out, emotionally taxed, family-oriented, middle-class churchgoers could "feel somehow significant again, or maybe for the first time" is based on a common understanding of faith-based voluntarism as a meaningful alternative to types of secular and even religious activities that are seen as largely egocentric. As Rebecca Allahyari has argued in her study of volunteers in religious charity organizations, people who become actively involved in charity work are engaged in a process of "moral selving," an effort at "creating oneself as a more virtuous, and often more spiritual, person ... in contrast to a situated identity" (2000: 4). To the evangelicals in my study, the pursuit of self-betterment through virtuous action was geared toward sacred aspirations that were defined partly in contrast to the situated identity of class, which was constantly problematized even when the advantages of elevated class status were taken for granted. The pursuit was motivated by religious precepts that shape evangelical subjectivity, including personal piety and proselytization. Identifying conventional markers of class and contemplating their theological relevance thus appeared to serve as an important step for suburban evangelicals entering the field of social engagement.

The connection that is assumed to exist between the egocentric tendencies of middle-class leisure and the selfless generosity of social outreach was made clear by Cheri Davenport, a middle-aged real estate broker and member of Eternal Vine. When I interviewed Cheri in her plush and tastefully decorated home, I asked her to describe how she initially became interested in social outreach ministries. She explained that despite her having become a born-again, Bible-believing evangelical in her midthirties, it took another twenty years before she realized the importance of social outreach as an expression of one's faith. Her realization came almost like an epiphany: "A few years ago, maybe four or five, my husband and I were both sitting in church and left that day and said to each other that we felt like chipmunks. With our cheeks full, you know? We were just going to church and getting ourselves fed, and we felt like it was time to start giving out. We wanted to reach out and help other people and share what all knowledge God had given us. So we started doing some volunteer work."

Cheri and her husband decided that being faithful Christians required more than just having their personal needs fulfilled and sins redeemed. She acquainted herself with other socially engaged evangelicals and became involved in local outreach ministries and faith-based organizations, especially those that worked with the urban poor. She volunteered frequently (occasionally joined by her husband) at downtown shelters and social service agencies located near public housing projects, and felt particularly drawn to the idea of ministering to poor families with young children. Cheri's manner of describing her motivations and the self-transformation she has undergone in the process echo the major elements of reflexivity and cultural critique expressed repeatedly by other suburban evangelicals.

I just got sick of sitting on this nice cushy couch here in my pretty little living room and knowing that there's people out there that are hurting, and that if they just knew Jesus, if they just knew hope, that it would make a difference in their lives. So I just want to do that with my time, and more of my time. It's like the more I do it the more I want to do it. The more things

I get involved in the more things I want to do. There's a lot of opportunity in this town, *a lot* of opportunity to minister.

Cheri's account offers a narrative in which, having achieved a life of relative comfort and financial stability, she began to worry about falling into patterns of consumer complacency. She found herself unsettled by the ethical implications of a bourgeois lifestyle that suddenly appeared (probably not for the first time) to contradict the moral imperatives of her faith. At the very moment when she felt adequately fulfilled in life and at church, she came to see her comfort and satisfaction as problems rather than desirable objectives. In short, in the process of becoming personally fulfilled Cheri internalized an intrinsic evangelical skepticism toward personal fulfillment as an end goal. Although the therapeutic tenor of contemporary Christian self-help pervades evangelical congregations like Eternal Vine, it is intersected by thematic cross-currents that lead some churchgoers to question, if not directly challenge, the cultural standards on which their ideas of self-realization are based. For evangelicals like Cheri this results in an intensification of moral ambitions oriented toward social engagement, including the desire to make meaningful use of one's time and resources by helping people in need and getting them to "know Jesus," all in a spirit of humility and service.

Suburban evangelicals in Knoxville claimed all kinds of personal motivations for getting involved in social outreach ministries. Some, as we have already seen, suggested that coming from a working-class background gave them an inclination to empathize with people struggling to make ends meet. Others described experiences of traveling to other countries and witnessing the effects of intense poverty, which made them feel compassion for the poor, in general, as well as a greater appreciation of the value of cross-cultural ministry. Norm Griswall, an elder at Marble Valley Presbyterian who helped spearhead the megachurch's efforts to reach out to the black community in the inner city, said that growing up as a "missionary kid" (the child of missionary parents) in Latin America instilled in him a lasting appreciation for cultural diversity and a heightened awareness of the kinds of social problems that exist beyond what he called "Yuppieville." Francine Daly, another member of Marble Valley and a very active outreach volunteer, was inspired to get involved after a visit to the Holocaust Memorial Museum in Washington, DC. She started reading about the holocaust and was especially moved by the stories of Christians who hid Jews from persecution. Soon after this she learned that a refugee agency in

Knoxville was looking for someone to provide temporary housing and assistance to a Muslim family arriving from Kosovo. After consulting with her husband, she offered them her home, where they stayed for several weeks. Francine interpreted all this as the moment when God inspired her to move in a new direction in her faith, one that forced her to change previous habits and priorities to reflect a deeper spirituality based on compassion for the needy and willingness to forgo the benefits of living entirely in her own physical and emotional comfort zone. Many similar accounts circulate among socially engaged evangelicals, and in just about every case that I encountered there was an element of reflection on issues of relative privilege and privation, and the idea that overcoming the spiritual injuries of class requires coming to terms with the existence of underprivileged, marginalized, or victimized Others.

As I noted earlier, evangelical concerns about class and consumerist materialism do not necessarily imply a critique of capitalism per se. The structure of socioeconomic stratification on which capitalism relies is neither questioned nor condemned by conservative evangelicals in Knoxville, but rather taken as natural and given. In light of this, one might speculate that the ruminations described in this chapter amount to little more than the cultural reinforcement of social and symbolic boundaries that maintain rather than complicate impermeable class distinctions (Lamont and Fournier 1992). Although on some levels this may be true, these ruminations reveal the significant extent to which conservative evangelicals in affluent suburban congregations periodically entertain the notion that an inherent relationship exists between their actions as members of an elevated social class and the misfortunes and deprivations of others who are less well off. When socially engaged evangelicals in Knoxville invoked the wider evangelical discourse of antimaterialism, they were essentially making the case that the dangers of living a bourgeois, materialistic lifestyle are not merely dangers of a personal nature but matters of far-reaching moral and religious consequence as well because they directly affect other people, whether they are other churchgoers who fall prey to similar patterns or the poor and needy, whose deprivations are left unattended as a result of middle-class ignorance and indifference. It is in this sense that a level of social consciousness raising and a decentering of moral individualism can be read from what otherwise appears to outsiders as the angst-ridden navel-gazing of the well-to-do. Examining the evangelical critique of materialism and its role in outreach mobilization more closely, as I do in the remainder of this chapter, we see clearly how suburban evangelicals self-consciously address and manage the contradictions that animate their religious lives. Moral dilemmas regarding one's lifestyle habits and the use of one's money and time are never easily dismissed nor completely resolved by theology or simplistic self-help panaceas. They are subject to continuous reflection and revision. Their mediation in words and deeds constantly reinforces conservative theological and moral beliefs while offering room for the development of new discursive and practical realms for working out the problem of how to embody the virtues of wealth, productivity, service, and sacrifice all at once.

MAKING SENSE OF MAMMON

The anthropologist Webb Keane describes what he calls the "moral narrative of modernity" as a quest for purification, an ideology of self-liberation that "characteristically involves a certain dematerialization of the human world, a denial of some of the ways human subjects are enmeshed with material objects" (Keane 2007: 271). European Protestant missionaries carried this ontological paradigm to foreign mission fields, bringing it into conflict with local traditions and indigenous customs that, in contrast, reinforced direct links between materiality and personal subjectivity. In the Sumbanese context analyzed by Keane, the resulting "clash of semiotic ideologies" produced a situation where the social values traditionally attached to material forms such as ceremonial objects, money, and status commodities became unstable, and traditional norms of personhood became ambiguous. Building on Keane's analysis, which addresses Christian acculturation in a non-Western setting, I would argue that similar instabilities and normative ambiguities exist even among Christians in Western cultural contexts. Although evangelical subjectivity is predicated on the idea of faith as an abstract liberation of the self from the weight of earthly and impure things, evangelicals in their daily lives struggle with the belief that there may well be social and even spiritual values derived from one's attachment to a world of materiality. In other words, North American evangelicals do not simply reproduce Western modernity's quest for spiritual purification; they also inherit the ambivalence intrinsic to that moral project. The desire to overcome or at least minimize the determinative influence of money and material wealth in one's life is complicated by positive connotations frequently attached to wealth that is earned, spent, and invested in line with sacred virtues. The problem of materialism is, for middle-class evangelicals, an effort to understand how it is that material wealth can both enhance and threaten the moral ambitions inspired by the dictates of Protestant faith.

Money is not a taboo topic of conversation among suburban evangelicals but it does raise for them a number of important and sometimes difficult questions. Most of the churchgoers I encountered at Eternal Vine and Marble Valley Presbyterian either were financially well off or sufficiently if not gainfully employed. Discussions about financial issues took place openly in a variety of formal and informal contexts, as people were eager to know how best to earn, spend, and invest money in accordance with biblical principles. They made no attempt to deny the everyday relevance of money and monetary practice; rather they made considerable effort to address it in relation to higher religious concerns, so that their motivations were always guided by spiritual rather than material interests. As other scholars have demonstrated (e.g., Bialecki 2008; Bielo 2007), evangelicals distinguish between monetary practices that conform to what are taken to be secular values and those that fall under the rubric of the sacred, and they seek moreover to re-enchant whole realms of economic activity by imbuing profane transactions with religious significance. Churches and parachurch ministries offer a range of counseling services and workshops, such as the widely popular "Financial Peace" seminars developed by author and media personality Dave Ramsey, aimed at teaching people how to achieve and maintain financial solvency with confidence and without compromising Christian ethics.[5] Contrary to public perception, these ministries rarely promote what is known as prosperity theology, which is based on the belief that God wants everyone to be prosperous and that all believers can achieve health and wealth almost instantaneously through disciplines of prayer and obedience. This approach is uncommon among most white conservative evangelicals, despite its strong media profile, and many of the pastors and churchgoers I knew rejected the movement as idolatrous and materialistic.[6]

Now and then, of course, situations arise when issues of monetary practice appear not so straightforward and spark disagreement or controversy among evangelical churchgoers. Questions about tithing, for example, have the potential to stir discord, as churchgoers differ over how the imperative to tithe should be regulated and enforced. For years, the leadership at Eternal Vine Church chose not to collect church offerings during worship services; members were encouraged instead to leave their offerings in locked drop-boxes just outside the doors of the main sanctuary. The idea behind this was to avoid the old main-line tradition of the public offering, which was perceived as ritualized peer pressure based on crass, legalistic norms that were not conducive to the spirit of authentic spirituality that was so central to Eternal Vine's mission as a church. The congregation got by financially for a long time without requiring a formal tithe or passing collection plates, but eventually the growth of the megachurch's ministries outstripped its annual revenue. The leadership decided to institute a change and announced that offerings were henceforth going to be collected during services, on the grounds that members needed to learn to take seriously the value of proper "stewardship," meaning their shared responsibility for resources that belong to God. To ease the transition, the senior staff chose to forgo the use of the conventional offering plate and instead started passing around green velvet sacks with small wooden handles. Aside from looking less "churchy," the sacks had the added benefit of allowing churchgoers to give their offerings without others seeing how much they gave. The transition was accomplished over time but not without discontent arising in the process. Some churchgoers were outraged by the sudden change in policy and the top-down nature of its implementation. Others were concerned that Eternal Vine was moving toward a more formal and less voluntary approach to offerings rather than standing firm in its efforts to be more distinctive. Still others objected to the ways that money was being spent at the megachurch, including some who complained about recent plans to purchase a large espresso machine for the hospitality room. Regardless of the specifics, the whole incident demonstrates that issues of money can be especially thorny when they involve financial practices that pertain directly to matters of church governance, aesthetics of worship, and standards of religious discipline.

Given the ambiguities surrounding money and wealth, especially in the context of an affluent megachurch, the critique of materialism offers a particularly relevant idiom for introspection. It also provides an outlet through which conservative evangelicals express lingering discontent with regard to modernity. Evangelicalism has generally resigned to modernity in that churches and denominations are more likely than their historical predecessors to become engaged by choice or necessity with modern technologies, aesthetic tastes, and intellectual trends. But the fundamentalist antimodernism that carried such force throughout the twentieth century has not receded entirely from the conservative evangelical imagination. It continues to underlie the reactionary sentiments of right-wing Christians opposed to political and cultural movements such as social liberalism, feminism, scientific evolutionism, and moral relativism. On an even more general level, conservative evangelicals criticize the culture of secular modernity where they believe moral values are determined not by divinely inspired principles and virtues but by vain desires and materialist ambitions. Like other Westerners who have yearned for means of escape from the disenchantment and alienation of the modern world (Ortner 1999), evangelicals denounce the lifestyle habits and social mores produced by a society ruled by money and commodities, in which risk and sacrifice are no longer viewed as their own rewards.[7]

Yet as earnest seekers of modernity's riches and comforts, they remain ambivalent. This will become even clearer in the following sections as I break down the evangelical critique of materialism into three major subthemes: consumerism, upward versus downward mobility, and issues of time management, especially in relation to family life. Each of these subthemes represents a problem or tendency that was identified by socially engaged evangelicals in Knoxville as symptomatic of modern materialism, and endemic to the middle-class suburban milieu to which they belong. In each case we will also see how such targets of cultural critique were utilized as catalysts for outreach mobilization among pastors and churchgoers.

Consumerism

Paul Genero once described "biblical Christianity" as a totally "God-centric" faith, characterized by utter dependence on God's will and expressed through active compassion and loving sacrifices. He contrasted this with what he called "consumer Christianity," which is "egocentric," status-driven, and focused on commodities rather than spiritual blessings. The negative effects of consumerism, he noted, can be seen throughout society but are especially problematic among local Christian churches. Since Paul's critique focused primarily on suburban congregations, it was laced with images of leisure-class privilege.

> What you tend to see is that there is less of a felt need for God. You know how it is. You have money in the bank, all your bills are paid, you got all your scholarship stuff coming in and you're just sitting fat and sassy. You start to feel smug about life: "Oh, I'm just sitting happy here." You know? It's the same with Christians. Everything's going great and we've got a full staff at church, and our buildings are full of people ... we have all the felt

needs in our life taken care of with money ... and our kids are all cute and they're doing well in school and there are no *unsolvable* problems. "I'm putting money away for retirement, and maybe I just got a raise at work, and I live in a nice neighborhood, etc." Then why do you need God?

Paul's comments are unmistakable in their negative comparison. Patterns of consumer complacency associated with suburban lifestyles are seen to be reproduced in local churches. By implying that suburban evangelicals fall prey to consumerism as they strive for financial security, property ownership, and high-quality education, Paul did not mean to dismiss or condemn everything that results from material wealth. After all, the modus operandi of his organization, the Samaritans of Knoxville, was to harness the resources of affluent churches and communities for purposes of organized benevolence. He did, however, identify certain aspects of consumerism as factors that limit the depth of Christian faith and impede the progress of social outreach and evangelism. "I'm learning to deal with all the casual disinterest I see. We have so many years of church life that have hardened our arteries, because we live in an affluent society that goes against our core principles." He paused for a moment and added, "It is the rare Christian who can in the midst of his affluence—in his castle—connect himself to the pain-filled world."

I often detected an implicit class commentary embedded in the ways evangelicals talked about consumerism as part of the larger critique of materialism. They tended to valorize the labor productivity of the working class as opposed to the conspicuous consumption equated with wealth. Pastors and ministry leaders peppered their discussions with industrial metaphors and suggestions that being a biblical Christian means being ready to "roll up your sleeves" and "take care of business." Frequent references to stereotypically masculine activities such as car repair, construction work, and hunting reinforced a "muscular" view of faith as something that should be practical and industrious rather than passive and frivolous (adding yet another gendered layer to the complexity of this critique). Socially engaged evangelicals drew on this tendency, like Paul Genero and Stacy Miggs, who both described themselves as having working-class backgrounds that taught them the values of working hard and helping people in need. Now and then, members of the Samaritans of Knoxville referred to the organization as "a blue-collar effort," which seemed to refer mainly to the spirit of the enterprise rather than its demographics. For suburban evangelicals in Knoxville, becoming socially engaged was conceived as a way of "keeping it real," of breaking free of the stagnation and pretensions of middle-class comfort and embracing a labor-intensive approach to evangelical religiosity.

A key concept operating within this class commentary is that of productivity. The problem with consumerism is that it promotes wasteful self-indulgence, at the expense of a radical faith capable of bearing fruit in the real world and inspiring missionary and entrepreneurial zeal. The members of Eternal Vine and Marble Valley Presbyterian have a lot at stake in maintaining clear distinctions between consumer-driven as opposed to faith-based action, especially given that both megachurches grew in part by strategically appealing to consumer sensibilities in the first place. In the words of one staff administrator at Eternal Vine: "We don't want people to come here with a consumer mentality; we want them to have a producer mentality." The "product" that megachurch leaders envision is a community of fervent Christians bound to one another spiritually and committed to promoting the gospel with conviction and humility. To quote a line from an announcement in Eternal Vine's Sunday bulletin: "The Father is calling us to transition from being spiritual consumers to being compassionate servants. In other words, God is calling us to exchange our prosperous, stuff-oriented lives for the life of Christ."

Consistent with the emphasis on productivity, the critique of materialism overlaps with evangelical discourse on "stewardship." The concept of stewardship in evangelical circles refers to the act of tithing or giving money to the church, but it goes further in its theological significance. Stewardship is conceived as a religious discipline that begins with the recognition that one's material assets are not one's own but belong primarily to God. Pastor Jerry of Marble Valley Presbyterian preached that "our attitude toward money and our use of money are prime indicators of our spiritual state." He explained that when money is idolized for the sake of personal gain it is dangerous, but "when money is seen as a resource for accomplishing God's purposes on earth, it becomes a useful part of our stewardship." Sermons and teachings on stewardship cite a wide range of Bible passages to remind churchgoers that supporting one's church financially and donating money to local ministries and foreign missions is a scriptural mandate, and an integral part of the sacrificial logic of redemption.[8] As Jon Bialecki has noted,

Christian stewardship entails a model of exchange in which monetary practices are "structured in such a way as to erase the importance of the subject as an agentive force, while at the same time stressing the accountability of that subject" (Bialecki 2008: 378). While the theological and historical roots of the concept are deep, its modern permutations suggest "an ethic of responsibility born of capitalism" (Schervish 1990: 80). Contemporary evangelical churchgoers are not only called on to submit material assets in service of God's kingdom, they are also expected to invest their assets in productive religious, social, and economic enterprises.

Socially engaged evangelicals highlighted social outreach as one such enterprise and built on conventional notions of stewardship, expanding their meaning in the course of mobilizing others. Calls for volunteers included statements urging churchgoers to take a step beyond the normal habit of writing checks for charities. One such announcement read: "We don't sense [God] is calling us just to give money to the poor. That is just an easy, middle-class way to relieve a guilty conscience. We believe God is calling us into relationship with the poor." The aim of mobilization of this kind was to steer the average churchgoer away from thinking of stewardship purely in terms of detached, impersonal monetary transactions. "In a busy world," Paul Genero told me, "the Body of Christ tends to lean toward commodity-based outreach," which "promotes dependency among needy people and doesn't get God's people involved relationally." The end result is that the church at best becomes "just a glorified social service agency," and believers remain isolated from relational "hands-on" opportunities to minister and evangelize. According to this view, the demands of evangelical stewardship require not just giving away money but participating fully in ministries and missionary activities that put God's resources to good use.[9] Writing checks is good, but simply writing checks and expecting them to make an impact in the world or advance the cause of Christianization is equated with the problem of consumer complacency, an unproductive habit that limits the possibilities of redemption and evangelism by reducing such imperatives to the logic of alienated commodity exchange. Evangelical churchgoers who have presumably been raised to accept the essential terms of consumer capitalism are invited to imagine an alternative framework for the moral domestication of wealth. Although not many churchgoers at Eternal Vine and Marble Valley Presbyterian responded to such calls with great commitment, the underlying message must have resonated strongly given that so many of them struggled with doubts and dilemmas about such issues as they climbed, or tried to climb, the proverbial social ladder.

Upward versus Downward Mobility

Contrary to common belief, evangelical preaching is rarely just about condemning the sinful ways of the unchurched world. It is more often a medium of moral instruction directed squarely at the people in the pews. On Christmas Eve, Eternal Vine's Pastor Tim gave an evocative sermon that tapped directly into the ambivalent sentiments I have described, relating them to a message about the importance of volunteering for local charity organizations. The sermon, titled "Christmas: Celebrating the Generosity of God," began in an unexpected way. Pastor Tim brought up the familiar complaint that "Christmas is too commercial," but defended the commercialism of the holiday season on the grounds that the buying and selling of gifts actually makes sense during Christmas, which celebrates the extraordinary generosity of God the Father. After all, the incarnation of Jesus Christ was a divine gift to humanity and, like the most precious of gifts, it required a sacrifice. Pastor Tim explained that the God portrayed in the Bible is an almighty creator who "refused to remain cloistered in a walled heaven." He is a God who, for the sake of redemption, took on a humble human form in order "to live in relationship with the messy world that he created."

Pastor Tim continued to build on the theme of incarnation and talked about the manger where Jesus was born, which he portrayed as a symbol of God's desire that believers engage in "incarnational" ministries of their own. As an illustration, he described his own personal experiences serving warm meals at a homeless shelter in the inner city and concluded by pointing out that, despite his initial reservations, he grew to love volunteer work because "God has allowed me to incarnate into a little painful place in the world." He urged churchgoers to accept the idea that living as a follower of Christ means willingly leaving your comfort zone to step into the "messy world" and confront all manner of physical and emotional suffering. He ended the sermon with a moral quip: "Go find a manger of pain and incarnate yourself into it."

A few days earlier, I had discussed similar matters with Jackie Sherman, a staff member at Marble Valley Presbyterian, in her office decorated at every angle with colorful holiday ornaments. She wore a bright red sweater and shiny Christmas tree earrings and regaled me with stories of her life as a Christian. She became somber, however, when we started to talk about all the wealth represented in the congregation. The presence of so much affluence was frustrating to her because she imagined that this made it that much more difficult for Christians to understand how they are supposed to follow in Christ's footsteps:

> Jesus Christ was for the broken, the oppressed. Foxes have holes, but the Son of Man has nowhere to lay his head.[10] Sometimes when I drive around and look at all the mansions that these Christians live in, and the chariots that they drive up here on Sunday morning, I'm asking, do you really know the Christ who said, "I came for the poor?" You know? That's the struggle I have.... You know, are we really living the radical Christian life in these affluent churches, where we almost have no minorities? We might give money to the church, but do we *sacrificially* give?

When I asked Jackie how she felt about the fact that the wealth she criticized also provided essential support for the megachurch and its dozens of ministries, she acknowledged that "there are some good things about having money." But she stressed that "if Christians were living a radical Christian life, we would have missionaries all over this city and it wouldn't have to take materialism to do it." Jackie cheered up instantly when she remembered examples like Margie and Harrison McKenzie and other churchgoing couples who used to live in the suburbs but chose instead to move to inner-city neighborhoods and minister directly to communities in need. "I believe that's the Christian life," she exclaimed. "Just think, that's what it's all about!"

When evangelicals choose to sacrifice comfort, wealth, or status to become missionaries or work in a less than lucrative field of ministry, they are held up by others as exemplars of Christian virtue. They represent Pastor Tim's image of incarnational faith put into action not only because they have chosen a path of full-bodied engagement but also because the path is seen to involve a voluntary pursuit of downward mobility. According to evangelical theology, Jesus Christ left the celestial realm, where he is united with God for all eternity, in order to be born into an earthly body. During his life and ministry, he spent much of his time among people in the lower strata of society. In the words of Ray Bakke, a well-known urban ministry activist who came to give an outreach workshop at Marble Valley Presbyterian, "Downward mobility is what Jesus was all about." Evangelicals who seek to emulate Jesus believe they have a responsibility to do likewise by modifying their lifestyles and essentially downshifting from positions of comfort and social privilege to positions of humility and service. As might be expected, the majority of churchgoers rarely go to extremes to accomplish this, and many would readily admit to being reluctant if not even a bit skeptical, but nonetheless they recognize the religious imperative to humble oneself and keep one's selfish or vain desires for upward mobility in check. This can be beneficial from the perspective of outreach mobilization because churchgoers are left looking for "mangers of pain" where they can minister to people in need and at the same time experience some of the spiritual advantages of self-imposed privation.

Yet the allure of upward mobility remains strong. One of the bestselling books in Christian publishing in 2000 was Bruce Wilkinson's *The Prayer of Jabez*, a short devotional study based on an obscure passage from Chronicles I of the Old Testament. Simply written, pocket-sized and inexpensive, the book was a runaway hit, selling nearly eight million copies in its first two years of printing. The main gist of the book is that God wants his people to pray and be blessed, and that it is not against God's will for people to pray for personal success and prosperity as long as they pray earnestly and use their blessings for the sake of God's kingdom. Wilkinson writes, "If seeking God's blessings is our ultimate act of worship, and asking to do more for Him is our utmost ambition, then asking for God's hand upon us is our strategic choice to sustain and continue the great things that God has begun in our lives" (2000: 49). At the height of its popularity, *The Prayer of Jabez* was featured prominently on display tables at secular as well as Christian bookstores across the country. Churchgoers in Knoxville talked excitedly about the book, circulated copies among their friends, and even thought of using it as a tool for evangelism since it was considered straightforward and inoffensive enough to be given to nonbelievers. With all their worry about materialism, they must have been relieved to read a book saying that there is essentially nothing wrong with wanting a life of plenty, so long as you attain it by humbly petitioning God.

The book also drew criticism from Christian circles, especially from conservative evangelicals who found its similarity to prosperity theology disturbing.[11] Evangelical critics took Wilkinson to task for reducing matters of faith to "individualistic optimism" and neglecting serious consideration for the theological importance of "enduring faithfulness at humble and thankless tasks" (Galli 2001). Local leaders echoed these criticisms as warnings to their congregations, although they did so diplomatically because they knew how popular the book had become among churchgoers. When Pastor Tim brought up the book during a sermon, he made sure to note its positive aspects before going on to describe the author's argument as "imbalanced." He compared Wilkinson's take on the prayer of Jabez to the Lord's Prayer, pointing out that "unlike the Lord's Prayer, the book focuses on asking God to bless me, and not as much on how I can be used in my community to bless the world." Churchgoers no doubt took such warnings to heart, but it is revealing that *The Prayer of Jabez* achieved such popularity among suburban evangelicals. The respective virtues associated with upward and downward mobility in the evangelical imagination are not easy to reconcile but they coexist nonetheless in the conflicted longings of churchgoers who are disinclined to give up their faith or the promise of prosperity but also believe, as one member at Eternal Vine told me, "You can't follow God and the American Dream at the same time."

"Busyness"

During a group Bible study one afternoon at Marble Valley Presbyterian, a discussion leader quoted 1 John 3:13: "Do not be surprised, my brothers, if the world hates you." He asked the group how they interpreted the meaning of the phrase *the world* in this passage. One man thought it referred to "the *culture* of the world," which stands in negative contrast to the Kingdom of God. An elderly woman suggested that *worldliness* refers to "anything that takes you away from God." A man in his midthirties named Greg then asked if it is ever possible to know what "the world" really is while we remain stuck in it. To illustrate his point, he brought up the science-fiction film *The Matrix,* which builds on the premise that reality as commonly perceived is a deceptive illusion that people can fully understand only once they separate themselves from it and embrace prophetic truths. Greg added that what Christians really need to do is take time to "step outside the culture of the world," so they can grasp the true nature of things and then "reenter" the world in order to change it. At this point, Jim Elroy of the Fuller Street Mission chimed in to say that this is precisely what happens to people who spend time working with the poor. He explained that outreach volunteers are similar to missionaries who, in a sense, withdraw from the world they know to do God's work, gaining a sharper and more spiritual perspective on the secular world in the process. Jim also pointed out, unapologetically, that too many Christians are so attached to their busy schedules and obsessed with "fixing themselves" that they cannot discover valuable opportunities to use their time in spiritually productive ways, such as sharing God's love with the poor.

When I asked ministry directors and volunteer coordinators about the most persistent problems they faced in gathering volunteers, almost all of them complained that no one seemed to have any time. Although they understood the reasons people gave for having to manage their time carefully, socially engaged evangelicals regarded the tendency toward "busyness" as yet another symptom of the culture of materialism. Not only were they frustrated about the amount of time that churchgoers were willing to allocate for social outreach, they also questioned the ultimate value of the various hurried or self-indulgent activities that took up the rest of their day. They argued that the more time people spend running around doing "busy stuff," the less time they have to "seek God's face" through prayer and acts of compassion. Furthermore, socially engaged evangelicals pointed out that when suburban church-goers worried too much about setting aside personal time for religious contemplation, they reproduced an unhealthy inclination to treat spiri-tual growth as something that occurs apart from the normal affairs of everyday life and their relationships with other people. A member of Eternal Vine who was active with the Samaritans of Knoxville told me that Christians today are wedded to a "false dichotomy" between the spiritual and the mundane. They fail to appreciate the spiritual value of simple acts like sharing a meal with someone from a totally different walk of life. He mocked the "hyperspirituality" of churchgoers who think that they are not having a religious experience unless they are having "quality time" with God.

Lifestyle habits, hobbies, and preoccupations that limit the amount of time churchgoers can devote to social outreach were particularly troublesome for socially engaged evangelicals who rely heavily on the availability of volunteers. Since suburban families typically choose from a wide range of activities, pastimes, and social networks with which to enrich their lives, social outreach ministries and faith-based organiza-tions must compete for their valuable time and energy. According to Carol Farlan, the director of a faith-based halfway house and a member of Marble Valley Presbyterian, this usually ends up being a losing battle:

The biggest problem is that time is one of the most valuable assets we have these days and there just doesn't seem to be enough of it for anybody. The years of people having a nine-to-five job are over.... So time becomes this very, very valuable commodity, and you're in there fighting for the same bit of time that's left over *after* somebody has worked all those hours and had their family time and taken all the kids to soccer practice and Brownies and Boy Scouts and all of that stuff, and has spent time with their spouse kind of working on their marriage. There isn't a lot left over.

Carol did not challenge the validity of the activities that consume people's daily lives, but like others she tended to see many of them as personal indulgences that were more about ego-gratification and status-seeking than total obedience to God's will. Raymond Andrews, a successful businessman who volunteered as a mentor for inner-city youths, described to me his commitment to social outreach as a process of reorganizing his personal priorities. He argued that a Christian's main duty is to give up his or her time and money, not just superficially but in "radical ways" that signify a willing "denial of self." Otherwise, he argued, the believer is indistinguishable from anyone else who "lives in a big fancy house and goes to soccer games." Raymond also based his volunteer efforts on the belief that relational commitments are just as valuable as financial charity, if not more so. This was an idea that he imparted to other churchgoers as well by emphasizing the intrinsic rewards of giving away something other than just material wealth. "There's *something* about how God blesses when people are willing to give their time."

As with virtually every aspect of the critique of materialism, the issue of how middle-class Christians organize their time is entangled with larger questions regarding the role of the family. Defending "traditional family values" (i.e., the heterosexual nuclear family) remains a subject of paramount importance to conservative evangelicals, which is reinforced in local congregations in preaching rhetoric and political crusades but also through ministries that promote strong marriages and close family relationships. Since the male-headed family household represents the primary site of moral discipline, developmental nurturing, and socialization, much emphasis is placed on maintaining the sanctity of its boundaries. At the same time, however, there is in evangelicalism a thread of reflexive commentary that raises the problem of family egoism, that is, a concern that when families spend too much time focused on themselves they become removed and isolated from the wider social world. While tight-knit nuclear families are seen as the building blocks of moral community, sanctioned by God and modeled after the relational unity of the Holy Trinity, the evangelical family is also expected to serve the needs of God's kingdom by avoiding inwardness and exclusivity. Unlike very fundamentalist families that are resolute about separating from the world as much as possible to protect children from secular influences, evangelical families struggle with a certain ambivalence that gets to the heart of what it means to commit to engaged orthodoxy. Evangelical families expect not only to live out their faith in private life but to promulgate it in public spaces, secular institutions, and extrafamilial relationships. Much as the missionary imperative to leave one's comfort zone entails some degree of personal sacrifice, the family is idealized as a selfless unit whose sacredness stems from its capacity for outward compassion as well as moral integrity. As indicated earlier, sacrifice and selflessness are also qualities linked to idealized conceptions of femininity and motherhood. This confluence of symbolic analogs reproduces an evangelical gender ideology that implicitly places on wives and mothers much of the responsibility of fortifying the Christian (suburban) home against materialism and the spiritual injuries of class, although the responsibility is meant to be shared by husbands and fathers, who are expected to make key decisions and set priorities on matters such as how the members of a Christian family ideally should spend their time.

Socially engaged evangelicals in Knoxville would point out that when families volunteer together or create their own outreach opportunities, they discover optimal ways to make the most of their time. Pastors and mobilizers represented social outreach as a distinctly "faith-based" activity that fits somewhere between leisure and education and therefore allows churchgoing families to reconcile their need for constructive "family time" with their religious obligations as witnesses for Christ. Homeschoolers and stay-at-home moms were especially encouraged to engage their children in volunteering and charity work so that the children will practice compassion and selflessness and learn to recognize such qualities as expressions of authentic faith and God working through them.[12] To all families, social outreach was presented as a chance to increase a family's sense of religious significance, since it held out the promise of achieving "transformations" and encountering "changed lives" in the larger community, the world of strangers waiting to be saved. This progression, which underscores rhetorical links between outreach and evangelism, was of great importance to socially engaged evangelicals, as Paul Genero explained when talking about incorporating his family into his work: "My family isn't the end all and be all of my religion anymore, but my family becomes part of what God wants to use to actually *bless,* to reach out to the rest of those who don't know Him. God just wants to love people through my family.... That's all part of the *secret* of the whole thing. They get filled up and overflowed by God and that overflow gets out to the community and the community feels the impact." In short, once evangelical families reject inward egoistic impulses, the time they spend together becomes something of an entirely different order, with no longer a minute wasted on selfish or frivolous things.

As an increasingly scarce commodity that must be managed and invested with utmost efficiency, time has become one of the great stress-inducers of late capitalism (Hochschild 1997). Anxieties pertaining to personal time management are so ubiquitous that whole sermons and seminars in evangelical megachurches are dedicated to the subject, as part of ongoing efforts to teach churchgoers how to organize their time "biblically," which is to say, how to sacralize time as much as humanly possible without feeling as though you are struggling just to keep up with the world. "Hold on loosely to our days," one pastor said, a reminder of the messianic and apocalyptic aspects of evangelical theology but also a practical argument for "not sweating the small stuff." The desire to live "in but not of the world" is chiefly concerned with temporality and the need to avoid the most pernicious elements of secular "worldliness" that work their way into daily life through something as simple as how one chooses to spend one's time. The impulse to be busy all the time, whether by choice or by necessity, is viewed as yet another example of the culture of materialism and the spiritual injuries of class affecting the lives of suburban churchgoers who find themselves caught in the whirlwind of a society constantly on the move. Ironically, ministries that exist in part to help churchgoers break the binds of secular time can be pretty time consuming in and of themselves, which again can be a problem for social outreach ministries that are likely to end up with shorter time commitments, if any at all, from overcommitted churchgoers who tend to feel that they have barely any time to spare.

During the final episode of *Survivor II,* Knoxville's Tina Wesson was asked what she planned to do with the one-million-dollar prize. She said that she would pay off her house and her best friend's house and establish a fund to help families in need. She also said that she had never earned more than minimum wage and looked forward to making a major contribution to her family's finances. In a nutshell, Wesson articulated widespread aspirations of success and self-fulfillment. Many of her fellow evangelical churchgoers would probably have answered the same way, also hoping to capitalize on good fortune for the sake of personal advancement (home ownership, status mobility) as well as for the sake of others (helping friends and needy strangers). At the same time, the fact that Wesson's born-again identity was known but relatively muted reinforced the discomfort that many suburban evangelicals feel as they try to figure out whether their material and social aspirations can be reconciled with the moral ambitions of their faith, including the desire to embody Christian virtues of sacrifice, humility, and benevolence.

I have argued in this chapter that the evangelical discourse of antimaterialism allows suburban churchgoers to reflect on perennial doubts and anxieties connected to a conflicted sense of class identity. Antimaterialist concerns revolve around issues of wealth, status, productivity, and consumption, and are extended to questions of class positionality relative to underprivileged communities. The problems of modern society that are believed to stem from materialism and the spiritual injuries of class are rarely analyzed in political-economic terms, but are regarded rather as distinctly moral and spiritual problems reflecting the scarcity, or at best superficiality, of religious virtue (i.e., "authentic faith") among the public values that define the middle class. Such sentiments are by no means unique to conservative evangelicals. Variations on this discourse appear among religious groups throughout the United States. Hasidic Jews in Brooklyn, for example, routinely portray secular materialism as something to fear and avoid, thereby distinguishing themselves and their pious lifestyle from the questionable and undisciplined morality of Gentiles and secular Jews (Fader 2009). For the evangelicals I studied in Knoxville, such distinctions were more complicated, since they did not consider themselves completely separate from the secular materialism that they were critiquing. Their critique was an exercise in reflexivity and not an outright assertion of moral superiority, although as Christ-loving born-again evangelicals they naturally assumed that they were better equipped than nonbelievers to confront and counteract the spiritual dangers of living in a comfort zone.

Socially engaged evangelicals built on these attitudes as they struggled to generate grassroots support for social outreach ministries. Their rhetorical aims were less about exploiting a guilty conscience than seeking to inspire or channel the moral ambitions of suburban churchgoers who were eager to discover new avenues of religious volunteerism and vocation. Although their appeals were evocative and probably convincing to many, the majority of churchgoers never fully embraced the idea, as evidenced by the fact that pastors and mobilizers remained frustrated by the lack of sustained volunteer participation. For most churchgoers, the pressures of daily life, including work and family, may be too great to risk the sacrifice of time, energy, and personal resources one might feel expected to commit to outreach ministries and faith-based organizations. Opportunities for spiritual growth through Bible study and fellowship with other churchgoers tend to be more readily accepted as priorities for the God-seeking evangelical believer. In Knoxville, those who did commit themselves to social engagement claimed to have found new meaning and purpose in their religious lives as a result of having loosened the shackles of materialism in their personal lives. Even in those circumstances, however, the specter of class was rarely absent. As I show in the next chapter, the spiritual injuries of class remained on the minds of socially engaged evangelicals, particularly because of the vertical power dynamics that inevitably entered into their interactions with the poor and distressed people they were prepared to serve.

CHAPTER 6

Compassion Accounts

But love your enemies, do good to them, and lend to them
without expecting to get anything back. Then your reward
will be great, you will be sons of the Most High, because
he is kind to the ungrateful and wicked. Be merciful, just as
your Father is merciful.

—Luke 6:35–36

Between the idea
And the reality
Between the motion
And the act
Falls the Shadow

—T.S. Eliot, *The Hollow Men*

The dismantling of the federal welfare state in the 1990s sparked renewed public interest in religiously inspired or "faith-based" charity work and welfare activism. Religious conservatives in particular were emboldened by the idea that the downsizing of government's role in the business of welfare would usher in a new era in which religious charities, social services, and local congregations would reclaim their rightful roles and legitimacy on issues of welfare and moral governance in community life. In addition to revivalist and missionary ideals, the moral ambitions of socially engaged evangelicals during this period were fueled to a large extent by the belief that faithful, discerning Christians (what George W. Bush called the "armies of compassion") were best suited to the task of reviving the spirit of civic responsibility and local charity that many felt had been undermined by the welfare state and its liberal policies of entitlement. Yet despite their activist enthusiasm,

153

conservative evangelical outreach workers and volunteers encountered ethical dilemmas and frustrations as they attempted to reach across the race and class divides in their home communities. They grappled with multiple and diverging aspects of evangelical theology and with the difficulties of managing the intrinsic power dynamics between themselves and the recipients of charitable aid with whom they sought to interact through social outreach.

Socially engaged evangelicals in Knoxville often talked about "compassion fatigue" as being one of the primary hardships they dealt with in the process of doing the actual work of social outreach. It was a recurring theme over the course of my research that came up during interviews as well as church discussion groups, workshops, and planning meetings. The concept of compassion fatigue has currency outside of evangelicalism as well, but its meanings vary depending on the group or social context in which it is invoked. One popular use of the phrase refers to the emotional desensitization that is believed to occur as a result of the shallow and formulaic manner in which humanitarian crises in remote regions of the world are represented in Western news media (Moeller 1999). In the lingo of the nonprofit sector, the idea of compassion fatigue explains why charitable donations from the general public drop after seasonal periods of accelerated giving (Allahyari 2000). Among evangelical pastors and churchgoers, the phrase carries a rather different meaning, although it is similar to other uses in that it evokes contemplation of the relationship between one's expectations and actions—or, more precisely, the gaps between one's moral ambitions and the conditions of existence that reinforce and simultaneously threaten to undermine them at every turn. When evangelicals speak of compassion fatigue, they refer to a condition of emotional exhaustion—also called "burnout"—that they attribute to frustrating experiences of being resisted or manipulated by irresponsible and unrepentant beneficiaries of charitable aid. Socially engaged evangelicals and outreach volunteers in Knoxville who got involved in the lives of poor people claimed to have had such experiences at various points in their involvement, and a few even cited compassion fatigue as the main factor in their need to withdraw, sometimes permanently, from social outreach activity.

That white churchgoing southerners should remain fixated on the potential difficulties and drawbacks associated with charitable social outreach makes sense in light of the conservative and segregationist tendencies that characterized their churches and denominations for so many decades. But other cultural factors are involved as well, and in this chapter I focus on the influence of a pair of twin imperatives, *compassion* and *accountability*, that ambiguously define the purpose of charitable giving in the context of evangelical outreach. Compassion, on the one hand, invokes an ideal of empathetic, unconditional benevolence. Accountability, on the other hand, imposes certain reciprocal obligations on the part of beneficiaries as a condition of continued benevolence (Bartkowski and Regis 2003). To an outside observer it may seem that compassion fatigue is simply an inevitable outcome of an obvious contradiction, but such a conclusion would not take into account that evangelicals explicitly recognize the paradox of compassion and accountability and see the relationship as dialectical rather than contradictory.

Conservative evangelicals are aware that putting theology into practice is never easy, and they know that the challenges of practical theology can be especially troublesome in interactions with cultural strangers and racial others affected by conditions of poverty, distress, and marginalization. And yet, when they do engage in social outreach, their sensitivity to the dynamics of social power often diminishes in the face of stronger cultural prejudices and religious intentions. Their prejudices may be expressed as suspicion toward charity recipients, and their intentions include the desire to embody "active and sacrificial compassion," a romanticized ideal of Christian charity based on a belief in the possibility of creating profound interpersonal bonds that transcend social boundaries and status hierarchies. As a result, evangelicals often overlook the degree to which the implementation of compassion and accountability reproduces conditions of "deep-lying incommensurability" (Simmel 1950: 392) between those who have the power to give and those who are burdened with the obligation to reciprocate, either through return gestures or with some other moral premium.

My aim here is not merely to point out ideological discrepancies or explain why suburban churchgoers encounter friction when they intervene in the lives of cultural strangers. I am interested, rather, in the conditions under which a conceptually manageable paradox becomes practically unmanageable for religious actors who uphold it. Why do evangelical ministry workers and volunteers have such difficulty balancing the relationship between compassion and accountability when their outreach methods assume these two concepts to be essentially compatible, even complementary? If we accept that socially engaged evangelicals earnestly operationalize compassion and accountability as a productive paradox, why should the stress of simultaneously embodying both virtues remain an impediment to their moral ambitions?

Much of the difficulty stems from the fact that the strategies of social outreach, like any other evangelical ministries, are always embedded within a larger ideological framework of Christian evangelism. This evangelistic framework, in turn, is rooted in a theology of exchange that is partially obscured by the romanticization of Christian compassion. When conservative evangelicals offer assistance and encouragement to poor and distressed people, they interpret their actions as unconditional gifts, free of the constraints of interest, debt, and power. However, their theology asserts that even the most "unconditional" gift of all (eternal salvation) is conditioned on the recipient's obligation to receive that which ultimately can never be repaid, and thus to remain a willing subject of divine authority. So while evangelical acts of compassion and charitable gifts are conceived as graceful gestures with "no strings attached," they invoke norms of reciprocity and indebtedness that are central to evangelical thought. The misrecognition that occurs here pertains less to the difference between interested and disinterested giving (Bourdieu 1990) than to a deep-seated concern among evangelicals to act like God without acting like they are God. In their "moral rhetorics of charitable action" (Allahyari 2000: 32), the conditions of giving are made prominent while the conditions of receiving are obscured to the point where the givers—enchanted by what Derrida calls the "madness of the impossible" (Derrida 2001: 45)—are often surprised or flustered to have to manage them at all.

The religious precepts of compassion and accountability are simultaneously consonant and at variance with prevailing notions of personhood and technologies of citizenship through which populations, rich and poor alike, are produced, empowered, and governed (Cruikshank 1999). Welfare privatization is represented within the discourse of evangelical social engagement as a historic opportunity to "restore" principles of biblical compassion and theocentric accountability to a public sphere seen as deprived of such values. This impetus is strongly tied to regnant neoliberal and neoconservative ideologies of personal responsibility, and reflects lingering antipathy among religious conservatives toward secular philanthropy and welfare entitlement. At the same time, the entry of socially engaged evangelicals into the welfare arena is conceived as an opportunity to redefine the very essence of altruism and refine the practices through which human social and spiritual relations are constituted. Evangelical acts of charitable giving, whether of goods or services, are similar to the ritual practice of "spiritual gifts" among charismatic Christians in that they are "linked to a Maussian concept of the gift as breaking down two forms of distinction: those differentiating persons and those distinguishing persons from objects" (Coleman 2004: 424). Socially engaged evangelicals complicate conventional modes of individualism because their methods and moral ambitions suggest a desire to collapse or transcend the boundaries of human intersubjectivity. Romanticization of compassion is among the most salient expressions of this desire. Worrying about compassion fatigue is among its most vexing preoccupations.

SAMARITANS OF KNOXVILLE

"We're not trying to run from the hard stuff," Paul Genero announced as he presided over the first open meeting of the Samaritans of Knoxville, in the conference room of a large Christian bookstore in West Knoxville. "What we're trying to do is build momentum, like bees around honey," he added, "and ultimately to infect our congregations with a desire to serve the people who are hurting in our community." Speaking to an assembled group of eighteen pastors, faith-based charity workers, and lay churchgoers, Paul chose his words deliberately to provide encouragement and also remind his listeners that outreach mobilization is a difficult task, full of obstacles and sensitive topics. He clarified that the purpose of their meetings was to allow Christian ministry workers and outreach coordinators—the people at the "front lines," as he called them—to network, share experiences and insights, and become better equipped to "serve" in their capacities as organizers, caregivers, and volunteers and in their efforts to mobilize grassroots support in their respective congregations.

After brief introductions and opening prayers, Paul distributed draft copies of a mission statement for the Samaritans of Knoxville, which he cowrote with his "leadership team," and asked for input and suggestions. The statement stressed the all-consuming importance of compassion, asserting that Christians have a unique calling to suffer empathetically with suffering people and take action on their behalf. The document also included a list of "Core Values," with items such as "Training," "Church," "Evangelism," and "Diversity," all described as crucial elements of a multifaceted approach to ministry and mobilization. Only one of the items sparked any real debate; it was the first item on the list: "Accountability." The value of accountability was described as follows: "We seek to observe biblical principles of accountability as it relates to each relationship, including the individual churches, the Samaritans of Knoxville membership, and the people we serve." This provoked a critical response from an urban pastor and social worker named Howard Singleton, who, notably, was the only African American in the room. Howard slowly removed his glasses, raised his hand straight up in the air, and asked—in a tone that suggested he already knew the answer—for someone to clarify what "the people we serve" means in this context. Raymond Andrews, a lay member of Paul's leadership team, answered that it refers to the people who receive charitable assistance from churches and individual churchgoers. Raymond added that it is crucial for recipients of Christian compassion to become morally and financially responsible individuals, willing to give up bad habits and sinful lifestyles that lead to poverty, crisis, and dependence. Another person pointed out that without proper standards of accountability, compassionate Christians are too easily manipulated or taken advantage of by others.

Howard was visibly frustrated but unsurprised by these responses. Citing years of firsthand experience in poor inner-city communities, he insisted that the wording of the statement was impractical and flawed. It failed, he argued, to make clear that volunteers can only force dependent people to be accountable if they (the volunteers) remain committed to the challenges of effective social outreach, including the need to sustain long-term relationships with dependent people rather than withdraw at the first sign of difficulty. "You don't have the right to hold someone accountable without a real relationship," he said, "and you don't state that here." He added that planning special outreach events at public housing projects (another item on the meeting agenda) is all well and good but "events are not the same as relational commitments."

Paul tried to ease the tension by acknowledging that the question of accountability is always going to be a "nerve issue," and he reminded the group that when standards of accountability are enacted according to biblical principles they are ultimately "all about grace." The conversation then shifted to other topics, but accountability came up again later in the meeting, prompting Howard to reiterate his point: "How do we make accountability a *real* value, rather than just a concept?" He suggested that the Samaritans of Knoxville implement a policy of organizing outreach volunteers into work teams focused on specific initiatives, so that a context for mutual accountability would be maintained and needy communities would not be vulnerable to the whims of less committed individuals and churches. "Speaking as a soldier who is at the front lines," Howard said, "I'm the one who has to clean up the blood of the messes you make when your churches just drop in, drop off, and leave the community behind."

Heads nodded uniformly in ready recognition. The "drop in, drop off" criticism was all too familiar to this group. Suburban evangelicals often criticize themselves for treating social outreach opportunities as short-term projects rather than long-term commitments, building false expectations and bad reputations. The language of accountability, moreover, pervades all aspects of evangelical life, as does Howard's emphasis on "relational commitments." Evangelicals see human relationships as ultimately redemptive, provided they are maintained in accordance with Christian virtues and biblical principles. Sunday sermons underscore the importance of relationships built on ethics of mutual love and responsibility, and pastors will periodically emphasize that the same relational ethics should apply to relationships that extend beyond the walls of the church. Few of those present at the Samaritans of Knoxville meeting that day would argue with Howard's suggestion that white suburban churches fail to adhere to the very standard they uphold. Nonetheless, the level of discomfort at the meeting was palpable on the heels of his vocal condemnation. His specific proposal was never explicitly addressed, and most people seemed content to let the awkward matter drop.

A subtext of racial alienation undoubtedly influenced the reception of Howard's comments. Although the region's history of racial tension is considered moderate compared with those of other southern cities, segregation and inner-city poverty remain stubborn social realities, adding to persistent urban development crises that have plagued the city's black population for decades. Suburban churches, especially the region's affluent megachurches, have been called to task for their failure to address systemic inequalities resulting from racism and "white flight." Much of the pressure has come directly from religious leaders in the black community, many of whom share the conservative theology of white evangelicals but advocate progressive views on issues of social and economic justice. Strong differences of opinion over the proper means of social welfare further exacerbate racial tensions.

For Howard, representing the position of many black community organizers, the problem requiring immediate and sustained attention was the inability or unwillingness of white churchgoers to make serious efforts to *empower* poor communities rather than merely provide handouts and enforce accountability. Everyone else at the meeting, however, was concerned about the risks of "enabling sin" by giving indiscriminate aid to undisciplined or immoral people. Holding "the people we serve" accountable was seen as a way to avoid being taken advantage of and exercising responsible stewardship. Although Howard's basic premise was one with which other Samaritans readily agreed, the racialized context of his intervention made it that much more poignant and difficult to address openly.

The factors that make the question of accountability such a "nerve issue" among socially engaged evangelicals are not restricted to racial politics, however. Of the various difficult or provocative issues that were brought into the open during the many outreach workshops and events I attended, few seemed to be as problematic as issues related to the challenge of reconciling compassion and accountability in the practice of social outreach. At times they were addressed head-on; at other times they were evaded. In general, they represent a source of insecurity and consternation for socially engaged evangelicals who romanticize compassion as an alternative to what are perceived as conventional norms of behavior in modern society. While carrying much of the ideological baggage of "compassionate conservatism" and harboring principled distrust toward "indiscriminate" charity (and, by extension, those who receive it), socially engaged evangelicals idealize the redemptive, bridge-building potential of compassionate action, and struggle with its implications. Ideally, organizers hope that moments like the one I just described will stimulate the kind of social reflexivity that allows religious groups to continually reexamine the character and consequences of their social engagement (see Lichterman 2005). All too often, however, the outcomes of social reflexivity are hampered by the very contradictions and power dynamics that call for reflexive intervention in the first place.

I asked Paul Genero to share his thoughts on accountability with me a few days after the meeting, the issue still fresh in our minds. He said that it is never easy to define the relationship between "servants" (those who give) and "the people we serve" (those who receive) in the practice of social outreach. It is a volatile subject because as much as Christians want to be patient and forgiving, they find it hard to help people who are not willing to help themselves. "We want to be wise with God's money so that we don't end up getting treated like doormats," Paul explained, "but at the same time we want to enter into relationships, be flexible, and remain compassionate to other people's suffering." Paul understood that the focus on accountability offends people who think it is harsh and unforgiving, but he was quick to point out that its effectiveness stems from an inherent "tenderness." Standards of accountability, he argued, are no different from "house rules" imposed on children by their parents. After all, parents love their children unconditionally and know their basic needs better than they do.

Such sentiments demonstrate the central paradox that evangelicals face in the moral economy of religious altruism. Whereas compassion is understood as unconditional, accountability is all about conditions and expectations that are deemed critical for compassion to *work*. Evangelicals who participate in social outreach ministries—whether through church-sponsored programs, faith-based organizations, or individual initiative—pursue the desire to be selfless and gracious, to give with "no strings attached." They seek, in short, to embody the radical sacrificial compassion of Jesus Christ. They also believe it is their mandate to instill godly virtues in others, particularly the virtues of moral, financial, and spiritual accountability, which they perceive as generally lacking among the poor and indigent.

THE LIMITS OF OUTREACH

One of the peculiar ironies of social outreach ministry is that well-meaning efforts are guided by expectations and preconceptions that become burdensome for everyone involved once they exert determinative influence over the way in which generosity is enacted. When charity recipients react with indifference (i.e., lack of gratitude), obstinacy, or resistance, the ideals of active compassion become harder for charity givers to rationalize and sustain. The risk of compassion fatigue is understood by socially engaged evangelicals to be especially high under such circumstances. Outreach volunteers become self-conscious that their judgment is clouded by anger or exhaustion, and they are faced with a choice either to withdraw or to persevere.

What follows are two personal narratives that were gathered during recorded interviews. They demonstrate how socially engaged evangelicals experience and recall the dilemmas of social outreach. In their tone and emphasis, they closely resemble anecdotes that socially engaged evangelicals share with one another during mobilization sessions and outreach workshops. They reveal in part the role of narrative in the construction of a religious identity based on ideals of service, perseverance, and grace. They also reveal the extent to which socially engaged evangelicals wrestle with questions of discernment and suspicion and an anxious concern to avoid bad judgment.

Stacy Miggs spoke often of a difficult relationship she once had with an alcohol- and drug-abusing single mother whom she met at a homeless shelter. Upon getting to know the woman and her child, Stacy decided to become involved in their lives, at first buying them food and clothing and eventually helping them move into a new home once the mother's situation stabilized. Stacy soon felt the Holy Spirit urging her to get more closely involved. She realized it was incumbent on her not only to help the woman with mundane affairs but also to put her on a path toward long-term health and self-sufficiency and ultimately spiritual redemption.[1] Stacy stepped up her investment in the relationship, gradually working herself into a position of credibility and authority so that she could take advantage of the opportunity "to impart some wisdom and offer some guidelines" in practical and spiritual matters. Over the course of a year, while the woman underwent drug treatment, Stacy and her husband contributed to her home and car expenses, using mostly their own money plus some extra funds provided by Eternal Vine Church. They also helped the woman cover the costs of day care for her daughter and night classes for herself so she could earn her GED and get a job. After all this, Stacy sadly recounted, the woman "chose to go back to the bottle, go back to the abuse": "We helped her to try to come out of this path. We tried to encourage her, we tried to help her in every way—physically, emotionally, spiritually. But she has still chosen ultimately to go back to the drugs and alcohol. Well, I don't want to enable that, and we've been enabling that. And I did not see it soon enough. If you choose that path, there's nothing we can do. So I've had to sever that tie. I *have* severed that tie."

Ending the relationship was emotionally draining for Stacy, and she thought about the situation every time she reflected on the difficulties of active compassion. While desiring to be an instrument of God's mercy and grace, she felt a need to set limits and boundaries to avoid getting "burned" by people who "choose" to remain on destructive paths and refuse to accept responsibility: "I wanted to help. I wanted to see how the Lord could use me in that. But the wrong thing to me would have been to continue to pour into that relationship without any commitment there on her part. There are too many people who say, 'I need help, and I want somebody to walk this road with me,' and I'm there ready to do that. But there is an issue of responsibility and accountability on the other end."

Evangelicals who consistently engage in this kind of social outreach, as individuals or members of organized groups, often develop their own guidelines to assess the sincerity and personal accountability of those seeking or receiving help or material aid. Their guidelines are informal and reflect a combination of experience and intuition, which they confirm through prayer and consultation with other experienced volunteers and activists. They are careful to avoid practicing indiscriminate charity but at the same time they try to remain open to the everyday realities of poverty and dependency. At times, evangelicals are so keen to avoid getting "burned" that, through misplaced suspicion or rash judgment, they will reject someone with potentially "sincere" needs instead of, as some would say, "erring on the side of compassion."

Steve Latham, also a member of Eternal Vine, has spent most of his professional life working for Christian nonprofits and faith-based organizations in downtown Knoxville. He deals with homeless people on a daily basis and believes strongly in the importance of balancing compassion with firm standards of accountability. Steve admitted, however, that it is often hard to draw the line between them. He described to me an occasion when he was working at a social service agency and a disheveled man, who was not one of the agency's registered clients, approached him for a handout. The man walked right into his office and announced, "I need gas money," prompting Steve, who was suspicious of the man on sight, to think to himself, "Yeah right, you need gas money. I've heard that so many times." Steve assumed that the expressed need was not genuine and the money would be used to buy drugs or alcohol. He turned the man away, claiming that he had no cash on him and could not simply give away money that belonged to the agency without proper procedures. As the man was leaving he encountered a female coworker of Steve's and managed to get money from her instead. Observing this, Steve decided to follow through on his suspicion:

> I got in my car and followed him to the gas station. I said to myself, this is gonna be a test of humanity. Sure enough, he actually bought gas. The sad thing was that he was buying gas for his truck, which was such a pitiful truck that he had to pour it into the tank and then siphon it straight into the engine because the gas tank was eaten out. I realized that, even as long as I've been in the business and thinking I'm galvanized by it all, there are still hurting people.

Steve remembered his momentary lapse of Christian intuition with regret, but in his telling of the story he highlighted the positive lesson to be learned: the only way to help people in need is to have relationships with them. In relationships, sincere needs are clearly ascertained and individual accountability is either more visible or more easily inculcated. Nonetheless, as both of these stories reveal, practicing compassion—whether in the context of a personal relationship or not—often entails the need for evangelicals to reconcile themselves with disappointments, surprises, false expectations, and errors in judgment. In the process of "incarnating" themselves into worlds of poverty and dependency, they face daunting realizations not only about the "people we serve" but also about themselves, their temperaments, and the extent of their willingness to make sacrifices in the name of compassion.

There are, to be sure, positive outcomes from the social outreach efforts of churchgoers like Stacy Miggs and Steve Latham. In their eagerness and commitment to help others, socially engaged evangelicals make tangible differences in the lives of people who are struggling to get by, and in some cases, strong and enduring interpersonal bonds are formed across racial, ethnic, and class lines. However, the clash of expectations that takes place at the intersections of compassion and accountability raises all kinds of possibilities for conflict, resignation, and withdrawal. An ostensibly productive paradox remains stubbornly irreconcilable.

As I mentioned, evangelicals conceive of the relationship between compassion and accountability as dialectical rather than contradictory. The complementarity of compassion and accountability is reinforced by symbolic parallels with evangelical gender ideology. There is a tendency to feminize compassion by emphasizing nurturing qualities traditionally identified with women's gender roles, whereas descriptions of accountability invoke notions of patriarchal authority. For example, a churchgoer from Eternal Vine who used to sponsor refugee families with his wife explained to me that "when you work with refugees you need to have an equal measure of the compassion [pointing to his wife] and the 'hey, don't be foolin' around now [pointing to himself]." Effective outreach does not require male-female pairs, especially as many volunteers work alone or in teams, but gender stereotypes nonetheless reaffirm the practical logic on which social outreach ministries are based.

Compassion and accountability are imagined as distinct yet mutually constitutive. When properly realized, they are meant to have the power jointly to transform individual lives and relationships, and to endow social networks and even institutions with sacred Christian virtues. In this sense the complementarity of compassion and accountability directly corresponds with the larger projects of evangelism toward which all purposeful actions are oriented. As I discuss later, the connection to evangelism complicates this relationship by introducing an underlying logic of redemption and paternalistic authority into situations that charity workers and volunteers prefer to think of as occasions of unconditional grace and egalitarian fellowship. To fully grasp the nature of the complication, we need first to examine the theological and cultural underpinnings of compassion and accountability, each in turn, as they pertain to altruistic projects to which socially engaged evangelicals commit themselves.

COMPASSION

Evangelical notions of compassion are informed by an array of scriptural and cultural reference points. The interpretation presented here (and in the following section on accountability) is based similarly on my own synthesizing of materials that include field notes, interview data, and literary sources that I came across or was referred to during and since my fieldwork. Consequently, what follows is my ethnographic reading of a vernacular theology, one that is at once context specific and informed by broader social and institutional fields. I have neither the desire nor any pretense to provide the kind of coherent systemic theology that one might expect from biblical scholars and theologians. The gaps and contradictions that appear in my description should be read as cultural artifacts in and of themselves. Vernacular theologies play a significant role in defining how religion becomes a lived reality for those who ascribe meaning to them. The discourse on compassion that permeates social outreach among conservative evangelicals must be seen as culturally significant if not totally accountable, as it were, by academic standards.

Paul Genero instructed me that the key to understanding Christian compassion is to study the life of Jesus Christ. This was the same advice that he and others frequently gave to aspiring outreach volunteers and mobilizers. The words and actions attributed to Christ—from the parable of the Good Samaritan and the Sermon on the Mount to his healing of the sick and compassion toward outcasts—are the primary models of active compassion that churchgoers seek to emulate. Although compassion is not the means of attaining salvation, it is understood as a sign of faith and, under the most challenging of circumstances, a test of faith. As with the closely related concept of mercy, the power of one's compassion is a measure of one's total commitment to the rigors of a Christian lifestyle (Keller 1997: 38).

The definition of *compassion* that circulated the most among members of the Samaritans of Knoxville during my fieldwork comes from the Catholic theologian Henri Nouwen:

> The word compassion is derived from the Latin words *pati* and *cum* which together mean "to suffer with." Compassion asks us to go where it hurts, to enter into places of pain, to share in brokenness, fear, confusion, and anguish. Compassion challenges us to cry out with those in misery, to mourn with those who are lonely, to weep with those in tears. Compassion requires us to be weak with the weak, vulnerable with the vulnerable, and powerless with the powerless. Compassion means full immersion in the condition of being human. (1982: 4)

I asked Paul if he had any misgivings about drawing inspiration from the writings of a Catholic priest. He simply shrugged his shoulders and said, "He was a man who loved Jesus, just like me," adding that no one ever expressed any objection to the definition or its source. Indeed, Nouwen's themes of suffering, "brokenness," and "full immersion" appeal tremendously to evangelical sensibilities. The Christ figure epitomizes righteous suffering for evangelical Protestants no less than for Catholics (although perhaps less graphically). The image of the Son of God as one who sacrificed himself to relieve the suffering of others is especially evocative because of how it is symbolically linked to the emotional structure of parental love. By reminding themselves of the compassion that parents feel for their children, suburban churchgoers—most of them parents themselves—identify with God the Father, who took pity on the world but also felt sorrow as Jesus hung "broken" on the cross. This theme of divine pathos in the gospel narrative directly influences the tone of evangelical social outreach.

"Brokenness" evokes a double meaning in evangelical parlance. It suggests, on the one hand, the Calvinist doctrine of total human depravity. On the other hand, it refers to an ideal human disposition characterized by selfless humility before God. Jesus epitomized brokenness in the latter sense because of his willingness to sacrifice himself in the service of God's will. The implication for thinking about compassion is that, as one outreach volunteer put it, "compassion ministry is an overflow of realizing where we all came from." In other words, as Christians realize their inherent sinfulness and embrace God's forgiveness with repentance and gratitude, they become endowed with a radical compassion for others that they did not previously possess. Bringing about such a transformation in oneself is a formidable challenge for churchgoers, as is the mandate to treat all human beings as equally worthy (and unworthy) before God. The tendency to rely on cultural biases and preconceived notions when looking to assess the urgency or sincerity of different people's welfare needs reproduces harsh but inevitable distinctions between the worthy and the undeserving, the reliable and the suspicious, the innocent and the corrupted, and so on. To counteract this, Paul repeatedly stressed theological training as part of outreach mobilization: "You need a strong theological understanding in order for people who are willing to do 'feel-good' kind of volunteering, who are willing to minister to cute little blond kids, to also become willing to work with guys with AIDS, cleaning their bedpans. That's the kind of compassion that's truly biblical. When we suburbanites talk about loving our neighbor it is largely superficial, because we are unwilling to embrace real humility and sacrifice."

The juxtaposition here between "cute little blond kids" and "guys with AIDS" conveys the desire to practice social outreach in an egalitarian mode. It also reinforces the importance of taking risks and stepping outside one's comfort zone, which is linked to Henri Nouwen's point that compassion necessitates "full immersion in the condition of being human." By being fully immersed in strange and unsettling sites of human experience, the compassionate Christian becomes something of a missionary, an instrument of divine mercy in urban ghettos, homeless shelters, and hospital wards, where people are seen to be in the grip of despair. Compassion, in this sense, is imagined not as a distinct emotion but as the interface of hope and desperation, wherein lies the domain of the sacred.

Crucial underlying themes in the discourse on compassion are derived from the parable of the Good Samaritan (Luke 10:25–37).[2] The parable tells of a man who is beaten, robbed, and left for dead on the desert road between Jerusalem and Jericho. A Hebrew priest and a Levite walk past him without offering help, presumably in observance of Levitical ritual purity laws. Later the man receives help from a passing Samaritan, who tends to his wounds, takes him to an inn, and covers the expenses for lodging and care. The parable ends with Jesus saying that it was the Samaritan—"the one who showed mercy"—who proved to be a true neighbor to a person in need. Jesus then instructs his audience to "go and do likewise."

For the purpose of mobilization, the Samaritans of Knoxville prepared and circulated a lesson plan about the Good Samaritan, to be used in adult Sunday school classes and outreach workshops. The lesson begins with a discussion of the two Jewish clergymen, who are described as having ignored the bloody victim because "their schedules were full" and because they valued "compassionless purity" over "dirty compassion." The lesson goes on to state that "none of Jesus' listeners expected the hero of the story to be a Samaritan," leading to the suggestion that the Samaritan must have been compelled by a profound impulse to do what he did, one that transcended human nature. To determine the source of the Samaritan's actions, the lesson focuses specifically on verse 33, which says that he "felt compassion" (some English translations use "pity" or "deep pity"). The Greek phrase is "unpacked" etymologically and compared against other Bible passages where the same phrase appears, such as 1 Kings 3:26 (in the Greek translation), where a mother cries out to King Solomon, relinquishing custody of her young child to spare the child's life. The mother's outburst is characterized in the lesson plan as "an overwhelming urge that wells up deep inside, to prevent harm or offer extensive help." Visceral compassion is described as unique among emotions because it "results in taking action on behalf of the one in need." The lesson concludes that the Good Samaritan did not merely *feel* compassion but, like the desperate mother before Solomon, was *moved* by it. He was forced by an overwhelming urge to take actions that were costly and potentially troublesome.

In the framework of the lesson plan, compassion is represented as both "action oriented" and risky; it is also described as "schedule changing, priority shifting, and reputation damaging." Once again, Jesus is held up as the exemplar. The lesson points out that Jesus' merciful deeds, from healing lepers and blind men to feeding the multitudes, were actions that made him that much more susceptible to the wrath of his detractors. Yet Jesus' "costly love" also led to "tangible results" in the lives of people who came into contact with him. The lesson concludes that modern-day Christians, if they are to walk in Christ's footsteps, must similarly perform risky, costly acts of mercy whenever they feel "deeply stirred" by the impulse to alleviate human suffering.

Alongside the emphasis on action in outreach mobilization and training, there is an equally strong emphasis on reassigning the locus of agency to a divine source. This too reflects biblical injunctions that are interpreted to mean that truly benevolent actions are those that are "Spirit led," that is, they should be motivated by deference to God's will rather than selfish motives such as the desire to earn one's way into heaven, impress other people, or assuage a guilty conscience. Evangelicals readily quote Bible passages whenever stressing the idea that compassion—and humanitarianism in general—should never be about opportunism, pride, or noblesse oblige.[3] To ensure that one's intentions are free of egocentric urges, socially engaged evangelicals highlight the importance of prayer. Every single outreach event or meeting that I attended in Knoxville began and ended with time set aside for group prayer.[4] In the words of Henri Nouwen, "Prayer is the very beat of the compassionate heart" (1982: 109). Prayer is valued as a means of putting God in complete control and allowing the human heart to be instilled with a divine, otherworldly passion. An outreach volunteer explained the effect to me this way: "Do you think I really care about people? It's not about that. *God* puts those feelings of pain in my heart. I've been praying for years, and God keeps working on my heart. Compassion is impossible unless the Spirit of God lives within you." When the Spirit is present, everything—from words of comfort, to the touch of a hand, to food donations, to the repair of a broken screen door—becomes a potential vehicle of grace. In the evangelical conscience, compassion represents both goodwill and good evangelism.

Finally, Christian compassion is conceived as unconditional, ideally enacted without reciprocal obligations, expectations, or rewards. However, true compassion is also understood as a gift of such extraordinarily evocative power for both giver and recipient that the latter will inevitably experience it as transformative. Evangelical volunteers are thus frequently troubled when charity recipients do not respond with proper gratitude or some comparable demonstration of personal reformation. Socially engaged evangelicals in Knoxville periodically addressed this issue when training others to avoid burnout. Pastor Jake, senior pastor of a Baptist church with an active outreach ministry, explained during a meeting of the Samaritans of Knoxville that he grew up hearing the Good Samaritan story over and over again but he never lived it out fully because he was always waiting for "thank you's" that never came. As his church became more involved in social outreach, he rediscovered the true significance of compassion. He remembered that Jesus was rarely thanked by those he healed and that he even showed compassion to those who betrayed and killed him. "I realized," Pastor Jake said, placing one hand over his heart, "that if grace and mercy was ever deserved, or earned, then it wouldn't be grace and mercy. And if I show grace and mercy to those who don't deserve it, I am more like Jesus than I've ever been." Pastor Jake explained that Christian compassion means more than telling troubled people that they are headed in the wrong direction, hoping they appreciate the advice, and expecting them to fly right. The modern church, he concluded, is guilty of hypocrisy:

> We preach against sin, but we don't want to do anything about it. We preach against abortion, but we don't do anything to help the women who we've convinced to keep their babies. Why don't we invest in housing for single teen mothers so they can get back on their feet after having children? We preach against homosexuality, but the church does nothing to care for people with AIDS.... Don't get me wrong, salvation is by grace, not works, but once we are saved it is our duty to give that grace and mercy to other people.

Pastor Jake's comments reveal how closely intertwined compassion is with evangelism and also that this entanglement is never easily managed. Loving one's neighbor like the Good Samaritan and being true to the Great Commission are not supposed to be at odds. But in practice it appears that they are, at least based on the common concern among churchgoers that too much compassion potentially undermines the impact of proselytization. The mediating factor that, in principle, ensures the link between compassion and evangelism is accountability. Accountability, however, is attended by tricky ideological and cultural baggage of its own.

ACCOUNTABILITY

North American evangelicals generally believe that human beings exist in the world as free moral agents. We are all equally accountable for our thoughts and actions, and it is ultimately God who holds us to account. Evangelicals readily cite chapter and verse from the Bible to support this belief.[5] The Bible is understood to be full of narratives and injunctions that essentially demonstrate the standards by which God evaluates moral and spiritual accountability. How those standards are interpreted forms the basis of evangelical religiosity and ethical comportment. As one public speaker said while counseling parents at a Christian high school on the subject of drug prevention, "Even our heavenly Father draws lines in the dirt." That this statement was made in the context of issues pertaining to parental authority illustrates the fact that the concept of accountability, like compassion, is crucial not only for understanding the believer's relationship to God but also the ideal way that human beings, especially Christians, are supposed to interact with one another. The faithful must watch others as closely as they watch themselves and stay mindful of all transgressions, rebuk-

ing those who sin and forgiving those who repent (see Luke 17:1–4).
Larry Kreider, an evangelical author and leadership consultant, defines
accountability as follows: "The meaning of accountability is *to give
an account to others for what God has called us to do.* We are first
accountable to the Lord regarding how we live out our commitment to
Christ.... Then we are accountable to fellow believers. These people are
often the spiritual leaders God has placed in our lives" (Kreider 2002:
36, original emphasis).

Accountability functions among evangelicals as a theological and
instructional paradigm that is applicable to every aspect of their lives,
from how they run their homes and businesses to matters of sexual
morality and family life to even broader notions of religious, civic, and
political responsibility. Church pastors constantly reaffirm its religious
importance, which is further reinforced by institutional practices such as
the organization of small groups—including Bible study groups, prayer
cells, support groups, and the like—which are sometimes known also
as "accountability groups." These and other mechanisms provide relational contexts in which evangelicals churchgoers become, as another
evangelical author put it, "regularly answerable for each of the key areas
of our lives to qualified people" (Morley 1997: 337). As an organizational principle, the concept of accountability helps to legitimize the
authority of church pastors and elders, especially in megachurches with
large budgets and influence. By delegating pastoral and administrative
responsibilities among teams made up of clergy, staff, and lay volunteers, megachurches maintain bureaucratic efficiency and also provide
visible structures of corporate accountability, which is desirable in light
of high-profile corruption and sex scandals involving celebrity pastors
and wealthy televangelists, which never fail to draw negative public
attention and media scrutiny.

At times when evangelicals talk or write about accountability, it
is not hard to detect a tone of nostalgia—two distinct modes of nostalgia, to be exact. The first I will refer to as *apostolic nostalgia,* and
the second as *nationalist nostalgia.* Both modes reflect aspects of the
current historical moment, particularly the political attitudes of religious conservatives toward liberal secularism and the role of the state
in social welfare. Apostolic nostalgia is expressed as a yearning for
"traditional" or "biblical" social values that are viewed as consistent
with the values upheld by first-century Christians, as depicted in the
New Testament. The spiritually vibrant lives of the apostles, and the
expansion of the church under their leadership, are understood to rep-

resent what happens when groups of people submit to a totalizing accountability structure that places the Word of God above all else (e.g., Kreider 2002: 37). The church consultant George Barna argues that people who are willing to become the kind of committed disciples of Christ that the apostles of the early church were are the most likely to "embrace the principles Jesus taught of obeying God's commands, loving people, expressing gratitude to God through service, strategically training new followers, holding each other accountable, and working in cooperation to achieve the ends of the kingdom" (2000: 25). Socially engaged evangelicals in Knoxville were keen to evoke the sentiments of apostolic nostalgia. They hoped to inspire a restorative spirit in their church communities, with modern-day Christians embracing the values of first-century Christians, specifically with regard to social welfare and caring for the poor.

Nationalist nostalgia is similarly embedded in evangelical discourse on accountability, in that it tends to glorify a U.S. national past when hardworking rural men and women assumed full responsibility for their lives and the lives of others. This nativistic perspective idealizes the memory of an agrarian (Christian) society where, as some would say, "people really knew what accountability meant." It also pertains directly to contemporary social politics by feeding the perception that before social services were taken over by the misguided efforts of "big government," all matters concerning welfare and poverty relief were effectively and judiciously supervised by religious charity organizations and community-based civic associations. An outspoken proponent of this view is Marvin Olasky, a conservative evangelical academic, editor in chief of *World* magazine, and author of several works, including the highly influential book *The Tragedy of American Compassion*. Olasky was a prominent right-wing advocate of federal welfare reform in the 1990s and later became one of the ideological architects behind the Republican political platform of "compassionate conservatism." Olasky's support for government withdrawal from the business of welfare was based on a specific reading of the history of welfare in the United States and his assertion that effective poverty relief takes place only when local communities are empowered to provide charitable services to people in need in a manner consistent with godly virtues.[6] Chief among those virtues is what he termed "benign suspicion," a quality of discernment that, in a bygone age, "came naturally to charity workers who had grown up reading the Bible" (1992: 107). According to Olasky, God-fearing welfare workers in the nineteenth century practiced benign suspicion in order to avoid the pitfalls of indiscriminate charity. In this way they shielded charity organizations from the demoralizing influence of fraudulent, immoral aid seekers, and enforced standards that discouraged welfare dependency among the poor.

The Tragedy of American Compassion was but one in a stream of right-wing antientitlement polemics published in the 1980s and 1990s, but it captured the interest of socially engaged evangelicals more than almost any other Christian scholarly text of the period. What set Olasky's work apart was his ability to present a moral and historical (some would say revisionist) narrative that encompasses notions of Christian faith, meritocratic individualism, communitarian ethics, and nationalist pride all at once. Furthermore, by emphasizing the compatibility of generosity and judgment, and asserting the right and obligation of local religious communities to assess the welfare needs and moral worth of the poor and indigent, Olasky contributed to an ideological movement that effectively detached poverty relief from social justice. Such arguments, reinforced by neoliberal conceptions and public policy rhetoric centered around personal responsibility, individual empowerment, and self-esteem (Cruikshank 1999; Goldstein 2001), played a key role in the conservative push for welfare reform and provided conservative evangelicals with concrete historical and biblical justifications for the faith-based activism of the postwelfare era.

The combination of apostolic and nationalist nostalgia charges the concept of accountability with theological and ideological properties, adding to its determinative influence in the lives of evangelicals. Everyday efforts to embody the virtues of God's grace bear the weight of social and intellectual histories that inform how institutions and social networks function, how social interactions are carried out, and how relationships are evaluated. Consequently, when socially engaged evangelicals perform acts of compassion for people who are dependent on social welfare, they do so armed not only with a desire to give selflessly but also an internalized sense of obligation that extends well beyond the realm of individual ethics. It is an obligation to "restore" biblical standards of discernment in the welfare sphere, both for the sake of wayward and needy individuals and for the sake of national renewal and reformation.

But in real-life interactions, what standards of discernment do socially engaged evangelicals rely on to assess the accountability of potential aid recipients in the first place? When I discussed this with Paul Genero, he admitted that it remains a difficult learning process.

The best thing to do, he explained, is "get lots of advice, pray a lot, and always err on the side of too much compassion." Still, evangelicals in Knoxville were cautious not to waste God's resources by allowing irresponsible, manipulative, or obdurate people to get by with a false sense of entitlement. Some churches and faith-based organizations dealt with this problem by developing formal protocols for needs assessment when questionable cases arise. For example, the Samaritans of Knoxville assisted in the creation of a citywide database for church staff to consult when they need to verify requests from "walk-ins"—people who walk into churches looking for handouts, such as grocery store vouchers or money for rent or utility bills. Churches that receive walk-ins did not want to turn away anyone in need, but they were wary of those who "work the system," those who solicit one church or social service agency after another and never make the effort to become self-sufficient or personally responsible. The database, which streamlined information about specific individuals gathered from local service agencies, became accessible through a hotline that church staff could call whenever they encountered walk-ins who appeared suspicious, unpleasant, or disreputable. Churches could then identify aid seekers who have been previously flagged as manipulators, miscreants, or addicts, and choose either to refuse their requests or to initiate some form of intervention.

The guiding assumption behind character assessments of this kind (which remain highly susceptible to prejudice, despite the pretense of objectivity) is the idea that God helps those who are willing—which is to say, those who *appear* willing—to help themselves, all else being equal. But all else is rarely equal. The interactions between suburban churchgoers and "the people we serve" take place within existing frameworks of social inequality, and the demands of evangelical accountability in such contexts mark the presence of lingering power dynamics. If the practical implications of compassionate social outreach include taking risks, breaking cultural barriers, and "loving the unlovable," the imperative of accountability reinforces benign suspicion as a privilege of power and affluence. Ennobled by their class status (which, as we saw in chapter 5, is also a source of ethical concern), suburban churchgoers project middle-class norms onto others, which affects the way they assess accountability in the context of social outreach. Temperance, humility, contrition, and gratitude (among other markers of gentility) are held up as moral premiums that "the people we serve" are expected to display in return for gifts of charity and compassion.

The following example is illustrative of how such dynamics are expressed in actual relationships. Raymond Andrews is a wealthy businessman who was actively involved in the Samaritans of Knoxville both as a major donor and periodic volunteer. He described to me how he and his wife once befriended an African American woman whom they repeatedly saw walking the entire length of a busy commercial road. They eventually stopped and struck up a conversation with the woman and learned that she was a single mother with a young disabled son. She walked to work every day because no public transportation was available and she could not afford to buy a car. Upon getting to know the woman and her son, Raymond decided to buy a car so she could drive to work and perhaps find a better-paying job. After some time, during which mother and son occasionally joined the Andrews family for Sunday services at Eternal Vine, the woman left her job for unspecified reasons. She started having car trouble and, despite various attempts to earn fast cash, fell deeply into debt. She approached Raymond asking for several hundred dollars. His reaction betrayed a sense of mild indignation:

> I wasn't going to give her the money at first because, I told her, "You can work. You're a healthy person. There's a million jobs out there you can get." But she's real picky. She's like, "I'm not gonna be a maid at the Super 8, you know, that's too hard." Or, "Well I don't want to wait tables, because I just don't want to do that." So I was going to hold her accountable. I'm not just gonna keep feeding her money. So what I did is I loaned her the money—I gave her the money, but I told her she had to bring me receipts that showed she's paid this off, and she did that. I told her I wanted the money back because, I told her, "I got you that car so you could work, not so you could just not work."

From Raymond's perspective, the car that he initially gave her was a token of his compassion, but it was also an inalienable gift that implicitly validated his moral authority and established his right to place conditions on further assistance. His frustration about her request for money was in response to her apparent refusal to apply for jobs that Raymond felt suited her needs. By insisting that she show him receipts and pay back his loan, Raymond redefined their relationship to ensure her compliance and indebtedness. He introduced a framework for accountability based primarily on his own assessments of her material needs and priorities:

> She brought me the receipts, and we sat down and did a budget. She didn't make much. But it's amazing, when you really sit down and do a budget for

a poor person, they can live off very little because they don't need health insurance, they don't need car insurance, they don't need life insurance. They get free medical care, you know, and they get food stamps. Rent is only, like, two hundred dollars a month, and she gets disability money for her son. When you compare a poor person's budget to someone who makes, like, forty thousand dollars, it's amazing how low the budget can really get to where somebody can actually survive because they don't need all these safety net things, since they have nothing to lose.

Raymond was able to justify his assumption that poor people do not need "safety nets" and "have nothing to lose" because of the nature of the relationship in which the conclusion was formed, a relationship defined in his eyes by what evangelicals call "vertical accountability." This means that the exercise of moral influence and guidance in the relationship was primarily unilateral and paternalistic, with Raymond, the dominant party in terms of wealth and status, staking privileged claims over the conditions of social exchange. Unlike "horizontal accountability," which is meant to exist mutually among undifferentiated individuals (such as the members of a congregational small group), vertical accountability implicitly assumes an imbalance in resources as well as wisdom and foresight.[7] Given that structural inequalities between suburban churchgoers and "the people we serve" are reinforced by the very enactment of compassion and accountability, the element of verticality in such relationships is rarely questioned by charitable givers, and it is challenged by recipients only at the risk of losing support and patronage that they are relatively powerless to reject. Thus it is all the more telling that conservative and socially engaged evangelicals romanticize the value of compassion to such an extent, as if to detach it from dynamics of power and reciprocity or to distinguish it somehow from the idiom of salvation from which it clearly derives.

REDEEMING TRANSACTIONS

"Salvation is free, but it comes at a price." This popular evangelical catchphrase underscores the logic of redemption in Christian soteriology. In an evangelical theology of exchange, sinners are "saved" when they accept that their sins have already been redeemed by the grace of God and the sacrifice of Jesus Christ, to whom they must remain eternally grateful and obedient. The insurmountability of cosmic debt is an object of devotion and penance throughout the life of the Christian, in anticipation of heavenly rewards in the afterlife. Crucial to this sense of indebtedness is the idea that every person lives what evangelicals call "an exchanged life" with Jesus. Christian piety is understood here as a reflection of one's willingness to receive the inalienable gift of divine grace—"a priceless gift that can never be repaid" (Sjogren 1993: 19)—and the spirit (or Spirit) with which it is given.

Pastors and churchgoers in Knoxville invoked notions of the spirit of the gift (in the Maussian sense) in their attempts to deepen their understanding of the nature of grace and apply it to a range of human experiences. Take, for example, the imagery conveyed to me by Cheri Davenport, who led a postabortion counseling program at Eternal Vine Church: "I like to use the example of Christ standing at the door knocking, and he's holding this big beautiful gift, all wrapped up with a bow. It's their forgiveness, their joy, their peace. All they have to do is go to the door, open it up, take the gift, and receive it, and then say thank you for it, which is part of receiving it. If you truly receive it, you're grateful, and you express gratitude. That's a sign that you've truly received a gift."

Evangelical ministries, whatever form they may take, are always evangelistic in the sense that they are meant to teach people to "truly receive" the gift of grace and this aim is directly related to the work of spreading the gospel. In social outreach ministries and faith-based organizations, altruistic motives for helping the poor and needy are secondary to the motives of evangelism. Although many evangelical social workers and volunteers in Knoxville were careful never to "cram the gospel down people's throats," they were strongly inclined to believe that charitable acts—as vehicles of divine grace—should ideally bring about transformative experiences and conversions in the lives of recipients. The moral ambitions of compassion and accountability are oriented toward the realization of redemptive transactions envisioned as occasions of pure, disinterested giving and simultaneously enacted as rituals of exchange. In the context of evangelical outreach, charitable givers begin to assume contested, even reluctant roles—from the expectant Evangelist to the gracious Redeemer—that potentially strain their interactions with charity recipients.

To get a fuller sense of how the line between service and salvation becomes blurred in evangelical outreach, we can think about the central significance of the theme of hope. Socially engaged evangelicals say that they have a desire to plant "seeds of hope" in the lives of those who may otherwise be deprived of hope. Whether or not someone professes to be a Christian (as did the woman in Raymond's account), conditions of poverty and distress are usually interpreted by evangelicals as evidence of spiritual as well as material deprivation. Possessed of economic and cultural capital, the suburban evangelicals see themselves as equally well possessed of authentic, Bible-based spirituality. They believe this advantage gives them a capacity for moral decision making superior to that of chronically struggling people who worsen their circumstances by making bad choices. If charity recipients showed signs of persistent irresponsibility or obduracy, then charitable givers were even more inclined to rationalize their interventions in evangelistic terms. Raymond Andrews's concluding remarks from the case described in the last section are illustrative:

> We kept her accountable. I told her I'm not giving her any more money. But I can tell you this—it's not easy. The fruit is not real quick to come. But I don't care. I do it just because I want to help somebody out. I've had a lot of experience working with people and trying to encourage them to work versus not work and be accountable for what they do. I do believe in accountability, I think it's biblical, and I think it's the only way to make—[pause] to help somebody actually, really have a good fruitful life.

Raymond viewed his actions as essentially disinterested and based on biblical principles, which was crucial to his belief that compassion and accountability help people lead "fruitful" (which is to say, faithful) lives. Social hierarchy is rendered inconsequential in this perspective by the theological valences of generosity and sacrifice, and by the implicit link to Christian evangelism as a project of giving people the hope they need to carry on, and to ultimately find God. Similarly, Stacy Miggs regretted that she had to terminate her relationship with the substance-abusing woman who refused to become accountable, but she consoled herself with the optimism that "a lot of seeds have been planted." She explained, "I know that the people here at church were the first people that had ever done so much for her. So I have to think that ultimately something will happen as a result of that in her life."

Hope is the motivational linchpin of evangelical outreach mobilization. It is a recurring theme intended to counteract frustration and dispel negative biases among conservative churchgoers, especially those who are ambivalent about social outreach in the first place or take a cynical view of antipoverty activism. Jim Elroy of the Fuller Street Mission explained to me how he tried to mobilize support among reluctant churchgoers by emphasizing hope and reward:

> I try to help people understand that there's hope. I don't just mean there's hope for the poor homeless person, because clearly there is, but hope in that if they get involved with a poor homeless person, *it's worth their investment.* People do change. They can change. The thing that will stop helping the poor quicker than anything else is if the public ever comes to believe that it's useless, it's hopeless, that there's no reason to do it because it doesn't make any difference. So what I want to do is communicate to people that what you do does make a difference. People change, people's lives turn around, alcoholics change, mentally ill people get stabilized, family violence victims don't live in violence anymore. I want to create a sense of hope about ministry to the poor.

Insofar as socially engaged evangelicals stress the point that social outreach carries the potential to turn people's lives around, the rhetoric of mobilization borrows heavily from the testimonial genre with which evangelicals narrativize their own conversions. But this is not the only reason why such arguments are deemed effective for mobilization. The idea that serving the needs of the poor could be a worthwhile "investment" of one's time and resources is appealing to suburban evangelicals who relate to the meritocratic idealism of the market economy yet aspire to devotional investments that transcend the individuating norms of modern capitalism. The channeling of compassion through charitable giving and other outreach initiatives is imagined as a radical departure from economic rationality, similar to the "boundless giving of oneself" that typifies the ideal of erotic love (Weber 1946a: 347). It is a sacralized mode of exchange (cf. Coleman 2004; Harding 2000), which is at the same time romanticized to such an extent that its qualities of generosity and sacrifice are presumed to be wholly distinct from the realm of exchange altogether.

The intersection of these overlapping and counterposed layers of meaning is a matter of consequence because this is the indeterminate space where the paradox of compassion and accountability becomes problematic. When charity and evangelism are one and the same, a conflicted code of exchange comes into play in which Christians are expected to give selflessly and sacrificially while recipients of charity are obliged to reciprocate in kind. It becomes that much more likely that "the people we serve" will be perceived as indebted to inalienable gifts that can never be repaid. As charity recipients continue to make choices that suburban churchgoers find unacceptable, and the paternalism inherent in vertical accountability intensifies, the potential for moral conflict is exacerbated. Although the concept of accountability, like compassion, is geared toward an ideal of interpersonal boundlessness—that is, a breakdown of worldly orientations that differentiate one embodied self from another—it has the capacity to reproduce dynamics of social power and alienation between suburban evangelicals and less privileged, objectified others.[8]

Charitable actions are rarely ever completely "pure and disinterested" or free of entanglements and premiums for giver and receiver alike. Yet for some charitable actors, the very elusiveness of the pure gift is a key motivating factor in their efforts to see it realized. The desire to prove that gifts can be given without reciprocal obligations of any kind is fueled by moral and theological outlooks that presuppose that they should be (Parry 1986: 458). Individuals who engage in religiously inspired charity, especially in the industrialized West, often proceed with the conviction that what they are doing represents an exception to the impossible and a challenge to the normative rational calculations of everyday life. This conviction is reinforced by symbolic linkages between disinterested charity and grand idealized objects such as "God" or "society," the presence of which charitable activity serves to mediate. Such linkages and underlying discourses are tremendously important because they stir the moral ambitions that make it possible for individuals to pursue religious and social initiatives despite perceived obstacles and impediments. As the sociologist Robert Wuthnow notes in his study of compassionate action, "The discourse in which such behavior is inscribed is no less a part of the act than is the behavior itself" (1991: 45).

According to Pierre Bourdieu (1990), socially structured practices of gift exchange are legitimated by cultural values that allow them to be misrecognized as disinterested. The subjective experience of charitable giving, in Bourdieuian terms, obscures the "objective truth" of reciprocity for those involved, which enhances the *charm* (and efficacy) of the gift itself. My analysis in this chapter also emphasizes the enchanting qualities inherent in the gift, which here means the power of altruistic gestures to obscure, in the eyes of givers, the unequal social relations on which those gifts are predicated. But I diverge from Bourdieu in terms of the particular form of misrecognition evident in this case. Evangelicals in Knoxville did not simply misrecognize interested giving as disinterested. Rather they internalized a complex assembly of moral ambitions that together support a worldview that represents charitable actions as conditional and unconditional *at the same time* but does not appear to provide sufficient methods to resolve potential crises and contradictions.

The problem that socially engaged evangelicals in Knoxville described as compassion fatigue is not, as critics might suppose, simply an expression of conservative evangelical intolerance or hypocrisy. Although it is also not entirely unique to evangelicals, I would argue that these particular instances should be read as a cultural phenomenon that reflects multiple coexisting layers of evangelical thought and practice. When socially engaged evangelicals set out to externalize the values of compassion and accountability, they are motivated by a plurality of compelling yet conflicted expectations about exactly what it is they are doing. An ideology of the pure gift intersects with the transactional logic of redemption; ideals of benevolence and equality are mobilized through practices of "benign suspicion" and incommensurability; the pathos of compassion meets the fervor of evangelism. If the challenge facing evangelicals were simply a matter of negotiating the paradox of compassion and accountability—that is, finding the perfect balance of "tough love"—then I suspect the "nerve issue" of accountability would not be quite so difficult for groups like the Samaritans of Knoxville to resolve. The reality is far more complex. Although certain aspects of evangelical social engagement stand at odds with competing social ethics and practices in the nonprofit arena (as Howard's interventions at the Samaritans of Knoxville meeting demonstrate), it is also the case that competing social ethics and practices exist within the very contours of the evangelical movement, surfacing in situations when the stakes of engaged orthodoxy are imagined to be at their highest.[9]

When Paul Genero announced to his colleagues that "we're not trying to run from the hard stuff," he was acknowledging the inevitable ambiguities and ambivalences that conservative evangelicals face as they take on what for many is the relatively unfamiliar work of social outreach in a civic sphere reconstituted by the politics of welfare reform. In his own way he also sounded a missionary charge, reminding mobilizers and volunteers that purposeful efforts undertaken by people of faith necessarily invite obstacles and hardships that must be identified and confronted if the power of Christ's redemption is to "infect" the culture of that reconstituted civic sphere. Motivational concepts that socially engaged evangelicals act on as they try to negotiate the blurry distinctions between redemptive power and social power are telling in this sense because they are indicative of broad cultural goals presupposed by evangelical projects of Christianization. In the excitement of postwelfare faith-based activism, evangelical aspirations, expectations, and frustrations are shaped by an array of cultural, theological, and political idioms, but they also converge around basic social aesthetics that conservative evangelicals have in mind they think about what a good society—which is to say, a "godly" society—should actually look like.

CHAPTER 7

Taking the (Inner) City for God

Listening to churchgoers at Eternal Vine and Marble Valley Presbyterian talk about Knoxville's impoverished inner city, it often seemed
as though the inner city was something of a missionary preoccupation. For those less involved in social outreach it is uncharted territory,
an alluring but harsh and unsettling element of the urban landscape.
For socially engaged pastors and churchgoers it represents "pockets
of despair" calling out for intervention, so close to home. It is seen as
a place where black children, dependent single parents, gang leaders,
and drug addicts await the goodwill and generosity of those who live
just a short drive away with their resources and messages of hope. The
megachurches I studied showed a particular fascination with the inner
city that was far more prominent than their interest in serving poor rural
white communities in the nearby Appalachian Mountains (although
churches throughout the region have active Appalachian ministries).[1]
Unlike Appalachia, the black inner city represents a mission field that
is at once proximate in location—the nearest "backyard" to the affluent suburbs—and culturally foreign for the majority of white suburban
churchgoers. As an image of localized otherness and disorder, the inner
city was the focus of constant emphasis and idealization on the part of
socially engaged evangelicals in Knoxville who needed to reaffirm their
bona fides as champions of a missionary cause.

   In this chapter I explore the religious and cultural significance of the
inner city for white suburban and socially engaged evangelicals, linking

it to coterminous evangelical concerns regarding the status of "the city" as an outpost of the Kingdom of God on Earth, and the importance (and difficulty) of achieving racial reconciliation, social harmony, and urban community development as markers of the kingdom. I begin with a discussion of the essential yet polysemic concept of the Kingdom of God, and the ways that evangelicals imagine its social implications while trying to work with and around its ambiguous temporal connotations. I then discuss the sense of exilic consciousness expressed among suburban evangelicals in relation to the city—that is, their complicated sense of being exiles from the urban center, with its moral and social dysfunction—and how this informs their belief that they are all the more spiritually obliged, and qualified, to advance the welfare of the inner city. In that section and the following one I also provide examples of the engagements and institutional relationships that stem from a preoccupation with the black inner city. The latter section is an in-depth case study focusing on Marble Valley Presbyterian's partnership with a small black church in an inner-city neighborhood undergoing a process of community development. Although the partnership was predicated on notions of racial reconciliation, relations between the two congregations were strained by preconceptions and prejudices on both sides, disagreements about issues of accountability and social justice, and the inevitable tensions that come about when the circumstances of an institutional partnership actually produce something more in the way of a system of patronage. These strains did not completely overdetermine the nature of the partnership or minimize the positive outcomes, but they were indicative of deep cultural rifts, some of which carry salient political implications. I conclude the chapter with thoughts on what such case studies reveal about the increasingly influential and authoritative role that affluent evangelical megachurches play in certain segments of civil society, especially regarding community service and the reorganization of local nonprofit sectors in the postwelfare era.

THE CITY AND THE KINGDOM

The city has historically been something of a moral conundrum for conservative Protestants. Nineteenth-century preachers and reformers believed that urban industrialization accelerated the breakdown of moral character and community in modern society. Twentieth-century fundamentalists inveighed against modern cultural trends such as liberalism, secularism, and relativism, which they believed were propagated by savvy urban elites intent on undermining traditional Christian values and authority structures. Urban centers were disparaged as places of vice, social decay, commercialism, rampant ethnic and religious diversity, and racial conflict. In the 1950s–1960s, white churches reacted to demographic and economic changes in U.S. cities by moving to the suburbs, justifying "white flight" on theological and separationist grounds (Dochuk 2003). Despite this aversion, modern-day evangelicalism would never have reached its current cultural prominence without movements of revivalism and mobilization that have taken place in contexts of urban engagement. Even Christian fundamentalism, so often viewed as inherently provincial and rural, emerged with the participation of urban communities and institutions, a fact that is overlooked by the populist antiurban sentiments that pepper right-wing religious rhetoric. In the neo-evangelical revivalism of the postwar era, major U.S. cities were targeted as sites of urban "crusades" that generated mass media publicity as well as mass conversions, and launched figures such as the indomitable Reverend Billy Graham into the national spotlight. For preachers and revivalists like Graham, the city itself was a platform on which to stage grand missionary dramas to reach and transform the national culture as a whole; it also became a battleground over issues of race, ecumenism, and biblical orthodoxy that left many conservative Protestants bitterly divided.[2]

The tendency to regard the city as both a breeding ground for sinful decadence and an optimal location for assertions of Christian cultural hegemony remains prevalent among conservative evangelicals, but the focus of these perceptions has shifted in the era of welfare reform. Beginning in the 1990s, evangelical activists were busy forging new strategies of political and social engagement, and for some this involved a renewed emphasis on urban ministry. Faith-based organizations dedicated to urban revitalization and community development started to increase their visibility, and evangelical ministry leaders in the field promoted practical theologies and local initiatives to enhance the church's role in addressing social concerns unique to urban environments (e.g., Bakke 1997; Carle and DeCaro 1997; Dawson 2001). Christian scholars and pastors called on affluent churches to overcome their hypocritical indifference toward the urban poor (Shank and Reed 1995; Sider 1999). Others stressed the need for local congregations to set aside their differences and come together in order to "break the dominion of oppressive spirits that obstruct the advance of God's Kingdom" and "win the *hearts* of the people of a city to know the love of Christ" (Haggard and Hayford 1997: 18; original emphasis).

What these various appeals had in common was a push to reimagine the city as a microcosm of the Kingdom of God, and to recognize complex urban problems as essentially religious or spiritual problems exacerbated by disunity and apathy on the part of God's evangelical emissaries. Making sense of what evangelical pastors and churchgoers mean when they refer to the Kingdom of God is no straightforward proposition. The concept entails different implications depending on how it is locally understood and the context in which it is invoked. Far from having a fixed, codified meaning shared among all like-minded evangelicals, the Kingdom of God summons a wide range of overlapping meanings and applications. In one sense it refers to a transcendent celestial realm, a kingdom that is "not of this world," as Jesus declared before Pontius Pilate (John 18:36). This is the kingdom of the afterlife, reserved for the faithful; it is also the kingdom of the afterworld, the universal postapocalyptic reign of Christ on Earth. From this premillennialist perspective, the Kingdom of God is an intangible yet inevitable reality and the purpose of evangelism is to convince as many people as possible to join the kingdom (through conversion) before the Final Judgment. In other usages the Kingdom of God is portrayed as immanent and temporal, something to be enacted and witnessed in the here and now. The line in the Lord's Prayer "thy kingdom come, thy will be done on Earth as it is in Heaven" is taken by many churchgoers to refer to the kingdom's direct relevance in earthly affairs. Evangelism from this perspective is not just about bringing people into God's kingdom but also bringing God's kingdom into the world. It is noteworthy that this particular angle verges on what is known as "postmillennial" theology, which posits that Christ's return will occur *after* rather than before the prophesied Millennium and that it is the responsibility of the church to herald an age of righteousness and justice immediately at hand. Because this theology assumes a more active role for humanity in the fulfillment of God's grand millennial scheme, and because of its association with liberal mainline traditions, conservative evangelicals adamantly reject postmillennialism. Nonetheless, there are elements of postmillennialist influence, however minor, in the ways that conservative evangelicals address the issue of the kingdom and in their activist orientations.

The popular evangelical author Philip Yancey addresses the dualism of the Kingdom of God as a theological concept in his book *The Jesus*

I Never Knew. Yancey acknowledges that the concept carries potentially radical implications for the present age but rejects outright the idea that it might justify radical political ideologies or liberationist social movements of any kind. He argues that the teachings of Christ were not meant to create "politics of polarization," but to convey an understanding of the Kingdom of God as both "Now" and "Not Yet" (1995: 250).[3] Echoing sentiments steeped in historical precedent, Yancey explains that since the "fullness" of the kingdom cannot be achieved before the Second Coming, the role of the church right now is to exemplify the values of the kingdom and thereby provide the world with a sense of what is to come.[4] Modern Christians distort theology by insisting that they can bring the kingdom into existence by sheer force of effort, as if to transform the corrupt and sinful world into something it simply cannot be. Although Yancey generally advocates limited forms of Christian social engagement, his skeptical and cautionary attitude toward ideologically driven activism is indicative of the antipathy that most white conservative evangelicals in the United States feel toward progressive social movements and interventions.

Insofar as conservative Protestants across doctrinal persuasions entertain notions of the Kingdom of God as a temporal paradigm, their interpretations vary as to what it should look like and the degree to which "the messianic, redemptive aspects of the vision gain predominance over any intermediary steps" (Bialecki 2009: 117). Suburban evangelicals in Knoxville did not tend to emphasize totally theocratic or radically egalitarian visions, but echoed various twists on the Augustinian notion of a worldly existence governed by the heavenly virtues of faith, spiritual unity, and social harmony. Marble Valley Presbyterian's Pastor Jerry delivered a Sunday sermon in which he argued that Christian love and evangelism were equally crucial components for the realization of God's kingdom as an earthly state: "When we pray, 'Your kingdom come, your will be done on Earth as in Heaven,' we are praying for God's love to seek and find us, and through us to seek and find others, beginning with those closest to us, and reaching out to those whom we would never even notice or care about, had God not first sought us and found us, and poured his love into our hearts." Yet even with elaborate statements like this, and with all the time that evangelicals spend reading and studying the Bible, pastors and churchgoers alike rarely presented totally uniform ways of interpreting one of Christianity's more puzzling theological abstractions.

In order to get a sense of how evangelicals in Knoxville translated their notions of the kingdom into concrete social implications, I once asked a group of churchgoers in an adult Sunday school class at Marble Valley Presbyterian to describe what they thought the city of Knoxville would look like if all local churches worked together and maximized their potential to advance God's kingdom on Earth. Here is a sample of their responses, which almost always took the form of a simple, one-sentence answer:

> "We would see God in people we don't expect."
> "Life would be deeper, more meaningful."
> "Needs would be met by the church rather than the government."
> "There would be less emphasis on denominations."
> "There would be more racial and ethnic harmony."
> "People would be living the gospel, not just talking it."
> "We would be like first-century Christians."

These responses clearly were not meant to serve as precise theological definitions, but they were nonetheless consistent with conservative evangelical ideas about what it would mean for the human condition today if the world were thoroughly Christianized.[5] As the broad scope of the responses suggests, the Kingdom of God can function in evangelical culture as something of an empty signifier (Barthes 1972). This is not to say that it is devoid of meaningful content. It is a discursive symbol that derives significance from its capacity to accommodate multiple concepts and interpretive applications relatively free of ambiguity, even if they appear vague or contradictory in juxtaposition.

When socially engaged evangelicals in Knoxville conveyed kingdom imagery and related concepts in outreach mobilization, they were more inclined than others to highlight specific social implications and to locate them in the urban social context. Eternal Vine's Pastor Tim occasionally used his sermons to articulate an explicit kingdom theology that took the city as its primary point of focus. On one such occasion, he delivered a sermon based on Isaiah 65:17–25, where God describes the "new earth" that awaits the faithful. Pastor Tim explained that the quality of life described in Isaiah's messianic narrative of Jerusalem's everlasting deliverance—including long life, equality, health, and security— is meant to serve as a model of what a righteous society should look like. He suggested, with just a hint of irony, that when Jesus Christ returns, the principles outlined in Isaiah will be the cornerstones of his "party platform." Pastor Tim then paused for a moment, chuckled, and said, "Wouldn't it be cool if there was actually a political platform that was based entirely on the Book of Isaiah? We could all drive around with campaign bumper stickers that say something like *My Way Is Yahweh!*"

Using PowerPoint slides projected on the sanctuary's giant video screens, Pastor Tim continued his sermon by listing eight distinct themes that could make up a political platform consistent with the vision of God's kingdom laid out in Isaiah. The themes were listed as follows: Good Healthcare, Housing, Justice, Jobs, Creative Expression, Equality of Opportunity, Spiritual Renewal, and Healthy Environment. After discussing the scriptural and theological relevance of each item, Pastor Tim went back over the list and proposed practical methods that evangelicals should consider when looking to apply the principles to life in Knoxville. For example, on the subject of healthcare he urged medical professionals in the megachurch to "make the most of your healing gifts" and not worry too much about making more money. On the topic of justice, he encouraged concerned churchgoers to stop simply complaining about social problems such as poverty and unemployment, and consider running for public office. "There is a real need for more Christians in the public square." On equality opportunity, Pastor Tim bluntly told his congregants that if they think that there is enough social equality in Knoxville they should imagine what life is like for children in the inner city whose mothers are in jail and whose fathers work at fast-food joints for meager wages. (Note Pastor Tim's reversal of the more common pattern of associating black fathers with prison and mothers with low-wage service work. Assuming this was a deliberate move, his reason may have been to avoid blatant racial stereotyping, or perhaps to minimize prejudicial responses by generating sympathy.) He added that if anyone is bothered by the fact that inner-city children go to worse schools than children in affluent suburbs, then they should get involved in efforts to improve the educational system throughout the greater Knoxville area.

Pastor Tim's demeanor and tone of voice as he neared the sermon's conclusion became sober and contemplative. "We are at a crossroads as a church," he said. "We can either be a nice big suburban church and ignore the needs of our own community or we can get involved in partnering with God in what he's doing in the world." The sermon was surprisingly concrete and instructional, venturing into a level of specificity that I was not accustomed to hearing at Eternal Vine. Pastor Tim's scriptural exegeses normally pertained to issues of personal faith and spirituality and, like many conservative evangelical preachers, he rarely expressed such detailed agendas (bordering on reformist) for evangelical social engagement. In the weeks following, it appeared that the sermon had provoked some consternation but not much public response, nor had it triggered an upsurge in outreach mobilization. As fodder for evangelical self-reflection, sermons like this provide churchgoers with concepts and mental images that both confirm and unsettle preconceived notions about the secular world and their relationship to it. The more explicit the implications are, the harder it is to act on them without first having to resolve lingering uncertainties and disagreements about whether it is even necessary or appropriate to interpret prophetic scriptures quite so comprehensively in matters of social welfare.

Mobilizers like Kyle Anderson, a staff pastor at Eternal Vine, negotiate the fine line between abstractions and explicit reformist aims. At an introductory meeting for prospective outreach volunteers, Kyle shared that his vision for major transformation in Knoxville was a society with no racial or economic segregation, and with low levels of crime, drug use, and unemployment. He imagined a "citywide church" where people from different backgrounds would celebrate Christian holidays together regardless of social status or ethnicity. Kyle said that when a society functions according to the principles of God's kingdom, "people who dress nicely will go to church with people who don't dress nicely." These sentiments, which were familiar to most pastors and churchgoers, had the effect of valuing a kind of Christian multiculturalism, taken as a mark of true equality. Socially engaged evangelicals went further than most in pointing out that socioeconomic disparities are linked to other forms of social boundary maintenance, but rarely was the airing of ostensibly egalitarian ideals accompanied by visions of a world where inequality actually ceases to exist. Appreciating cultural diversity and bridging the divide between rich and poor are essential components of living in God's kingdom, but this framework does not imply that socioeconomic disparities or the structures that produce them are likely ever to be completely eradicated.

I found similar tendencies among evangelical ministry activists. Tom Frick is a major figure in Knoxville's Christian nonprofit community who at various points in his life attended both Eternal Vine and Marble Valley Presbyterian. For Tom, visions of urban community development and integration are central to his understanding of the Kingdom of God on Earth. He explained to me that for those visions to be realized through the actions of churches, community organizations, civic associations, and political and economic entities, the residents of a city must collectively learn to share what the author Ray Bakke calls "a conscious theology of place" (1997: 60). Tom outlined his own imagining of such a prospect:

> If I had my ideal dream—you know that would never happen—but it would be to have four or five blocks of folks here that are all different sizes, shapes, poverty levels, economic levels, cultures, all having a common central theme of Christianity, living in the middle of the city and infiltrating the rest of the city, through the political arenas, the business arenas, the school arenas, all those different levels, mixing it up based on who they are, fleshing their faith out in that way. For me, that would be the ultimate utopia.

Despite Tom's admission that his ideal dream "would never happen," he remained a forceful and energetic leader of a nonprofit organization that collaborates with area churches and government agencies to create social integration and economic development in low-income urban communities. His efforts were guided by a utopian optimism tempered by a more skeptical evangelical realism, but this did not stop him from embracing his moral ambitions with an urgency and commitment that enhanced their practical relevance. Tom's notion of a "conscious theology of place" conveys a religious agenda that is grounded, emplaced, and immediate, while it is also oriented toward a utopian future that can only be anticipated rather than fully realized. His comments are revealing on another level as well: Tom presents a template for a missionary narrative in which diverse, integrated communities inevitably "infiltrate the rest of the city," spiritually reviving public and private sectors and institutions, and thereby transforming theologized spaces into Christianized places.

Evangelical visions of urban renewal in Knoxville often stressed the importance of multi-institutional, interdenominational, and interracial cooperation, reflecting the expansionist nature of their revivalist and missionary overtones. Socially engaged evangelicals placed considerable emphasis on the need to bridge the region's formidable urban-suburban divides, culturally and institutionally. The fact that this proved difficult time and again only fed the perpetual aspiration. "Yeah, this is hard work," said one active volunteer, sharing his thoughts on the challenges of civic bridge building, "but it is *kingdom* work." The challenges were even more apparent when it came to the problem of how the approaches to issues of social welfare adopted by white evangelicals differed from those of other groups and communities with which the evangelicals sought to partner, including black church leaders and community organizers in the inner city. In an interview with Howard Singleton, whose intervention on the topic of accountability at the Samaritans of Knoxville meeting I recounted in chapter 6, I asked whether he felt that urban-suburban, cross-racial partnerships in Knoxville were likely to have a positive impact, bridging long-standing cultural and socioeconomic gaps in the region. "Yes and no," he answered. "The *no* is that this has been done before and it will be done again. The *yes* is that there are some sincere people here that are in a struggle, and willing to struggle. That's where my hope comes from." Although Howard shared the conviction of his white evangelical counterparts that hearts and minds could be changed through building relationships between structurally alienated segments of society, and that this could eventually lead to larger societal transformations, he tended to view recent trends as only slight improvements in a history of well-meaning yet critically flawed efforts at racial reconciliation. As a representative of the urban black community, Howard qualified his optimism in recognition of the fact that collaborative endeavors are often conditioned on the benevolence of white church communities and the particular funding streams and organizational resources that they are willing to make available. The perception among inner-city activists that white prejudices, social inequalities, and institutional power dynamics tend to be reproduced rather than minimized under these circumstances led to persistent intergroup tensions and miscommunications. Among white evangelicals, such difficulties made it even harder to mobilize enthusiastic support for long-term collaborative projects, and (perhaps paradoxically) reinforced their usual inclination to downplay structural factors and see the challenges of "kingdom work" as essentially rooted in cultural incompatibilities.

I return to these points later in the chapter when I discuss the specific case of a partnership between Marble Valley Presbyterian and a small, inner-city black church, a partnership that centered around notions of "racial reconciliation" and "Christian community development." Before that, I briefly turn to another aspect of the white evangelical preoccupation with social outreach and engagement in the inner city, namely, the identification of poor black communities as sites of white alienation, and the accompanying feelings of exile and risk that engaged interventions seem to involve.

ENGAGING THE EXILIC FRAME

Of the Bible verses cited in connection with evangelical outreach initiatives concerned with urban community development and revitalization, one that I came across very frequently was Jeremiah 29:7. Addressing the Jewish people in Babylonian exile, the prophet relays God's instructions to "seek the peace and prosperity of the city to which I have carried you into exile. Pray to the Lord for it, because if it prospers, you too will prosper." The passage was especially popular among local pastors and ministry leaders, members of the Christian nonprofit community, and participants in the citywide Pastors' Prayer Network described earlier. The verse was read as a reminder that God's people are expected to be constructively engaged and concerned for the general welfare of the cities where they live. There was a lot of reflection on the instructional meaning of the verse but, curiously, I did not witness an instance where the particular relevance of the word *exile* was openly addressed. Do suburban evangelicals imagine themselves as "exiles" similar to the Jews of the sixth century BCE? If so, where were they exiled from and where do they expect to return? (What is their Jerusalem?) Clearly, the symbolic parallel between the city of Knoxville and ancient Babylon is meant to be taken metaphorically—as an allegorical provocation rather than a direct comparison—but it is nonetheless revealing. It raises the possibility for the city to be portrayed as a place of oppression and sin, where the righteous dwell in a state of estrangement, detached yet spiritually elevated. For suburban evangelicals in Knoxville, reengaging the city meant rediscovering that the fate and fortunes of the city are irrevocably tied to their own, but at the same time recognizing the city as a perilous place where they do not intuitively belong.

The sociologist Omar McRoberts (2003) has demonstrated how the theme of "in but not of" in some Christian churches serves as an expression of exilic consciousness and as a pivotal framing device that "moves beyond the common belief that religious adherence ensures one's place in the hereafter and addresses the earthly isolation one must endure in the meantime" (2003: 65). In churches composed mainly of ethnic minorities and immigrants, the extension of the exilic frame to matters of worldly concern makes it possible for everyday experiences of marginality and alienation to attain strong religious significance. The exilic frame also assumes a key role in the construction of congregational identities that are at once inwardly focused and outwardly oriented, thus facilitating church recruitment as well as various forms of religious activism and mobilization. Among white evangelicals in suburban churches such as Eternal Vine and Marble Valley Presbyterian, the exilic frame serves as a reminder of their collective identity and distinction as a community of faith, but it also serves as a call to action; specifically, it is a call to engage in prayerful, practical, and missionary action directed at distant yet not-so-distant urban spaces of poverty and distress.

We can begin to get a better sense of how such conceptions are internalized and acted on, and the experiences that the resulting style of urban social engagement can lead to, by looking at the specific example of one individual who reorganized his professional and personal life around a religious vision of urban revitalization centered around the inner city. Damien Richards is a middle-aged white entrepreneur who made much of his substantial wealth as the founder and CEO of a large consulting firm. At the time of my research, he was a member of the board of elders at Eternal Vine, where he performed key leadership and administrative roles. When I met him, he and his family lived in a large house in one of Knoxville's most affluent communities, but in previous years they had lived in a restored Victorian home situated close to a fairly impoverished and crime-ridden inner-city neighborhood. Damien's initial decision to relocate to the inner city came about in the mid-1990s, when he felt a desire to apply his wealth and expertise to new ventures that would more fully reflect his faith. As he explained to me, "I had kind of done a lot of what I wanted to do as a for-profit and realized, boy, I could sure transfer a lot of those skills and relationships—my network of relationships in the town became pretty strong—into an area of need and use that leverage to help make a difference there. So it was the heart that led."

Damien was especially keen to get involved with redevelopment projects that were already under way in neighborhoods located within Knoxville's federally designated Empowerment Zone. He focused on a public housing project that was targeted for redevelopment through public-private initiatives funded in part by a Clinton-era U.S. Department of Housing and Urban Development (HUD) program known as HOPE VI. Established in 1993, the HOPE VI program was designed to revamp public housing in selected cities, as part of a range of policy initiatives intended to increase private homeownership and reduce welfare spending. Public housing authorities were encouraged to work with real-estate developers, local businesses, and nonprofit agencies to replace urban projects with mixed-income, mixed-use communities with affordable housing options, social services, and economic growth opportunities available to a limited number of low-income residents and working families. In 1999, Knoxville's largest housing project was razed and 250 families were displaced to make way for construction on 225 new single- and double-occupancy homes. Former residents either were relocated to other projects or found other places to live. Low-income renters who would be able to return to the newly built homes had to meet certain qualifications for residence and, unless they were elderly or disabled, were required to sign a contract pledging that they will find gainful employment or enroll in job training and other service programs. After a period of five to seven years, subsidized renters were required to rent or purchase nonsubsidized homes or move to a different housing project.[6] The remaining homes were to be sold to working families requiring minimal public assistance and people in higher income brackets, ideally raising overall property values.

An enthusiastic advocate of economic privatization, Damien was optimistic about such initiatives and believed they held great promise to boost urban revitalization and community development. He bought and renovated a three-story home on the outskirts of the project, prior to the implementation of the HOPE VI plan, and moved there with his wife and three young children. His move inspired a small number of socially engaged evangelicals, including Tom Frick and, as we saw in chapter 4, Margie and Harrison McKenzie, later to follow suit. Damien was motivated both by the desire to embrace a more altruistically oriented Christian lifestyle and by a practical understanding that to participate fully in the ministry field he needed to integrate himself completely into the social environment he hoped to influence:

> If you really want to have a significant impact you have to live there, especially as someone who would be characterized as an affluent person. You know, [people are always] going in and helping, then leaving. That's great, but you don't live here. The school isn't your school. The crime isn't your crime. The drug trade and how it affects everyone isn't affecting you, because you leave. So you need to live there, and [then] all of a sudden the community's issues become your issues and you become enmeshed in the community through that.

Damien's immersion in the life of the community was facilitated by his widely publicized working relationship with Pastor Terrence, the leader of an independent black church in the neighborhood. A former drug dealer turned charismatic preacher, Pastor Terrence had been struggling for years to implement church-based outreach programs to provide job training and leadership opportunities to inner-city youths, as well as other community services. Getting these programs off the ground partly depended on his ability to garner the support of local faith-based organizations, charitable foundations, and affluent white churches. Damien Richards became a valuable resource for Pastor Terrence. Damien's influence and clout in the business community and in the nonprofit sector were vital; he also offered a direct link to Eternal Vine, which eventually helped to fund the building of a new church building and community center for Pastor Terrence's congregation. The professional partnership between the two men flourished for a few years, producing innovative social programs and services geared to the needs of the inner city. Their relationship was also a fascinating study in contrasts: an urban black preacher committed to community empowerment and preaching the prophetic discourse of social justice, paired with a wealthy, mild-mannered white entrepreneur who believed in the virtues of benevolent faith and believed almost as strongly in strategic planning and corporate efficiency as the means of achieving them. They needed each other in order to fulfill their aims—Pastor Terrence needed access to people and resources in the white churches and business community; Damien needed new ministry opportunities and someone to grant him credibility in the urban black community. Despite clear differences in personality and style, their partnership was hailed by locals as a model of interracial bridge building and collaboration, the kind which many felt was previously inconceivable in Knoxville.

By most accounts, including those of members of both churches, the relationship between Damien and Pastor Terrence was eventually strained because of differences in approach, exacerbated by concerns among congregants in the black church that their autonomy was being compromised by the priorities of white conservative evangelicals. Damien gradually withdrew from his leadership role alongside Pastor Terrence and started his own Christian philanthropy, the goal of which was to ensure that financial resources being channeled into urban ministries were distributed in ways that produced, in Damien's words, "the biggest bang for the buck." Looking back on the partnership, Damien felt that the black community's concerns and suspicions were misplaced but reasonable responses that turned out to be major obstacles to what he was trying to do in the community. He knew that certain aspects of planning and implementation probably should have been executed with greater sensitivity and patience, and admitted that these were qualities that white evangelicals tend to neglect when they impose their cultural standards and practices on others. At the same time, he was frustrated and bitter that his well-intentioned efforts were stymied, and he complained more generally that the political and civic culture of Knoxville effectively made it almost impossible to bring any real prospects for social change to fruition.

An issue that left Damien particularly frustrated was the state of public education in the inner city. Around the same time he moved into the neighborhood, Damien was directly involved in an attempt, ultimately unsuccessful, to convince the city government to turn one of the neighborhood schools into an Edison School, which meant outsourcing its administration to a private, for-profit company called the Edison Project (founded by the media entrepreneur and Knoxville native Chris Whittle). After two years of campaign and negotiation, the effort failed under political opposition mostly from the local teachers union. The defeat shattered Damien's hopes to establish a precedent for reforming the public school system, and it was a personal setback as well because he wanted to enroll his children in public schools but was not prepared to do so given the shape that they were in. Faced with the dilemma of whether to send their children to chronically underfunded, low-performing public schools or high-performing but socially insular private schools, Damien and his wife chose the latter, as did most other white evangelicals who moved closer to the inner city and faced the same choice (though some opted for homeschooling instead). In the end, personal family concerns won out over the desire to make social engagement a totally immersive familywide endeavor.

Damien finally moved his family back to the suburbs, although he continued to be actively involved in Christian philanthropy through his foundation. In this capacity and as an elder at Eternal Vine, Damien stayed committed to an evangelical call to action embedded in the exilic frame inspired by Jeremiah 29:7, which he cited frequently. I asked him to explain how he understands the significance of the passage. He responded:

> It's a hugely important scripture for the church, because it is countercultural to how mainline evangelicalism has operated.... If you really look at the evangelical church, and most of the popular literature in evangelicalism, the mentality is: "The world is going to hell, you need to prepare yourself, remove yourself from the danger of the world, and be a separatist." Jeremiah 29:7 is completely the opposite. It says the world is what it is—it's got evil, it's got good. You may not even be in a place you want to be, but God's

word to the people was "seek the peace and prosperity of the community to which I've called you." Immerse yourself, marry these people, learn their language, get in the midst of them. That's huge, because very few churches are encouraging their members to engage culture and be loving there. Most churches have an Us vs. Them mentality. You can't transform culture [that way] because everybody's on the defense; you create distance. But if you are into engaging people in relationship and say, "I'm allowing Christ to live through me in whatever arena he's called me," you can transform culture.

Damien's comments indicated a double-edged critique. His critique of "mainline evangelicalism" was rooted in an understanding of scripture he gained while taking courses at an evangelical seminary, where he learned that the Kingdom of God is "present and yet to come," and that Jesus "is slowly advancing his kingdom through his people." This convinced him that the strict premillennialist worldview held by so many conservative evangelicals—including many of his fellow church members and staff—needs to be reformed at the church level. At the same time, his references to a larger "culture" in need of being transformed indicated an implicit critique of secular public culture and, more specifically (given his investments in urban ministries), the culture of the inner city with its ever-present social ills and moral hazards. Damien's theology of social engagement was deeply altruistic yet its particular prophetic tone was largely determined by an exilic frame, which was reinforced by encounters with urban ministry and his ambivalence about those experiences.

To the extent that the moral ambitions of socially engaged evangelicals focus on the problems of the inner city, they are at once intensified and complicated by feelings of alienation and potential risk. Spaces of urban distress are also seen as places of urban danger and unsettling otherness. In his study of church activism among mostly minority congregations in the "rough" Boston neighborhood of Four Corners, McRoberts observed that local churches tend to regard "the street" in three distinct ways: "as an evil other to be avoided at all cost, as a recruitment ground to be trod and sacralized, and as a point of contact with persons at risk who are to be served" (2003: 82). Among middle-class churchgoers (especially suburban commuters) fear of the street is often a barrier to urban outreach, but in some cases it is also viewed as a barrier to be overcome (2003: 97). Overcoming fear is the ultimate test of faith, after all, and few local ministries appear to offer so powerful a combination of personal piety and uncertain risk for the average middle-class churchgoer as those that involve sustained urban engagement. White suburban evangelicals in Knoxville expressed all of these sentiments and ideas, emphasizing the intimidating challenges of urban ministry while repeatedly stressing that those very challenges reaffirm why, as one churchgoer put it, "we need the poor."

Yet such understandings among white evangelicals are frequently compounded by prejudices and concerns about the racial otherness associated with the inner city. In a manner reminiscent of racial stereotypes that informed Western missionary activities in colonial contexts, and persist to this day (though more implicit) in the racial politics of the Christian Right (Kintz 1997) and in evangelical constructions of the moral body (Griffith 2004), the divide between normalized "whiteness" and marginalized "blackness" is an ontological distance that white evangelicals traverse with caution. The effects of racialization are deeply embedded in the ideas and institutions that sustain racial alienation and complicate most well-intentioned efforts to overcome the cultural barriers that separate historically white and black church communities (Emerson and Smith 2000). By routinely portraying black inner-city communities as "dark" recesses of dysfunction desperately awaiting spiritual and relational intervention, white evangelicals in Knoxville effectively reproduced their own racial anxieties and racialized hierarchies of value. Their moral ambitions reflected a complex mix of intentions and perceived risks that did not necessarily hinder social engagement and racial reconciliation but introduced enough dissonance to make it hard for some to sustain the progress toward long-term goals that they hoped to see accomplished.

The extended case study that follows provides another illustration of how the issues described here play out in the course of institutional and intrasectoral partnerships in which megachurches play prominent if not decisive roles. Such partnerships reveal the ways that complex and contradictory desires affect the practice of evangelical social engagement at an institutional level. They also reveal how regional power dynamics are often reproduced through some of the very ministry initiatives that megachurches engage in as they seek to "take the city for God."

PARTNERSHIPS AND PATRONAGE

In 1997, Marble Valley Presbyterian established an official partnership with Harvest Glory, a small black inner-city congregation. The newly formed church was composed of members who split off from another congregation, reportedly because they felt its social ministries were ineffective in addressing community problems such as poverty, inadequate housing, and gang violence. Under the youthful and charismatic leadership of Pastor Leon, Harvest Glory needed partners and financial backers in order to get its new ministry initiatives off the ground. As members of Marble Valley Presbyterian became aware of the situation, a group of elders and engaged churchgoers urged the leadership to get involved. An agreement was eventually reached between the two churches that they would begin a gradual process of getting to know one another. Active members of both congregations were encouraged to participate in a series of mediated workshops that were meant to foster interracial dialogue and reconciliation. After a short time, the board of elders at Marble Valley Presbyterian voted to approve a fundraising campaign to underwrite a third of the costs of building a $1.5 million facility that would serve as Harvest Glory's new worship and ministry center. A number of the white churchgoers who took part in the racial reconciliation workshops were real-estate developers, bank executives, and architects, who ended up donating valuable skills and resources to the construction of the new facility and to the development of twenty-three acres of adjoining property, purchased with additional financial backing from the megachurch. The adjoining property was to become the site of a "Christian community development" initiative, which I describe shortly.

The most public expressions of the new partnership were joint worship services that were staged once or twice a year, usually in the megachurch's sanctuary. At these services, Pastor Jerry and Pastor Leon shared the pulpit while choir singers from both churches stood side by side and sang a mixed repertoire of gospel music and classical hymns. These occasions were felt to have an enormous emotional impact. An elderly woman at Marble Valley Presbyterian commented to me that the image of a mixed-race church choir reminded her of "what heaven must look like," even though she also admitted that she never felt entirely comfortable with the exuberance of black gospel singing. As the affinities grew, the congregations soon began to refer to one another as "sister churches." The use of this term was significant both for what it indicated and for what it obscured. On the one hand, it reflected the ideals of egalitarian kinship and doctrinal fellowship, with a gendered emphasis that highlighted the symbolic feminization of all churches in relation to "the lordship of Jesus Christ." On the other hand, the term obscured vertical power dynamics intrinsic to such partnerships, as they are predicated on existing socioeconomic disparities. This aspect of the sister-church link, at once unspoken and glaringly apparent, caused certain tensions to emerge in the partnership of Marble Valley Presbyterian and Harvest Glory over issues having to do with the management of financial resources, and conflicting expectations about the exact nature of the partnership and the megachurch's authority to make practical demands.

The potential for tensions to develop in spite of best intentions must have been evident from the start. The difficulties of racial reconciliation in the South are rooted in generations of institutionalized racism and violence, as well as conflicting perspectives on what racial reconciliation ultimately entails. Black churches like Harvest Glory share conservative Protestant values of relational transparency, repentance, and forgiveness, but they combine this with an emphasis on the politics of race and social justice. White evangelicals, by contrast, typically downplay structural social critiques and think about racial matters from the perspective of what Emerson and Smith refer to as "accountable free-will individualism" (2000: 76). This divide was evident as members of Harvest Glory and Marble Valley Presbyterian engaged with their racial counterparts and realized the extent of their diverging views on social, economic, and political issues. As the partnership evolved, the issue of accountability emerged as a major source of contention, especially as the leaders of Marble Valley Presbyterian became frustrated with what they perceived to be a lack of adequate mechanisms of financial accountability at Harvest Glory. This frustration was in many ways predetermined by the expectations of church leaders from the beginning of the partnership. When the board of elders approved the fundraising campaign for Harvest Glory, they did so assuming that the church eventually would raise its own funds to cover the remaining balances. At the time, several prominent elders expressed concern that this would not happen and warned of the possibility that the megachurch would get stuck with having to alleviate the black church's financial burdens. As it happened, their fears were somewhat justified. Harvest Glory struggled in its early years to become financially solvent, and the relationship between the "sister churches" was frequently strained because of the perception among members of Marble Valley Presbyterian that Harvest Glory was willfully irresponsible with its finances. A string of crises nearly caused the partnership to collapse, including one instance when the megachurch ended up paying Harvest Glory's outstanding property taxes. Problems like these only compounded negative preconceptions among white evangelicals, including the stereotype that black communities do not wish or know how to uphold the virtues of accountability and fiscal solvency.

There are, in fact, several cultural stereotypes that influence the attitudes of conservative white evangelicals in Knoxville toward African Americans. For example, it is widely assumed that persistent poverty and social dysfunction in the urban black community are due to the absence of a healthy civic and entrepreneurial spirit. Echoing "culture of poverty" theories that have circulated in academic and political discourses for decades, white evangelicals tend to believe that poor black communities perpetuate poor conditions by valuing economic dependence over self-sufficiency, defeatism over meritocratic ambition, and identity politics over personal responsibility. Somewhat paradoxically, a number of white evangelicals confessed to me their impression that African Americans are in some ways more inherently and viscerally "spiritual" than they are. Such discrepant yet equally alienating assessments complicate white evangelical perspectives on racial matters, and add to the difficulties they face in promoting racial reconciliation while harboring major doubts about the ability of inner-city leaders and community organizations to effectively generate moral and social uplift on their own terms.

Although these stereotypes came through in a variety of comments and observations made during the course of casual conversation, most churchgoers were uncomfortable talking about them openly. I did, however, manage to have a very candid and informative discussion with Norman Griswell, an elder at Marble Valley Presbyterian who was an early and avid supporter of the partnership with Harvest Glory. He confessed that despite his enthusiasm he did share some of the doubts and concerns expressed by other churchgoers. The main problem, he noted with a hint of resignation, stemmed from a fundamental point of disagreement between the two churches: "We wanted to hold them accountable, and they didn't want to be held accountable." In the course of our conversation over lunch at a local diner, I discovered Norman to be a relatively open-minded and tolerant person, especially with regard to social welfare and multiculturalism. But like many of his fellow white churchgoers, his views on racial reconciliation were marked by racial biases that were reinforced through his encounters with the black community, even as he struggled self-consciously to look past those biases. Norman explained, for example, that in getting to know the black community he observed "a spiritual depth and reliance on the providence of God" that he felt was virtually absent among suburban middle-class whites. He observed that African Americans, to their credit, do not obsess about money and material possessions "the way us WASPs and capitalists do," allowing them to enjoy some of the "spiritual advantages" of having a less materialistic outlook on life. However, he saw significant disadvantages to this. Black communities, he explained, are culturally predisposed to downplay financial responsibility, and consequently black churches are forced to "live from one financial crisis to another." Norman attributed this to two behavioral factors that he felt characterize black culture as a whole. First, he noted that African Americans tend to blame all of their problems on racism, leading to the development of a false sense of entitlement and preventing poor families from appreciating the rigors and realities of economic self-determination. As an illustration, Norman pointed out that black people are quick to complain about being turned down for bank loans but refuse to acknowledge that banks have every right to deny loans to people who cannot provide collateral. Second, he argued that black churches typically do not value tithing as highly as white churches do, making it difficult for them to build up sufficient revenue on their own. He said that this was especially problematic in churches that minister to prostitutes and drug dealers, who may decide to change their sinful ways and join the church but are not likely to become generous tithers anytime soon. Norman's generalizations are revealing as abstract impressions culled from subjective experience, and perhaps less so in terms of accuracy.[7] They are significant because they represent widely held assumptions among white evangelicals in Knoxville, the kinds of assumptions that affect the paternalistic manner in which congregations like Marble Valley Presbyterian cultivate partnerships with financially dependent black churches.

It would be a mistake to conclude from this that the members of Marble Valley Presbyterian were anything less than completely sincere in their desire to approach the process of interracial cooperation in a spirit of equality. Representatives of the megachurch who took direct part in the relationship with Harvest Glory—including a retired accountant who volunteered to help the church keep its finances in order—were emotionally invested and committed to the idea of a relationship rooted in mutual trust and, most of all, Christian fellowship. If the partnership became contentious, it was not for lack of good intentions on both sides. Yet the very conditions through which the partnership developed were such that it almost inevitably took the form of a patronage relationship in which the expectations and stipulations emanating from institutions of white privilege and economic power held sway. The extension of the partnership into a small-scale community development initiative further facilitated the creation of social and institutional networks whereby conservative evangelicals gained the leverage necessary to exert control over the reconstitution of civil-society infrastructures in urban communities.

In 2000, Harvest Glory designated five acres of empty real estate—part of the twenty-three acres purchased with the help of Marble Valley Presbyterian—to be developed as a mixed-income residential subdivision. The project was part of Harvest Glory's vision to stimulate economic development in the inner city by creating opportunities for homeownership for middle- and working-class black families, thereby providing a boost for social ministries spearheaded by the church. The subdivision was given the name Harvest Homes, and the prescreened residents were all African Americans who belonged to Harvest Glory. The construction of twelve houses, a mere stone's throw from the new church building, was completed over the next two years. Of the twelve houses, eight were built by white contractors who subsidized most of the construction and received nominal fees to help cover the cost of labor. The other four homes were built by Habitat for Humanity with volunteer teams from several churches, including Marble Valley Presbyterian (in fact, the person who ended up in charge of coordinating the construction teams was a volunteer from the megachurch). The Habitat homes were offered to low-income working families who met the organization's qualifications for housing assistance. As a condition of moving in to Harvest Homes, each family signed an agreement to join a neighborhood homeowner's association and participate in ongoing community initiatives.

The Harvest Homes project was inspired by a faith-based redevelopment model known as "Christian community development," coined by John Perkins, a popular black author, activist, and ministry leader. A veteran of civil rights struggles in the Deep South, Perkins has founded numerous ministry organizations over the years, including most notably the Christian Community Development Association, to address poverty and racism at the grassroots. The Perkins strategy follows the basic logic of urban renewal associated with community development corporations (CDCs) since the 1960s: promoting affordable housing, mixed-income neighborhoods, entrepreneurial incentives, and job creation. The added twist of "Christian" community development is an explicit emphasis on the value of Christian faith as a pillar for civic health and community building (Perkins 1993). In addition to raising up "indigenous" leaders in poor neighborhoods, especially church leaders and activists, the Perkins strategy seeks to encourage middle-class Christian families to reside in developing areas in order to help "fill the vacuum of moral, spiritual, and economic leadership that is so prevalent in poor communities" (Perkins 1993: 73).[8] "Urban communities need our best and brightest. They need strong two-parent families. They need to see with their own eyes disciplined families with a strong work ethic and meaningful values. They need to experience families that are not only concerned about their own families, but who also take an active interest in children whose families are not so fortunate" (1993: 77).

Perkins neatly summarizes his ministry philosophy with what he calls "the three Rs of community development": relocation, reconciliation, and redistribution (1993: 6–7). *Relocation,* as just indicated, calls on well-to-do families (including those who rose up from poverty) to stimulate economic growth and civic pride in poor communities by taking residence. *Reconciliation* refers to the process by which "the love and forgiveness of the gospel reconcile us to God and to each other across all racial, cultural, social, and economic barriers." Lastly, *redistribution* refers to the sharing of "skills, technologies, and educational resources in a way that empowers people to break out of the cycle of poverty." This is achieved through forming business cooperatives, securing corporate and government subsidies, and facilitating low-interest home loans for working families. As might be expected, the politics of redistribution are understood to pose the greatest challenge, especially insofar as redistributive practices require the participation and goodwill of institutions that are likely to be situated at a considerable physical and social distance from neighborhoods undergoing redevelopment. It is for this reason that nonprofit organizations, CDCs, and local churches are called on to play vital intermediary roles.

One of the key intermediary players in the development of Harvest Homes was the Koinonia Partnership of Knoxville (KPK), a Christian nonprofit run by Tom Frick, whose thoughts on theology and urban social integration were discussed earlier in this chapter.[9] As a former member of Marble Valley Presbyterian, a voluntary inner-city resident, and one of the few white members of Harvest Glory, Tom was an early proponent of the partnership between the two churches. As the Harvest Homes project took shape, his organization became the primary CDC, managing logistics among various agencies and corporations and raising the necessary funds to help qualified low- and middle-income families obtain mortgages. Inspired in large part by John Perkins, Tom wanted to encourage "indigenous" leadership in the inner city and create opportunities for homeownership to boost morale as well as commercial viability. "It all starts with a family or a group of families, living in a neighborhood, who value that place," he told me. "At some point, then, the market forces take over and the property values start to climb." Threads of neoliberal ideology are clearly evident in Tom's formulation of urban ministry, including his emphasis on private property and marketization as the preferred engines of social change. His views were not defined exclusively by this one perspective, as he frequently advocated progressive ideas on redistributive justice as well. However, the progressive attitudes that he and his associates at KPK held were restricted, to a considerable degree, by the organization's largely conservative donor base. Although KPK received philanthropic grants and HUD subsidies, it relied heavily on private donations and support from local churches, including funding from Marble Valley Presbyterian's missions budget. Implementing social programs and development initiatives in the inner city while satisfying (or at least not offending) the moral sensibilities of white conservative evangelicals was a delicate balancing act of which Tom Frick, like many socially engaged evangelicals, remained constantly aware.

The importance of intermediary agencies like KPK, and for that matter Marble Valley Presbyterian, was never lost on anyone, least of all the incoming residents of Harvest Homes. At a public ceremony marking the completion of the initial construction phase, major partners and contributors to the project were honored with plaques and words of recognition from Harvest Glory's Pastor Leon and a few of the prospective homeowners. A young father who had recently moved his family into their new home addressed the crowd of donors and news reporters. He praised the tireless efforts of the various agencies that had helped to make Harvest Homes a reality. He compared their combined efforts to a story in Mark 2:1–12, in which a group of people bring a paralyzed man to Jesus to be healed. As the men arrive at the home where Jesus is staying, they find a large crowd of followers blocking the doorway. They decide to lift the paralyzed man over the house and lower him down through a hole in the roof. Jesus is moved by their actions and performs the healing miracle. By making this story analogous to his own situation, the young father expressed his gratitude to organizations like Harvest Glory and KPK that "helped us reach the people that have turned us down before." Yet the comparison also seemed to me to convey a peculiar double meaning. On the one hand, the speaker insinuated that low- to middle-income African Americans in Knoxville who aspire to become homeowners still encounter resistance from lending institutions, resistance that is only overcome through the mediation of reputable agencies with access to economic and political resources. On the other hand, the parallel he drew to the biblical story implicitly positions those very lending institutions symbolically in the role of Christ the healer.

After its construction, Harvest Homes was hailed as a model of successful community development and proof of a political climate increasingly favorable to the creation of affordable housing in Knoxville. Within a few years of my fieldwork, the Harvest Homes neighborhood association, composed of twelve households, received an award in recognition of its "civic achievements" from a municipal planning agency. Although the "official" partnership between Marble Valley Presbyterian and Harvest Glory came to an end shortly thereafter, it was regarded by many as a success in terms of racial reconciliation, and the two congregations have maintained good relations. But the story included many bumps in the road, as we have seen, and reveals just how tenuous the cultural politics of racial reconciliation can be. Living in a socially conservative and racially stratified environment, where public policies ensuring adequate resource distribution and community empowerment are relatively scant, urban black communities in Knoxville must rely to a large extent on the goodwill of white institutions and political power brokers, including businesses, philanthropies, and civic organizations. They cannot depend on a broad base of black-owned businesses, CDCs, political lobby groups, and media outlets with which to partner, putting them at a disadvantage compared to black communities in some other metropolitan regions (Silverman 2001).

Black community organizers and church leaders told me that they were optimistic about the increased investments of white evangelical churches in the affairs of the inner city and hoped to see them produce positive changes on the ground. They complained, however, that white evangelicals from the suburbs had a tendency to approach urban community affairs with a "missionary mentality," as though they were there to "rescue rather than serve" the inner city, as one person put it. Others complained that suburban megachurches relied too heavily on "corporate philosophies" that privileged efficiency and growth over community empowerment.[10] Those who worked closely with white churches and institutions criticized what they perceived to be a double standard in the preoccupation with accountability. One community organizer explained that it is hard for disempowered groups to become truly empowered if dominant classes insist that they jump through administrative hoops and conform to external standards of professionalism that they cannot be expected to master without adequate time and resources. He found it especially egregious that when resources did become available, they were funneled through intermediary agencies, often located outside the inner city, thereby creating new political and bureaucratic hurdles and placing additional restraints on grassroots organizations. Addressing a meeting of the Samaritans of Knoxville, another community organizer said: "We have no time to risk leaving the trenches to come to you to get our resources. Our clients could be dead by then, and we could be killed by exhaustion." From this perspective, partnerships with white intermediary institutions effectively perpetuate existing power dynamics, but they also represent one of very few accessible options for overcoming them. Diplomacy is crucial for black church leaders, many of whom share the conservative theological orientations of white evangelicals and feel that they have some stake in maintaining harmonious relations with them for religious as well as institutional reasons.

For individual white evangelical patrons, the presence of intermediary faith-based agencies like Marble Valley Presbyterian and KPK reinforced the religious incentives for supporting Harvest Glory and the development of Harvest Homes. Aside from the tax deductions and good publicity they offered, sponsoring and facilitating the development project were conceived as acts of Christian stewardship, which made them especially appealing for Christian business executives who were eager for opportunities to demonstrate that they were good and virtuous stewards of earthly resources that they believe ultimately belong to God. Charitable contributions and altruistic deeds were meant to improve the conditions of the inner city, and to strengthen relational and institutional networks that might advance God's kingdom in Knoxville. At the same time, the generosity of white patrons was *contingent* on the role of these intermediary agencies, since they were seen to represent the ideological concerns and normative standards of the conservative evangelical community. Part of the reason the members of Marble Valley Presbyterian were willing to support the congregation's investments in Harvest Glory and Harvest Homes was because they appreciated that the megachurch was in a position to hold all parties—including KPK as well as Harvest Glory—directly accountable. The patronage structure that made the whole operation possible satisfied their charitable impulses, and it also satisfied their implicit desire to exert a measure of moral control over social and philanthropic initiatives that otherwise might have seemed too controversial or "risky" to undertake in the first place. In a religious subculture where the imperative to "take our cities for God" (Dawson 2001) invites a range of possible interpretations, and the relatively unfamiliar realm of inner-city welfare activism brings with it morally unpalatable notions of social and racial justice, the power of evangelical megachurches to monitor and steer the direction of urban social engagement carried out in the name of Christian community development is a source of comfort and encouragement to conservative evangelicals who are keen to produce social change but not always certain how.

MEGACHURCHES, CIVIL SOCIETY, AND CHRISTIANIZATION

The strategies and intentions that defined the urban social engagement described in the preceding pages were tied to religious concepts and utopian visions that pertained specifically to the inner city and issues of racial reconciliation and community development. They were also relevant to broader aspirations concerning the revitalization of civil society as a whole. But what exactly is entailed by such aspirations, for which the Kingdom of God is a constant reference point? If the immediate ends are envisioned according to abstract notions of social harmony, Christian fellowship, compassion, and accountability, what are the implications for civil society writ large? And what difference does it make, if any, when those who implement religiously inspired visions of revitalization are affiliated with powerful corporate entities such as megachurches?

The structure and vitality of civil society in the United States has emerged as a focal point of intellectual concern among American scholars in recent years. Prominent social scientists have contemplated the apparent decline of volunteerism and civic participation, looking for ways to salvage cherished Tocquevillian values considered essential for modern liberal democracies to function (Bellah et al. 1985; Fukuyama 1999; Putnam 2000). Churches and religious organizations are believed to stand out among the voluntary associations that promote civic engagement. They are regarded as exemplary "mediating structures" (Berger and Neuhaus 1977) that strengthen moral communities and empower individuals as free and responsible citizens. Studies have demonstrated that local congregations are indeed highly effective in helping everyday people become socially connected and involved in the affairs of community life (Ammerman 2005; Chaves 2004; Cnaan et al. 2002; Wuthnow 2004). According to Cnaan and coauthors, congregations achieve this by "operating as sources of skill acquisition, social interactions, mutual exchanges and obligations, and trust, all of which promote social activism and civic engagement" (2002: 255–256).

From a neo-Tocquevillian perspective, the growth of evangelical megachurches is an auspicious trend in that such congregations are veritable factories for the production of social capital—interpersonal bonds of trust and reciprocity—to be invested in civic and religious enterprises. This was noted even by Robert Putnam, who argued in his book *Bowling Alone* that social capital in the United States has been in a state of perpetual decline, but in a follow-up study included megachurches like Rick Warren's Saddleback Church on a list of "success stories" that suggest the spirit of civic engagement may still be alive and well (Putnam, Feldstein, and Cohen 2003). Putnam's analysis of Saddleback reveals that through mechanisms such as small groups, megachurches produce strong relational ties within the same religious, social, or ethnic groups, what he calls bonding social capital. Indeed megachurches do excel in this area, arguably more than in creating relational networks across lines of social difference or bridging social capital. Yet there are megachurches that do manage to become quite diverse, and more significantly, just about all evangelical megachurches emphasize "reaching out" through evangelism and community service as a core aspect of their congregational identity and mission (Thumma and Travis 2007). Although most of their ministry services may be directed inward—for purposes of church recruitment and member retention—their evangelical character compels members to look outward, to imagine the secular world as a space of missionary intervention, starting right at home. As the efforts of socially engaged evangelicals suggest, evangelicals are rarely content with the idea of simply building up insulated and homogenous communities, and megachurches represent to many the chance to pursue ambitious strategies of social engagement.

However, in formulating the impact of evangelical megachurches on civil society, it is far too reductive to claim that by fostering civic participation and cooperation they inherently promote some generalized model of citizenship or universal notion of the common good. In trying to assess the impact of social action, it is necessary first to understand the range of diverse meanings and norms that cultural groups attach to the specific social networks and institutional practices they set in motion as they engage the civic sphere (Lichterman 2005). In other words, measuring the amount of social capital generated by this or that form of voluntary association is not nearly so revealing as asking "for what purposes are [voluntary] associations coming into being, and to what ends are the resultant networks and skills being mobilized?" (McRoberts 2003: 144)

One should not assume too readily, moreover, that the production of social capital naturally and automatically serves the interests of liberal or pluralistic values, or even reflects those values in every case.[11] Although civil society is idealized as an open democratic arena for civic discourse and empowerment, independent of political and economic powers, it is hardly as neutral or depoliticized as pluralistic idealism would suggest. At various points in U.S. history, for example, voluntary associations and cultural institutions have come up in support of exclusionary and oppressive practices against marginalized populations, including women, gays, and racial and ethnic minorities (Arneil 2006). Today, as the state's mediating role in matters of social welfare shrinks, local communities are becoming increasingly dependent on private interests to provide services that the public sector no longer enforces or guarantees. As Talal Asad has noted with regard to the public sphere, civil society is "a space *necessarily* (not just contingently) articulated by power. And everyone who enters it must address power's disposition of people and things, the dependence of some on the goodwill of others" (2003: 184, original emphasis). It is not sufficient, then, to accept without qualification that all cultural contributions to civil society benefit the common good in the same categorical ways, even the contributions of religious organizations that prioritize charity and benevolence toward others. To understand the influence and impact of evangelical megachurches, it is necessary to identify how they are positioned relative to existing dynamics of social, economic, and political power, and to assess how purposeful actions emanating from these institutions reflect specific religious and ideological motivations.

I would argue that instances of far-reaching social engagement initiated under the auspices of evangelical megachurches, such as the instances discussed in this chapter, are best understood as practices oriented toward systemic cultural Christianization. This is not a religious conspiracy to install a right-wing theocracy in place of liberal democracy, nor does it mean that the altruistic intentions of conserva-

212 I Taking the (Inner) City for God

tive evangelicals are superficial or a smoke screen to conceal "real" objectives that might seem less than charitable. It does mean, however, that megachurches like Eternal Vine and Marble Valley Presbyterian advance the project of Christianization, or rather one particular version of this project, by supporting ministries that expand their cultural influence and authority in local communities and nonprofit sectors.

As they facilitate and sponsor cross-cultural partnerships, faith-based coalitions, and intrasectoral alliances, megachurches enter into networks of cooperation that are meant to transcend social barriers and straddle the divides between religious and secular culture, and between the public and private sphere. Megachurches usually hold considerable leverage and prestige within these network because they have the resources, the staff, and the public profile to take a leading role in the efforts (Thumma and Travis 2007: 80). One potential outcome of the ability to "call the shots" is the circulation of norms, discourses, and practices consistent with their own Christian ideals. This circulation may not always happen in any pronounced fashion, and when it does there are plenty of potential obstacles, gaps, and frictions to take into consideration. It may also be the case that socially engaged evangelicals playing key network roles diverge from their home congregations in how they represent their ideological concerns. But the point is that the enterprising and missionary activism of megachurches is such that their social ministries, however modest in scale, contribute to continual efforts on the part of evangelicals to institutionalize evangelical religiosity in ever-widening spheres of civil society, and to make it a more visible and formidable force in public culture (cf. Deeb 2006).

Methods of evangelical social engagement are guided by altruistic aims—the best of real-world intentions—but they are also conceived by church leaders and activists as strategies of evangelism, meaning that their primary purpose is to extend the purview of Christianity and interpellate friends and strangers alike as subjects of its totalizing presence. The language of "kingdom" is apt in this regard—every kingdom must have subjects—and although evangelical megachurches are by no means unique in their efforts to "take the city for God," they are, advocates might say, uniquely well suited to the task of expanding the realm of God's kingdom into new territories, such as the impoverished inner city, where it is assumed to be nascent or unrecognized. At the same time, and in a manner similar to neo-Pentecostal megachurches in Guatemala studied by Kevin O'Neill (2010), evangelical megachurches in the United States provide churchgoers with opportunities to perform their citizenship through Christian practices that redefine the secular city—and by extension the nation as a whole—as a stage of spiritual and cultural transformation.

The predominantly white and socially conservative members of Eternal Vine and Marble Valley Presbyterian enter the civic sphere with a set of ideas and doctrines concerning what the world is and what the world can (and will) become. Some of these ideas and doctrines are rooted in centuries of theological discourse, others emerge and resonate with distinctly contemporary social movements, public policies, and economic trends. In times of neoliberal restructuring and the unyielding influence of right-wing politics in public life, the prevailing norms of moral governance in mainstream society have become increasingly amenable to conservative evangelical sensibilities. This has made it possible for evangelicals to embrace social engagement as a viable exercise of religious and civic responsibilities. The fact that, for evangelicals in Knoxville, the actual practice of social engagement involves persistent setbacks, frictions, and disagreements testifies to the enduring presence of alternative sensibilities and counterhegemonic currents—the very things that make hard work out of "kingdom work." These are challenges that inspire the moral ambitions of socially engaged evangelicals, while reminding them of just how much they look forward to the more perfect world to come.

Epilogue

One of the more unexpected surprises of my fieldwork came when I was invited to accompany a group of high school students on a biennial "spring break mission trip" to Washington, DC, organized by the youth ministry at Marble Valley Presbyterian. I was invited by Margie McKenzie, whose career as an outreach coordinator began as a result of having attended this same trip years earlier. I happily agreed to come along and planned to be little more than a fly on the wall, observing some thirty teenagers as they spent the week visiting homeless shelters, day-care centers, and various goodwill agencies in the impoverished inner-city neighborhoods of the nation's capital. Fate had other plans, however. Contrary to my expectations, I had been thrust into the role of a chaperone, one of a handful of adults who assumed the responsibility of supervising the youths and transporting them from place to place. After nearly a year of participant observation in evangelical churches and ministries, I was used to performing unfamiliar roles. But I honestly never imagined I would one day be the driver of a big church van, shuttling pubescent soldiers of Christ through the streets of DC on their mission to do God's work.

In many ways the mission trip was just as unusual an experience for the youth group; indeed, that was its function. The majority of the teenagers had little or no previous firsthand exposure to urban poverty. Most of them lived in the affluent suburbs of Knoxville, attended well-funded schools, and had only an abstract and detached awareness of

Knoxville's inner city just a few miles from their own backyards. Their enthusiasm in anticipation of the trip to DC was palpable, as was their fear of the unknown. During a preliminary meeting, as they were briefed on what to expect and how to behave, a redheaded girl with braces and pigtails asked if she should be careful to avoid wearing colors that might get her in trouble with violent street gangs. Her friends laughed at the idea that she could possibly be misidentified as a gang member, and realizing this she blushed and started laughing too. Still, no matter how far-fetched a scenario that was, it was clear to me from the conversations I heard that day that these teenagers, sheltered as they were from the harsh realities of urban deprivation, were quite unsure and a little nervous about what to expect.

The purpose of the trip, aside from getting high schoolers more involved in the megachurch's programs, was to provide evangelical teenagers with a short-term, "low risk/high grace" opportunity to experience what it means to be engaged in Christian ministry and missionary work. Each day was packed with volunteer activities coordinated with faith-based and charity organizations in the DC area, and ended with group discussions and the singing of worship songs in the recreation room of the inner-city community center where we slept. All of the activities and interactions with poor people, most of whom were African American or Latino, were to be interpreted by participants as part and parcel of the work of Christian evangelism. The teenagers were told not to proselytize for converts unless someone was openly receptive or an opportunity presented itself with minimal risk of offending, but they were taught that acts of charity and compassion were expressions of God's love and potentially effective testimonials to the saving grace of Jesus Christ. The trip was also meant to provide the teenagers with opportunities to grow spiritually, and many of them appeared to be deeply affected by the experience. As I watched them interact with the poor and needy individuals they were there to serve, they reacted with a mix of enthusiasm, empathy, revulsion, and bafflement, but they remained strikingly earnest even in the most awkward moments. Ennobled by biblical inspiration and peer encouragement, they were well prepared to assimilate their encounters through self-conscious narratives of revelation and redemption.

The experience proved to be quite humbling for the teenagers, many of whom realized by comparison how much comfort and privilege they took for granted in their lives. This realization, almost more than anything else, was the aspect of the trip that became most relevant to their evolving sense of what it means to be a Christian in the modern world. One evening near the end of the week, the full group was broken up into smaller groups for the usual evening discussion, and to my surprise I was asked to lead one of them through a list of reflection questions. The kids who were assigned to me were pleasant, somewhat impish youngsters with whom I had already formed a bond. "Guys! We're gonna be in his book!" one of them shouted when he saw me pull out my tape recorder and place it on the landing of the narrow stairwell where we convened. I took us through the questions that were given to me by the trip leaders, supplementing them with questions of my own. Their answers were insightful and full of youthful candor, but I couldn't help but notice that they were remarkably similar—in content and tone—to those of adults whom I had interviewed previously. To the written question, "What did God show you today?" a precocious and deeply committed high school senior named Laura answered, "I think God shows us stuff every day because we are in a place we're not used to being. If we were just walking through the Washington Mall and looking at the White House, we wouldn't necessarily see God. But I think because we're out of our comfort zone and we're hanging around homeless men, then it's more obvious to see God."

As the conversation moved on, they talked about how impressed they were by the strong religious faith of some of the social workers and welfare clients they had met, which they attributed to the fact that some people who live in difficult circumstances find little else to rely on in life other than trust in Jesus. The teenagers started to think about themselves and described feeling a sense of worry that their dependence on God was less intense than that of the urban poor. They complained about living in the suburbs where kids are always preoccupied with material things like clothes and cars, and being popular at school, making it hard for teenagers to put God at the center of their lives. "The world has a stronger pull on us," Laura said, as if to suggest that the gravitational pull of materialism exerts a weaker force on those who have nothing to lose. At the same time, however, teenagers and trip leaders throughout the week also indicated their belief that the poor and needy, by virtue of being poor and needy, lack something essential in their lives, some elusive source of fortitude to lift them out of grave circumstances. The perception of a spiritual vacuum that needed urgently to be filled made it possible for these budding young evangelists to recognize their chari- table gestures—every warm meal, every hammer and nail, every hug, every word of encouragement—as spiritual offerings, special gifts in a redemptive economy of salvation.

At the end of our discussion I asked my group if they expected to take the lessons they learned in Washington back to Knoxville. They replied affirmatively, automatically taking a cue from trip leaders and local ministry workers who repeatedly advised that they should not let the momentum fade when they returned home. They were eager to show their optimism on this point but harbored doubts as well, since they knew that their parents and peers back home did not share the emotional experience they just had, and they suspected, even at such a young age, that most people were simply not committed to making care for the poor a regular part of their lives. As I listened to them, I wondered if they knew just how much they sounded like their parents. Recapitulating the style of evangelical self-criticism described throughout this book, many of the teenagers on the mission trip complained about apathy and social insularity among white middle-class Christians and accused suburban evangelicals of caring too much about their own comfort, security, and social reputations. They were, in short, learning to express the sentiments and virtues that evangelicals associate with authentic Christian spirituality. They were cultivating moral ambitions—the habits of knowing what it is that Christians can and should be doing in the world—regardless of whether or how they will choose to act on those ambitions when they become adults.

The next generation of evangelicals in Knoxville may very well be less entrenched than recent generations in their skepticism of and resistance to Christian ministries that entail a broad and inclusive social conscience, and more inclined to support activities based on direct links between social welfare and evangelism. Across the United States, it is already evident that younger white evangelicals have begun to draw positive attention to issues previously associated with liberal activism, such as social justice, human rights, and the environment. The upcoming generation of evangelicals is also said to be more likely than previous ones to avoid close identification with one political party, and has proven more amenable to political centrism on domestic issues and multilateralism in international affairs (Gushee 2008). Where these trends will lead, whether they will draw political momentum away from right-wing fundamentalists, and whether they will increase the institutional leverage of socially engaged evangelicals in conservative churches, all remain to be seen and are not within the scope of this ethnography.

What is foreseeable, if history is any guide, is that the field of evangelical social engagement will remain complex and internally fraught. We can see a recent example of this in the conflicted evangelical response to controversial statements made in March 2010 by the media host Glenn Beck, who warned Christians to "run as fast as you can" from churches that talk about social and economic justice, which he called "code words" for radical ideological extremism. Beck's tirade drew support from right-wing pundits and preachers, but enraged liberal and moderate evangelicals and even drew cautious responses from prominent conservatives—including Albert Mohler, president of the Southern Baptist Theological Seminary, and Richard Land, president of the Southern Baptist Convention's Ethics and Religious Liberty Commission—who questioned the wisdom of Christians distancing themselves so vigorously from ideas of justice that remain crucial to the spirit of the gospel. It is also noteworthy that many conservative evangelicals who took issue with Beck's comments are equally inclined to criticize evangelicals on the political left, such as Reverend Jim Wallis, who has made no secret of his progressive social views and would be an even stronger role model for socially engaged evangelicals if he were not seen as such a polarizing figure in the movement. Inasmuch as social engagement inspires evangelicals, it troubles and provokes them as well. It will continue to do so as long as evangelicals struggle among themselves—and within themselves—to determine how best to carry out the Great Commission in local communities, and how to convince others, as the parable of the Good Samaritan instructs, to "go and do likewise."

As socially engaged pastors and churchgoers attempt to reach out to local communities, their cultural practices reveal the range of attitudes and assumptions that inform and sometimes hinder their efforts. They also demonstrate that evangelicals are committed to moral visions that extend beyond the ethics of individualism that otherwise feature prominently in their worldview. I would not dispute that evangelical ministries are chiefly guided by what Christian Smith calls the "personal influence strategy," which is based on the belief that "the only truly effective way to change the world is one-individual-at-a-time through the influence of interpersonal relationships" (1998: 187). This approach, which Smith describes as "profoundly individualistic" (1998: 189), orients evangelicals toward personalized or individuated forms of outreach that bring volunteers into direct contact with people whose lives are meant to be transformed by their goodwill and compassion. Smith argues that because of this emphasis, evangelicals are left "largely incapable of seeing how supraindividual social structures, collective processes, and institutional systems profoundly pattern and influence human consciousness, experience, and life-chances" (1998: 189). Although my analysis partially reinforces Smith's observation, the ethnographic material I have presented reveals important exceptions to this tendency. However personal, modest, and informal the efforts of the socially engaged evangelicals may appear, they do recognize or presuppose the existence of social structures, collective processes, and institutional systems that facilitate or impede evangelical aspirations and conceptions of the public good.

By suggesting that some conservative evangelicals are in fact capable of thinking beyond the restrictive framework of moral individualism—predominant as that framework may be—I do not mean to say that they are necessarily inclined toward social progressivism, although that is sometimes the case. I do, however, argue that, despite prevailing assumptions, these evangelicals readily acknowledge and insist on certain advantages to thinking about social welfare in systemic terms. They remain opposed to the welfare state and reject the idea that social justice should require government to play an active leading role. Yet for socially engaged evangelicals like those I observed in Knoxville, there are perceived benefits to promoting systemic nongovernmental initiatives that rely on social and institutional networks in which evangelicals assume prominent roles. On the one hand, such networks emerge from voluntaristic relationships and broad-based collaborative partnerships that revitalize civil society and make it easier for community organizations to work collectively to improve social welfare. On the other hand, to the extent that such networks are seen by evangelicals to enhance the public circulation of Christian beliefs, norms, and values, they advance the cultural project of Christianization, not in a generic sense but according to distinctly evangelical ideals and intentions.

The modern proliferation of resourceful megachurches, and the political and cultural currency of "faith-based initiatives" in the era of federal welfare reform, together signaled for socially engaged evangelicals a historic opportunity to establish evangelical religiosity as a dominant influence in realms of public life where religious influences were previously marginalized. Contrary to much public opinion, such expansionism is not necessarily meant to serve the same theocratic objectives associated with Christian Dominionism and other right-wing movements whose political machinations provoke liberal alarmism (Goldberg 2006; Hedges 2006; Phillips 2006). Local strategies of outreach mobilization and institutionalization would be grossly misunderstood if they were assumed to represent no more than veiled attempts to usurp the functions of the state or undermine the principles of liberal democracy. However, these efforts on the part of conservative evangelicals and the political activism of the Christian Right are roughly consistent in their basic orientation toward essentially missionary and revivalist ideals. These include the desire to limit the breadth of moral heterogeneity in modern society and complicate (but not necessarily erase) the conventional boundaries of religion and secularity. Whether they talk about "taking the city for God," "putting God back in the public square," or "infecting" churches with the impulse to serve God by humbly serving others, socially engaged evangelicals are concerned to wrestle against the principalities and powers that subject the world to spiritual darkness (to paraphrase the Book of Ephesians). In addition to waging spiritual warfare, denouncing social liberalism, and asserting Christian nationalism, theirs is a cultural mission. That mission, broadly speaking, is to propagate (or "restore") strictly biblical theocentric principles in place of unbiblical humanistic principles on which secular renderings of self and society ostensibly rely.

I have focused on the concept of moral ambition in this book to draw attention to the cultural, historical, and institutional factors that shape the ways that individuals, in this case fervently religious individuals, enact personal virtues that by their very definition incorporate the lives of others, from fellow churchgoers to the targets of social outreach to the wider local and national public. Because I include the discourse and practices of outreach mobilization as well as social outreach itself under the category of social engagement, my ethnography is filled with stories of frustration, doubt, and discord, some of which are intrinsic to the aspirational nature of evangelical thought and action, others that illustrate the difficulties that white, middle-class conservative evangelicals typically face as they venture into relatively uncertain terrains of social ministry. As goal-oriented habits and sentiments, the moral ambitions of socially engaged evangelicals are neither vain nor delusional but are expressions of something akin to what T. O. Beidelman (1993) has called the "moral imagination." Confronted by internal disagreements and inconsistencies, evangelical pastors and churchgoers exercise "strenuous imaginative effort"—one of evangelicalism's more abundant cultural resources—to create possibilities for self-realization, and in order to "appreciate and transcend these seemingly limiting differences and contradictions, if only in part, within their minds" (1993: 202).

I have also described social engagement as transformative for those who have strong commitments to this kind of externalizing and immersive work. In the course of assuming activist orientations, socially engaged evangelicals in Knoxville promoted the overarching ideological and evangelistic aims of their religious community, but they did not remain fixed on one set of social attitudes and prejudices, nor did they ignore their personal failings and contradictions. Although evangelical outreach volunteers tended to hold onto their cultural preconceptions—for example, about the urban poor, the inner city, people with HIV/AIDS, and "liberal do-gooders" in the welfare arena—those who were very active were more likely to integrate diverse perspectives and question previous assumptions. They saw the merits of accommodating tolerance and sensitivity, and recognized that they could be faithful emissaries of Christ and still run the risk of succumbing to the sins of selfishness, arrogance, and the desire to always be right. Such critical reflexivity is prevalent in many areas of evangelical ministry (including missiology) and hardly unique to the experiences of socially engaged evangelicals. But socially engaged evangelicals, be they pastors or lay churchgoers, stand out in their churches as members who intensify this reflexivity and channel it into social outreach, striving all the while to help other evangelicals put their relentless soul-searching to socially and spiritually productive use.

The moral ambitions of evangelical social engagement are simultaneously normative and progressive. They are wedded to an authoritative doctrinal tradition, yet they reflect the plasticity of evangelicalism as lived religion. They demonstrate the inventive ways that religious virtues are institutionalized, performed, and shared among evangelicals, albeit imperfectly. The common colloquial description of churches as "places of worship" is strikingly narrow when we remember that churches are sites of socialization and indoctrination as well as creative agency on the part of members intent on realizing their religious potential. Socially engaged evangelicals aspire to realize the potential of evangelical subjectivity by pushing its limits. They hope to collapse the divide between expectations and actions, and to minimize the distance between what Max Weber called "heroic" or "virtuoso religiosity" and the everydayness of "mass religiosity" (1946a: 287). Evangelical megachurches encourage such efforts by inspiring religious innovation and social enterprise, and inviting members to imagine what it could mean for them individually and collectively to minister to the world's needs in a Christlike fashion. Yet like most conservative evangelical institutions, they rest their symbolic foundations on moral judgments of "the world" outside their walls, a world that threatens to engulf them even as it calls out for moral and spiritual rescue. This combined with a host of other factors described in this book contribute to the conditions that at once fuel moral ambitions and leave evangelicals grasping for lofty ideals that often prove difficult to achieve.

In his *Confessions,* Saint Augustine of Hippo described ambition as a dangerous vice, a worldly desire for the "honor and glory" that belongs only to God. In the New International Version translation of the Bible, there are several passages (for example, in Philippians, Galatians, and James) that refer to "selfish ambition" as a conceit that believers do well to avoid, lest they be found wanting in God's judgment. By now it should be clear that my use of the term *ambition* is value neutral and is in no way meant to reify such religious or ethical connotations. I regard ambition as a generic human disposition that manifests itself in a wide range of social proclivities, which need not be associated only with egoism, avarice, unbridled opportunism, or the will to power.

Motivations that usher individuals to paths of uncommon drive and commitment do not preclude altruistic aims, and altruistic aims do not preclude individuals from being ambitious in their pursuit. Although evangelical theology rejects any reliance on "good works" as a means of salvation, and whereas subjectivity is idealized as an abnegation of the self in favor of total submission to God's will, living out one's born-again faith implies an active rather than passive state of being. Whatever ambivalence is felt toward the outside world, the cultural projects of evangelism and Christianization remain central, and such projects inevitably orient Christians in the direction of others—other people, other communities, and the general public at large. Some evangelicals, like those portrayed here, stake the full power and authenticity of their faith on their efforts to embody this outward orientation with virtuosity and uncompromising zeal. They are ambitious actors in a culture of relentless striving, and whatever else can be said about ambitious people, they rarely keep their ambitions to themselves.

Notes

1. INTRODUCTION

1. To protect the anonymity of informants and interviewees who prefer not to be identified, the names of individuals, churches, and Christian organizations in Knoxville appear in this book as pseudonyms. In some cases biographical or other identifying details have been altered as well.

2. The idea of "loving the poor" and serving one's community is hardly novel in the ethos of North American congregationalism, conservative or otherwise. Most religious congregations in the United States offer social services or outreach programs of one kind or another. These include informal services provided by members, such as youth mentoring or caring for the sick and elderly; formal programs, such as food pantries and homeless shelters, that may require paid staff, volunteer labor, and partnerships with external agencies; and highly specialized ministries that offer professional services such as free health care, job training, and skilled labor for low-income housing construction (Cnaan et al. 2002). However, "for the vast majority of congregations, social services constitute a minor and peripheral aspect of their organizational activities, taking up only small amounts of their resources and involving only small numbers of people" (Chaves 2004: 93).

When theology is factored in, we see that theologically conservative congregations are statistically less likely to sponsor social service programs than liberal mainline congregations (Chaves 2004: 53; Wuthnow 2004: 55). We see also that conservative evangelical churches are generally "less likely than other churches to address, either politically or through community services, pressing social and economic problems," and more likely to "concentrate their energy on evangelism or meeting the needs of congregational members" (Greenberg 2000: 389). It is possible, given the data, that evangelical megachurches made up of mostly middle-class members with college educations are more altruistically inclined than other evangelical churches (Chaves 2004: 52). Also, statistics vary among different areas of outreach ministry. For example, theologically conservative churches are only slightly less active than liberal churches with regard to prison ministries, distributing food to the poor, and job training programs, but the gap widens considerably for programs that serve inner-city communities and people with AIDS (Wuthnow 2004: 56).

3. In describing the subjects of my research as socially engaged evangelicals, I have self-consciously appropriated the terminology of "socially engaged Buddhism," a religious movement that "aims to combine the cultivation of inner peace with active social compassion in a practice and lifestyle that support and enrich both" (Jones 2003: 173). Comprising social action networks and affinity groups across the spectrum of global Buddhism, socially engaged Buddhists calls for a wide range of this-worldly interventions, from care for the poor, sick, and elderly, to civic and community voluntarism, to "radical social activism" (including lobbying and mass protest) on issues of nonviolence, social and economic justice, and environmental responsibility (2003: 175). There are, of course, many differences between socially engaged Buddhism and the style of evangelical engagement described in this book. Whereas Buddhists view human suffering as a consequence of self-delusion, and compassion as the outward manifestation of wisdom (Eppsteiner 1988), evangelicals link suffering to sin and believe that compassion is an outflow of divine revelation born of faith. Evangelical social engagement, which is not a distinct movement so much as an orientation, also tends to be less concerned with nonviolence and notions of justice than with compassion and mercy as catalysts for evangelism and moral uplift.

Nonetheless, I would argue that there are important similarities that justify making an analytical connection between these two instances of religiously inspired activism. Socially engaged Buddhists and socially engaged evangelicals share certain goal-oriented sensibilities, including the strong desire to educate, organize, and mobilize coreligionists on a scale not presently realized. They both seek to advance and refine their methods of engagement through, among other things, practices of ritual piety (e.g., meditation for Buddhists, prayer and Bible study for evangelicals), thereby creating direct affinities between their social concerns and core spiritual doctrines. Both groups also tend to represent a significant minority relative to their religious communities, even if their efforts are valorized by the majority. Finally, they share a tendency to associates themselves with causes that may be regarded as controversial among fellow adherents, especially if they involve radical social agendas or, in the case of conservative evangelicals, programs of social reform that are seen as being too politically progressive.

4. The logic of holism is common among faith-based organizations in the United States (Bartkowski and Regis 2003), as well as Christian nongovernmental organizations (NGOs) involved in global humanitarianism. For evangelical agencies working to alleviate poverty in the developing world, such as World Vision International, the idea of "development" encompasses both material and spiritual transformations. Among Christian aid workers, the goal

of stimulating economic development is inseparable from the goal of promoting evangelism, and both are seen as integral components of the ideal Christian lifestyle (Bornstein 2003).

5. In a 2006 survey, the Barna Research Group, a Christian polling organization, found that 38 percent of adults identified themselves as "evangelical," but when the survey applied a "nine-point theological filter" the figure dropped to 8 percent (see "Survey Explores Who Qualifies as an Evangelical," www.barna .org, January 18, 2007). This illustrates the high degree of variability among people who embrace evangelical tenets and the unreliability of the label as a fixed unit for quantitative analysis. Statistical inconsistencies about evangelicalism are an inevitable consequence of the slipperiness of the term, as well as the fact that multiple researchers have developed survey instruments that differ from one another in significant ways (Lindsay and Hackett 2008).

6. It has been argued that the mainstream popularization of evangelicalism in the latter half of the twentieth century was made possible by strategic efforts among church leaders to integrate a wide constituency of born-again believers while avoiding any overt association with liberal or fundamentalist extremes, and that as a result evangelicalism lacks a precise and fully distinguishable movement identity (Stone 1997). Others have gone so far as to suggest that evangelicalism is "a face void of any discernable features" that "needs to be relinquished as a religious identity, because it does not exist," except to serve the opportunism of "savvy religious leaders, academics, and pollsters" (Hart 2004: 17). In contrast, Christian Smith has argued that, however imprecise it may seem as a sociological category, evangelicalism is meaningful as a basis of subcultural identity for a large segment of American churchgoers. According to Smith, "What the evangelical movement *did* accomplish was to open up a 'space' between fundamentalism and liberalism in the field of religious collective identity; give that space a name; articulate and promote a resonant vision of faith and practice that players in the religious field came to associate with that name and identity-space; and invite a variety of religious players to move into that space and participate in the 'identity-work' and mission being accomplished there" (1998: 14, original emphasis).

7. The core tenets of conservative Protestantism can be elaborated as follows: (a) The Bible is the infallible Word of God. (b) Jesus Christ is the Son of God, who died for the redemption of human sin, was resurrected, ascended to heaven, and will return to defeat Satan and rule over "a new heaven and a new earth." (c) Eternal salvation is achieved not by sacraments but through faith conversions, which entail being "born again" in Christ. (d) Priestly intermediaries are not necessary for the administration of God's grace, which is available to all who seek and receive it (this is commonly known as "the priesthood of all believers").

8. The Personal Responsibility and Work Opportunity Reconciliation Act made severe cuts to federal welfare spending and imposed new limits and restrictions on public assistance, with the intention of forcing welfare recipients to find jobs and facilitating the privatization of social services. The Charitable Choice provision, written into the bill by Senator John Ashcroft (future U.S. attorney general under George W. Bush), was included to allow religious charities and

service organizations to compete with secular agencies for federal grants. In aiming to redefine the boundaries between church and state, Charitable Choice provoked heated legal and ethical debates despite strong public support for congressional efforts to reduce the welfare rolls and promote personal responsibility and civic voluntarism.

On his first day in office in 2001, President Bush issued an executive order creating the White House Office of Faith-Based and Community Initiatives, and establishing individual Centers for Faith-Based and Community Initiatives in five cabinet agencies. By 2006 the list was expanded to eleven. The goal was to set up an administrative infrastructure in the executive branch of government whose purpose was to make possible the distribution of federal tax dollars to community and faith-based organizations, and to encourage cooperation between policymakers and religious leaders in developing new policy initiatives. However, the Bush administration's efforts to expand Charitable Choice legislatively consistently failed to overcome growing resistance based on strict constitutional grounds, and so faith-based policies were enacted almost exclusively through the use of executive orders. In 2002, President Bush issued another order mandating that faith-based organizations receiving government funds should be allowed to use religious criteria when hiring new employees, and should otherwise feel free to express the religious nature of their work. While stipulating that faith-based organizations could not discriminate against clients on the basis of religion or use public funds for "inherently religious activities" (i.e., religious worship and instruction), the order was meant to appease religious conservatives who felt that sectarian agencies needed protection from regulatory arms of government that might limit their right to free expression. The question of regulation was a sticking point even among conservatives who otherwise favored the initiatives but cautioned against the risk that faith-based organizations would be forced to compromise their mission in order to meet restrictive demands of the state.

9. A new vanguard of conservative Christian lobbyists and political strategists came of age in the 1990s, many of whom "became aware of the problems of framing issues in moralistic, sectarian terms" and began to "recast a range of issues in the liberal language of rights, freedom, and equality" (Moen 1997: 25). One of the better known was Ralph Reed, who was executive director of the Christian Coalition for much of the decade and instrumental in pioneering a new politics of pragmatism and compromise, in tone if not in substance (Rozell 2003: 34). With the Republican takeover of Congress in 1994 and the centrism of the Clinton administration, a political climate developed in which religious conservatives could promote certain legislative priorities with minimal resistance. These included federal welfare reform legislation, which virtually dismantled the welfare state established under the New Deal and expanded by the Great Society initiatives of the 1960s. In the case of welfare reform, the aim of political conservatives to fight against "big government" was easily aligned with the desire of religious conservatives to remove the secular state from the business of social welfare.

10. At the forefront of urban social ministry in the late nineteenth and early twentieth centuries was the Salvation Army. In addition to operating

settlement houses for the poor and unemployed, the evangelical denomination treated the problems of urban life as essentially spiritual problems and sought to draw attention to them through high-profile "open air" crusades and other public rituals. Such efforts were instrumental in raising Christian social consciousness and were even more significant as spectacles of urban evangelism (Winston 1999).

11. Christian fundamentalism crystallized in opposition to the perceived threats of secular humanism, scientific rationalism, Darwinian theory, and liberal interpretations of the Bible. The name was derived from a series of essays titled *The Fundamentals*, published between 1910 and 1915, which defended strict literalist readings of the Bible against the intellectual challenges of academic scholars, scientists, and liberal theologians. Fundamentalist preachers called on Christians to withdraw from secular society and disengage from politics and popular culture. Although they also supported religious charity organizations and missionary societies, fundamentalists assumed an apocalyptic worldview and rejected the reformist efforts of liberal and moderate Christians as misguided and unbiblical.

12. Neo-evangelicalism took off in 1942 with the formation of the interdenominational National Association of Evangelicals (NAE), with Harold Ockenga as its first president. Although doctrinal and denominational rifts among its members remained, the NAE founders promoted the idea of a united evangelical front, insisting that "disparate religious subcultures could somehow be mobilized as a cooperative force" (Carpenter 1997: 155). The movement continued to develop around new evangelical institutions such as Fuller Theological Seminary (established in 1947) and the Evangelical Theological Society (1949), and media outlets such as NAE's flagship magazine, *Christianity Today* (1956). The famous Billy Graham Crusades from the late 1940s onward were particularly important in popularizing the movement's attempts to balance conservative theology, positive media visibility, and limited ecumenism.

These various venues were meant to forge an ideological middle ground between Christian liberalism and ultraconservatism, and to encourage open dialogue with alternative points of view, all in the name of making the work of evangelism more culturally relevant. The neo-evangelicals were also concerned to raise the intellectual profile of the movement by becoming more conversant with secular academic and scientific fields. These latter efforts have produced especially mixed results, due to an abiding tendency toward anti-intellectualism that has held sway throughout conservative Protestantism over the past century (Marsden 1987; Noll 1994; Wolfe 2000).

13. Carol Greenhouse addresses this directly in her ethnography of community and social order among conservative Baptists in the American South: "For a Christian, 'others' are not adversaries, or competitors, but constitute the very motive for spiritual maturity; one witnesses to others, one does good works among others, and so on. This is a substantially different concept of the individual than the one that Christians identify among non-Christians; one cannot call it individualism" (1986: 100).

14. In thinking about how religiosity informs activist orientations it is important to remember that although a community's theological orientation is highly

significant, it does not automatically dictate the form or style of social action undertaken by socially engaged members (see McRoberts 2003: 107). In his study of Hindu nationalism in India, Arvind Rajagopal writes: "While movements may have an ideology, these are usually produced for specific purposes, as strategic representations resonating with particular publics. What is necessary then is to map different accounts, views, and reflections of the movement and comprehend the manner of their mutual articulation.... Examining actual practices permits a detailing of parts without presuming their identity in advance, and thus discloses contradictions that may be instrumental to the movement's functioning" (2001: 212).

2. AWAKING SLEEPING GIANTS

1. The implementation of a new team-based administrative structure at Marble Valley Presbyterian came on the heels of a decision in 2001 by church leaders to end their affiliation with the Presbyterian Church of America (PCA) and join the Evangelical Presbyterian Church (EPC), a denomination that was known to be less restrictive on matters of local governance, autonomy, and doctrine. In previous years, as Marble Valley Presbyterian had become increasingly independent and self-sufficient, relations between the megachurch and the PCA had been somewhat strained. Tensions reached a boiling point during a peculiar episode in which Pastor Jerry was accused by PCA representatives of having allowed a female staff member to preach from the pulpit before a mixed audience during a special weekday program that took place in the main sanctuary. Interestingly, the question of Pastor Jerry's culpability hinged on a rather tenuous distinction between religious *teaching*, which ostensibly is open to anyone regardless of gender (and was what the megachurch claimed actually occurred), and *preaching*, which most conservative evangelicals consider to be an authoritative style of oration under the exclusive purview of men. In the end Pastor Jerry managed to avoid censure from the PCA but the damage was done, and an already frayed relationship between the megachurch and the denomination only worsened. The intention to leave the PCA was not supported by all members, and public forums preceding the final decision were heated, full of emotional pleas and diatribes from longtime members lamenting what they perceived as the megachurch's move away from its historical and doctrinal heritage. Those who felt no great affinity with the PCA, including mostly newer and younger members, welcomed the move. They saw it as a positive change that would facilitate autonomy and innovation without compromising doctrinal integrity. Despite the EPC's less dogmatic approach compared to the PCA, the denomination is recognized as being essentially conservative in its adherence to Reformed theology. After a concerted PR campaign by the Session, the membership voted by a wide margin in favor of the new denominational affiliation.

2. According to George Mosse, the notion of "respectability" as a marker of class identification emerged to prominence in modern Europe as the middle classes endorsed particular manners, tastes, and standards of ethical comport-

ment in light of the instabilities accompanying accelerated shifts from agrarian to industrial capitalism (Mosse 1985). Linda Kintz (1997: 145) takes up Mosse's claim that similar trends have emerged in the shift from industrial to financial capitalism by arguing that religious conservatives reproduce salient notions of middle-class respectability in order to secure their status positions and moral authority in the context of a national political economy in flux.

3. A propensity for doctrinal minimalism has continually resurfaced throughout the history of Protestant revivalism in America. Whether brought about by direct intentions or implicit cultural practices, doctrinal minimalism has often been a critical factor in the popularization, democratization, and institutionalization of evangelical Christian religiosity. In the twentieth century, postwar neo-evangelicalism inspired a resurgence of essentialized, populist approaches to conservative Protestant theology, reinforced by the decentralized and interdenominational character of the movement. By proposing that the "essentials" of Christian doctrine can be neatly delineated and shared across a wide cross section of evangelical church traditions, neo-evangelical revivalists aimed to create a united front around a common sense of orthopraxy (emphasizing a Christ-centered devotional lifestyle) as opposed to the dogmatic and divisive orthodoxies of the past (Watt 1991).

Among the grassroots elements that were instrumental in this regard were youth-oriented organizations such as Youth for Christ (the group that sponsored Billy Graham's early crusades), and Campus Crusade for Christ, founded by Bill Bright in 1951. Campus Crusade for Christ has played an especially influential role because of its hugely popular campus ministries and missionary programs, and because of the global dissemination of a brilliantly concise evangelical tract known as *The Four Spiritual Laws*. First published in 1965, and translated into more than 140 languages, the Four Spiritual Laws are: "1) God loves you and offers a wonderful plan for your life. 2) Man is sinful and separated from God. Therefore, he cannot know and experience God's love and plan for his life. 3) Jesus Christ is God's only provision for man's sin. Through Him you can know and experience God's love and plan for your life. 4) We must individually receive Jesus Christ as Savior and Lord, then we can know and experience God's love and plan for our lives" (see www.campuscrusade.com). The historian David Watt has noted that the minimalized gospel contained in tracts like *The Four Spiritual Laws* helped to recast evangelicalism as a product for popular consumption because it was "delivered in a way that embodied rather than questioned the commodification of the Christian tradition" (1991: 31).

4. A number of scholars of American Christianity have argued that individuals tend to be most drawn to churches and religious communities that, on the one hand, uphold strict moral premiums and maintain a strong, almost exclusivist sense of group identity and solidarity and, on the other hand, provide members with the cultural resources to remain embedded and engaged in mainstream society and public culture (Miller 1997; Smith 1998; Warner 1988).

5. "Megachurches Add Local Economy to their Mission," *New York Times*, November 23, 2007.

3. A REGION IN SPITE OF ITSELF

1. Gena Lewis, "Freedom Writers," *Metropulse*, March 1, 2001.

2. The Appalachian Regional Commission, a development agency created by Congress in 1965 as part of the War on Poverty, defines Appalachia as a geographic region covering two hundred thousand square miles along the Appalachia Mountains, spanning parts of twelve states (from southern New York to northern Mississippi) and all of West Virginia. The region's population is estimated at twenty-two million, with 42 percent of the population designated as "rural."

3. Harold W. Odum, doing research based at the University of North Carolina beginning in the 1920s, was among the earliest proponents of regionalism as a framework for scholarship and social reform in the South (see Odum 1947). The work of Odum and his colleagues was influential, especially in the development of government-sponsored programs in the aftermath of the Great Depression. More recently, social activists in Appalachia have invoked regionalist paradigms as a way to inspire social solidarity among disparate and impoverished communities. Despite good intentions, however, such efforts are often impeded by barriers of race, class, and gender, indicating the practical limitations of regionalism as a strategy of collective action (Fisher 1993).

4. Jack Neely, "Taking on a World's Fair: Cities Had Their Way with Knoxville, 1982," *Metropulse*, May 9, 2002.

5. At one point, development consultants proposed a plan to build a $160 million planetarium in downtown Knoxville. The proposal—known as Universe Knoxville—never came to fruition in part because of public resistance. Residents insisted that a high-tech planetarium did not represent the city's character or history in any way and would probably amount to no more than an expensive and misguided attempt to increase local tourism. As with other such proposals, Universe Knoxville was also criticized for having been devised by committee without any real public input at the outset.

6. Sources: *State of the South* 2000, report released by MDC, Inc. (www .mdcinc.org), and U.S. census data published at *CensusScope* (www .censusscope.org).

7. The popular Home and Gardens Television Network, or HGTV, is based in Knox County. The media corporation Whittle Communications had been based in downtown Knoxville before the company fragmented into several subsidiaries—including Channel One News and Edison Schools—and went out of business in the mid-1990s.

8. In addition to urban development, municipal agencies and nonprofit organizations in Knoxville started to work together to produce viable long-term strategies for addressing a broad range of comprehensive and systematic concerns. One such effort was a five-year program launched in 2000 called "Nine Counties. One Vision." Issue-oriented task forces composed of citizens, community organizers, real-estate developers, business executives, environmental activists, and religious figures were commissioned to develop concrete proposals to improve specific aspects of regional life, including transportation, education, health care, and economic growth, to name a few. The initiative, modeled

after a similar process in Chattanooga and sponsored by private foundations and corporations, was intended to facilitate public participation in and assuage popular distrust of a political system that many Knoxvillians believe remains under the control of a small but powerful group of elite, narrow-minded decision makers.

4. THE NAMES OF ACTION

1. Steve Sjogren is the senior pastor of Cincinnati's Vineyard Christian Church, and has produced numerous publications and on-line resources dedicated to promoting Christian ministries of social outreach as "servant evangelism." Sjogren defines servant evangelism as "demonstrating the kindness of God by offering to do some act of humble service with no strings attached" (1993: 17). He encourages churches to engage in "low risk/high grace" outreach activities—such as free carwashes, health screenings, food deliveries, street corner charity drives, and coffee or Popsicle giveaways—that allow Christian believers to interact casually with nonbelievers, especially those who are in need. The driving idea is that such acts of kindness provide churchgoers with opportunities to embody the virtues of unconditional grace, and in turn they facilitate interactions among strangers that can be gradually steered toward conversations about God, Jesus Christ, and Christian faith.

Describing the rationale behind a ministry strategy that assumes a central role for loving kindness both as context and catalyst for evangelism, Sjogren writes: "The first 90 percent of bearing witness to God's love is 'precognitive.' The Holy Spirit is doing a deep work in the *heart* of the person being drawn to the Lord. It is not so much a matter of sharing *information* as sharing *love*" (1993: 26, original emphasis). Like other evangelical pastors writing on themes of mercy and compassion (e.g., Keller 1997), Sjogren emphasizes that religious conversions are heavily dependent on peoples' affective responses to altruistic gestures rather than purely intellectual reactions to the logic of Christian salvation. In line with Vineyard theology, he also emphasizes the agency of the Holy Spirit, reinforcing the notion that when Christians do good deeds they should do so, ideally, because they have become humble vessels of divine grace through faith, not because they seek to prove their merit or gain eternal reward. For more information on Steve Sjogren's publications and ministries, see www .servantevangelism.com, and also www.servecoach.com.

2. Although most social workers and activists working on behalf of refugees in Knoxville were happy to have the support of affluent megachurches, they complained about what they viewed as arrogant or counterproductive tendencies among suburban conservative evangelicals. According to some agency representatives I spoke to, evangelicals tended to want to use refugee sponsorship as a platform for proselytization. A coordinator at the ecumenical nonprofit that specializes in refugee assistance claimed to have experienced several clashes with members of Eternal Vine precisely over this issue.

Furthermore, megachurches in particular had a reputation for producing volunteers and mobilizers who approached new ministries with such bold enthusiasm that they ignored the expertise of seasoned professionals, insisting instead on following their own impulses. This actually was a criticism I heard expressed by a number of welfare workers and community organizers. Not surprisingly, it was also a critique that socially engaged evangelicals occasionally directed at themselves. They knew full well that they sometimes had a propensity for overzealousness in the face of exciting outreach opportunities, and for diving into areas of social service in which they may yet lack sufficient knowledge and credibility, thereby alienating people with proper expertise. A similar critique, voiced by churchgoers and nonbelievers alike, reinforced the negative stereotype that middle-class evangelicals are more interested in immediate gratification and personalized results than in long-term social engagement, which is used to explain the perceived tendency among suburban megachurches to treat outreach initiatives as short-term projects without real commitment.

3. The parable is worth quoting in full: "When the Son of Man comes in his glory, and all the angels with him, he will sit on his throne in heavenly glory. All the nations will be gathered before him, and he will separate the people one from another as a shepherd separates the sheep from the goats. He will put the sheep on his right and the goats on his left. Then the King will say to those on his right, 'Come, you who are blessed by my Father; take your inheritance, the kingdom prepared for you since the creation of the world. For I was hungry and you gave me something to eat, I was thirsty and you gave me something to drink, I was a stranger and you invited me in, I needed clothes and you clothed me, I was sick and you looked after me, I was in prison and you came to visit me.' Then the righteous will answer him, 'Lord, when did we see you hungry and feed you, or thirsty and give you something to drink? When did we see you a stranger and invite you in, or needing clothes and clothe you? When did we see you sick or in prison and go to visit you?' The King will reply, 'I tell you the truth, whatever you did for one of the least of these brothers of mine, you did for me.' Then he will say to those on his left, 'Depart from me, you who are cursed, into the eternal fire prepared for the devil and his angels. For I was hungry and you gave me nothing to eat, I was thirsty and you gave me nothing to drink, I was a stranger and you did not invite me in, I needed clothes and you did not clothe me, I was sick and in prison and you did not look after me.' They also will answer, 'Lord, when did we see you hungry or thirsty or a stranger or needing clothes or sick or in prison, and did not help you?' He will reply, 'I tell you the truth, whatever you did not do for one of the least of these, you did not do for me.' Then they will go away to eternal punishment, but the righteous to eternal life" (Matthew 25:31–46).

5. THE SPIRITUAL INJURIES OF CLASS

1. In their influential study of the cultural values that sustain class inequality, Sennett and Cobb argue that every American "is subject to a scheme of values that tells him he must validate the self in order to win others' respect and his own" (1972: 75). This dominant scheme of values effectively obscures systemic forces that limit freedom and social mobility. The capitalist system of production that sustains hierarchical class distinctions is perpetuated by "a morality

of shaming and self-doubt" (1972: 74) that is especially potent among the working class, for whom upward mobility is often little more than an aspiration. Evangelical concerns about the culture of capitalism and the conditions of class stratification obviously differ tremendously from this theoretical perspective. Evangelicals do not consider status ambitions to be harmful because they obscure structural forces that actually restrict meritocratic potential, but rather because they lead people to internalize material desires that distract them from truly meaningful spiritual pursuits. If the two viewpoints have anything in common, it is their similar critique of dominant value systems that are interpreted as deceptive and misleading.

2. Women and men rate fairly equally on statistical measures of civic (nonpolitical) participation in the United States, but women on average are more likely to be involved in voluntary activities connected to religious organizations (Verba, Schlozman, and Brady 1995: 257–259). For women in conservative evangelical churches (especially stay-at-home moms), volunteering at church offers valuable opportunities to build social capital and pursue goal-oriented initiatives outside the home or workplace. Social outreach ministries in particular allow evangelical women to widen the scope of their moral ambitions and cultivate religious virtues in an area of ministry where men typically do not assert direct or total authority. Social outreach also allows evangelical women to combine their desires to be socially engaged with their domestic child-rearing responsibilities, since mothers will bring children along on outreach activities whenever possible.

3. The term *Mammon* is a New Testament Greek word derived from an Aramaic word meaning "riches." It is used in Christian terminology to connote avarice and other negative aspects of wealth, and it appears as the personification of a false god in some translations of Luke 16:13, which is quoted as an epigraph to this chapter. Although I quoted a New International Version translation, which uses the word *Money* instead of *Mammon*, the latter is very common in evangelical parlance.

4. The actual gender dynamics that take place in evangelical households are not always as straightforward as the patriarchal overtones of evangelical gender ideology suggest. Although it is clearly taught that men are meant to act as authoritative heads of households and women are to submit willingly and gracefully to their authority, research has shown that the symbolic traditionalism of evangelical marriage often belies the reality of "pragmatic egalitarianism" between husbands and wives (Gallagher and Smith 1999). Moreover, the doctrine of wifely submission should not simply be seen as an absolute blueprint for hierarchical male-dominance because submission to male authority has been shown to function at times as a vehicle for women to gain considerable authority and control in their personal and religious lives (Griffith 1997). In addition, as more and more evangelical families are forced to maintain dual incomes, the division of labor in the typical household does not necessarily follow the traditionalist prototype but rather shifts according to social, cultural, and economic variables, adaptive strategies, and individual negotiations (Bartkowski 2001). Nonetheless, it remains pertinent that the symbolic roles that men and women are expected to play in marriage reinforce the idea of women as essen-

tially docile, nurturing, and confined to the home, which it is their custodial obligation to maintain.

5. See Bielo 2007 for a detailed ethnographic analysis of one seminar designed and taught by a Christian entrepreneur who blends the language of modern business ethics and management with the religious logic of born-again subjectivity.

6. Prosperity theology has gained visibility and notoriety in North America because of multimillion-dollar ministries led by high-profile televangelists like Joel Osteen, Creflo Dollar, Joyce Meyer, and Jimmy Swaggart. Such ministries have exploded internationally and led to the formation of global networks that promote conservative and charismatic brands of Protestantism in the non-Western world while also providing ideological support for the advance of neoliberalism (Brouwer, Gifford, and Rose 1996; Gifford 1998). Prosperity theology has become prominent in developing countries throughout Latin America, Africa, and Asia (Gifford 1998; Jenkins 2002; Martin 2002), where the promise of untold health and wealth for those who are strong in their faith is especially appealing to poor and structurally marginalized populations seeking avenues of empowerment and upward mobility (e.g., Hackett 1995; Maxwell 1998). It has also become increasingly popular among Europe's expanding middle classes, including white-collar professionals and capitalist entrepreneurs (e.g., Coleman 2000; Wanner 2007). Among mainstream conservative evangelicals in the United States, like those in my study, prosperity theology remains controversial because of what many take to be its conspicuously materialistic style and tone. Churchgoers I spoke to were uncomfortable with the idea that one's faith might be linked to the expectation of material reward; they saw this as inaccurate theology—at best tacky, at worst heretical. They also criticized famous preachers in this tradition, who are seen to take pleasure in flaunting their personal wealth with gaudy suits and fancy cars.

7. Sherry Ortner has argued that the aspirations of Western mountaineers climbing Mount Everest and their attitudes toward their Sherpa guides have been consistently shaped by feelings of disdain for the "crassness of modernity" (1999: 37). In the romantic mindset of the mountaineers, modernity is a regressive phenomenon that is regarded as vulgar, boring, and materialistic. The condition of modern life is seen as full of "noisiness and busyness," depriving people of the "ability to commune with the self, nature, or God" (1999: 37). In this sense, climbing Everest is less about conquering nature (though this too is a motivation) than it is about subjecting the modernized yet world-weary self to risks and challenges associated with experiences of spiritual transcendence that apparently other Westerners, in their zest for material prosperity, have left behind. It is of course noteworthy that most of the mountaineers who climb Everest are themselves affluent members of society, who can afford to complain about the pitfalls of material wealth as easily as they can afford to spend tens of thousands of dollars for a trek up the world's tallest mountain.

8. Some of the Bible verses that are frequently quoted in reference to the concept of stewardship include: Luke 16:1–15, Mark 12:41–44, 1 Timothy 6:6–10, and Matthew 6:24.

9. Interestingly, the concept of stewardship has been taken up more recently by evangelicals involved in environmental activism. Activists promote the idea that human beings are stewards of God's Earth and that Christians need to be bold and proactive in their efforts to protect and preserve the natural world that God created. For more information, consult the Evangelical Environmental Network at www.creationcare.org.

10. The phrase refers to Matthew 8:20: "But Jesus said, 'Foxes have dens to live in, and birds have nests, but I, the Son of Man, have no home of my own, not even a place to lay my head.'"

11. "A Book Spreads the Word: Prayer for Prosperity Works," *New York Times,* May 8, 2001.

12. Homeschooling is a complicated issue for conservative evangelicals, who feel torn between the cultural strategies of separationism and activism. Although homeschooling is widely encouraged as an alternative to secular and public schools, some evangelicals worry that this reinforces isolationist tendencies and believe that evangelical families should not be abandoning educational institutions but working to improve and reform them from within (see Smith 2000: 131). Opinions were varied on the subject at Eternal Vine and Marble Valley Presbyterian, and the few evangelical homeschoolers I spoke to varied in their levels of commitment. Some parents chose to homeschool their children up until college, while others homeschooled their children for only a few years before junior high school or high school. Decisions were usually guided by factors such as personal preferences, the experiences of evangelical friends and neighbors, and whether or not a family could afford to have the mother stay home and give up the income she would earn in a paid profession. One mother described herself to me as a "fence-sitter" on the issue—she and her husband believed in homeschooling but wanted their children to be socially well adjusted and not to grow up sheltered. So some years they homeschooled the children and other years they enrolled them in local schools, reevaluating the matter on a yearly basis. However they went about it, evangelical homeschooling parents in Knoxville were serious in their desire to protect their children from ungodly influences while they tried hard to avoid being overly protective to the point of complete social detachment. For some families, the way to achieve the balance was to integrate civic and community-based activities into the homeschool curriculum.

6. COMPASSION ACCOUNTS

1. In her account, Stacy did not refer to the woman's ethnic or religious identity, a fair indication that the woman was white and at least of nominally Christian background. White evangelicals that I interviewed and spoke to typically used explicit identity markers in their stories only when the people described are nonwhite or non-Christian.

2. The parable of the Good Samaritan has undergone countless interpretations throughout the history of the Christian church, each reflecting the social and cultural nuances of its specific context. Naturally—and contrary to the assumptions of scriptural essentialists—the meanings and moral lessons derived from the parable are multiple and diverse (see Wuthnow 1991).

3. For example, see Philippians 2:3–4: "Do nothing out of selfish ambition or vain conceit, but in humility consider others better than yourselves. Each of you should look not only to your own interests, but also to the interests of others."

4. Evangelicals who criticize secular charities do so precisely on the basis that they lack a solid foundation in Christian prayer. The perceived inadequacies of state welfare agencies—that is, that they enable sin, fail to inspire social change, and promote moral relativism—are seen as direct results of the fact that welfare workers are prevented from integrating "spirituality" into their work.

5. For example, Romans 14:11–12: "It is written: 'As surely as I live,' says the Lord, 'every knee will bow before me; every tongue will confess to God.' So then, each of us will give an account of himself to God." Another frequently cited source on the topic of accountability is II Corinthians 5:10: "For we must all appear before the judgment seat of Christ, that each one may receive what is due him for the things done while in the body, whether good or bad."

6. Marvin Olasky built on the same themes in later books, notably *Renewing American Compassion,* published in 1996 with an introduction by Newt Gingrich, and *Compassionate Conservatism: What It Is, What It Does, and How It Can Transform America,* which was published to coincide with the 2000 presidential election and includes a foreword by then-candidate George W. Bush.

7. Typically evangelical churchgoers are expected to defer to the authority of pastors and elders, but never as a substitute for the vertical accountability that is meant to exist between believers and God. I often heard pastors and preachers caution churchgoers against placing undue authority in the hands of religious figures, or claiming undue authority over others. Nonetheless, confusion and slippage between vertical and horizontal accountability occur frequently in church life, particularly in times of crisis or transition when church leaders assert their authority to maintain order and prevent schism.

8. Practices of exchange are almost always linked to "deep-lying incommensurability" (in Simmel's words) of one kind or another, whether in the context of social relationships or larger institutional structures and hierarchies (see Weiner 1992). Organized philanthropy, in particular, has been identified as an institution of exchange whereby wealthy benefactors "[establish] a claim to moral righteousness and superiority, which ideologically justifies and fortifies [their] superior social status and power" (Blau 1964: 260). Studies have shown how elite philanthropies reinforce the interests and hegemonic dominance of the wealthy, even when benefactions are motivated by charitable or redistributive impulses (Odendahl 1990). Structural arguments contribute the most, however, when they help us to account for the specific *cultural* contexts in which transactional practices are situated, especially insofar as the meaning and significance of exchange are never limited to status competition and economic self-interest (Kapferer 1976). Even in capitalist societies where market competition and meritocratic individualism are dominant norms, the cultural relevance of altruistic ideals that offer radical alternatives to dominant norms should not be underestimated. It is the ubiquity of such ideals that makes their practical shortcomings all the more frustrating for those who believe in them.

9. In thinking about how the cultural dynamics of a social group may be characterized by multiple coexisting influences that create internal tension and irresolvable moral conflict, I have found Joel Robbins's work among the Urapmin of Papua New Guinea especially helpful. Robbins explores the "contradictory demands that emanate from the Christian moral system and the traditional conception of social action" (2004: 248), and identifies among the Urapmin two competing ethical paradigms, which he frames in Weberian terms: (1) an "ethic of conviction," rooted in a millennialist Christianity that condemns the will as sinful and mandates its renunciation at any expense, and (2) a pre-Christian "ethic of responsibility," which stresses the positive social value inherent in the exercise of individual will. The conflict between these coexisting ethics is heightened by the predominance and intensity of the Christian moral system, which "virtually creates the conditions that ensure people's failure to live up to its demands" (2004: 249). Understanding the nature of this conflict is, for Robbins, crucial for analyzing the specific conditions of culture change and discontinuity experienced by the Urapmin following the introduction of charismatic Christian revivalism.

7. TAKING THE (INNER) CITY FOR GOD

1. East Tennessee has a long history of religious and social activism dedicated to rural Appalachian poverty relief and community improvement. Marble Valley Presbyterian supported a few programs in Appalachia through its missions budget, carrying on a long-standing tradition among Presbyterian-Reformed churches in the region (Yeuell and Myers 1999), but they were not discussed or valorized nearly as often as ministries in the inner city. At Eternal Vine, Appalachian ministries were virtually nonexistent aside from informal efforts that I rarely heard anyone talk about. When the suburban churchgoers I knew talked about Appalachia at all, it was sometimes in reference to native customs and folksy aphorisms, but more often it took the form of derisive or self-effacing jokes. Attempts to identify with and simultaneously distance themselves from the stereotypes of "hillbillies" and "rednecks" were common among Knoxvillians, especially those who originally came from rural East Tennessee communities. Complex emotional and moral structures underlie such attitudes. John Hartigan (2005) has observed that self-conscious jokes and comments about the Appalachian poor reflect how seriously the category of "white trash" complicates the racialized moral order normally imagined by the white middle class. From this perspective, the fact that some suburban white evangelicals should focus more attention on the black inner city than on Appalachia may reflect an almost willful tendency to ignore the scope and severity of white rural poverty. The logistical and geographical challenges of ministering directly to the needs of Appalachian mountaineers are factors as well, although I hasten to add that countless other local churches and organizations in Knoxville in fact do support active relief programs on behalf of these communities.

2. In addition to the publicity they attracted, Billy Graham's famous urban crusades provoked much controversy among conservative Protestants in the 1960s–1970s. A recognized leader in the budding neo-evangelical movement,

Billy Graham alienated many white conservatives by opposing segregation and promoting racial cooperation in his revival meetings. He also offended Christian fundamentalists by reaching out to liberal Protestant churches and organizations and advocating interfaith dialogue. Fundamentalist critics accused Graham of risking the integrity of biblical orthodoxy by partnering with liberals, and they dismissed his sophisticated use of mass media as catering to secular popular culture. Even within the neo-evangelical movement there were hints of reservation about how far the movement should go in its strategies of engaged orthodoxy. Harold Ockenga, a cofounder of the National Association of Evangelicals and other major evangelical institutions, warned at one point that the movement was in danger of being overtaken by "that terrible octopus of liberalism" if interfaith fellowship became too much of a priority (quoted in Stone 1997: 123).

3. Philip Yancey's dualistic understanding of the Kingdom of God reflects common and long-held theological traditions in Western Protestantism, yet it should not be confused with Martin Luther's famous "doctrine of the two kingdoms." Whereas Luther distinguished two kingdoms by which God rules the world—the kingdom of "law" governed by secular authorities and the spiritual kingdom of grace represented by the Christian church—contemporary evangelicals like Yancey seem to be concerned with working out the distinction between the Kingdom of God as a divine metaphysical order to be loosely emulated in the present versus a utopian promise of an actual world to come.

4. Describing the significance of the Kingdom of God for revivalists and preachers during the eighteenth-century "Great Awakening," H. Richard Niebuhr wrote in 1937: "The good news was not only that there was light beyond darkness, but even more that in Christ men had been given the opportunity to anticipate both threat and promise, to bring the future into the present and receive a foretaste of the coming kingdom, a validation of the promise" (Niebuhr 1988: 140).

5. Interestingly, one female respondent answered that in a world modeled on the Kingdom of God there would be more "gender equity." Such sentiments were not unheard of at Marble Valley Presbyterian, but they were not common either. The speaker was known in the congregation as a committed Christian with something of a maverick streak, who seized almost any opportunity to challenge her fellow churchgoers to reexamine the assumptions of evangelical gender ideology. She was particularly outspoken in her belief that conservative evangelical churches deprived themselves of a vital resource by using the doctrine of submission as an excuse to limit the roles of female members.

6. Out of 149 cities with HOPE VI projects, Knoxville was one of only three to impose a five-year limit on subsidized rentals, the other two being Charlotte, NC, and Spartanburg, SC ("The High Cost of High Hopes," Knoxville News-Sentinel, March 25, 2001).

7. Norman's first point is arguably more a subjective assessment based in politically motivated rhetoric than a studied empirical observation. Conservative social critics often reduce social and economic problems to questions of personal responsibility and dismiss critiques based on systemic inequality and institutionalized racism as misleading or unproductive. Norman's second point,

that black churches place less value on monetary giving, may reflect his personal experiences, but as a general observation it is a misconception disproved by statistical evidence. Research has shown that no significant difference exists between white and black congregations in terms of how successful they are at generating money from voluntary offerings. Variations that do occur are likely to represent congregational differences along lines of income and denomination rather than race (Pressley and Collier 1999).

8. Perkins notes that a potential drawback of Christian community development is that without careful oversight it can become a smoke screen for gentrification, displacing rather than empowering the poor. His solution to the problem focuses on questions of intention: "The difference between relocation and gentrification is motive, pure and simple" (1993: 76). For Perkins, effective and redemptive urban ministry requires that participants focus constantly on the importance of grace and avoid acting selfishly. They must be generous with their resources and talents, and take care to ensure that communities are empowered at the grassroots. Only through disciplined commitments and authentic relationships, Perkins argues, can Christians become true "urban servants" rather than merely glorified caseworkers (1993: 160).

9. *Koinonia* comes from a Greek word whose meaning connotes aspects of "communion" or "community." It is often translated in English versions of the New Testament as "fellowship," and appears in church teachings as a concept to describe the relational unity of Christian followers and the spiritual intimacy of ritual communion. It is a popular inspirational concept among contemporary evangelicals, and is one of several Greek (or Hebrew) words from the Bible that evangelicals use repeatedly in their efforts to authenticate their faith.

10. These criticisms were familiar to white evangelicals because they heard them on occasion directly from leaders in the black community, as well as from white nonevangelicals in the nonprofit sector, and also because they were frequently inclined to lodge such complaints against themselves, in line with the critical reflexivity that animates so much evangelical discourses. It should be noted, however, that this rarely diminished their resolve to pursue outreach ministry initiatives in a manner suiting their conservative beliefs and moral standards.

11. As Robert Hefner has argued in an eloquent critique of Putnam: "The political impact of civic associations depends not just on their formal structure but on the discourse and practice they help promote. In assessing whether associations 'make democracy work,' then, we have to look carefully at what their members actually say and do. In particular, we have to examine the way their members relate to one another *and* to outsiders, and ask whether the overall pattern contributes to a public culture of inclusion and participation or uncivil exclusivity" (2000: 24, original emphasis).

References

Abzug, Robert H. 1994. *Cosmos Crumbling: American Reform and the Religious Imagination.* Oxford: Oxford University Press.

Allahyari, Rebecca Anne. 2000. *Visions of Charity: Volunteer Workers and Moral Community.* Berkeley: University of California Press.

Ammerman, Nancy Tatom. 2005. *Pillars of Faith: American Congregations and Their Partners.* Berkeley: University of California Press.

Arneil, Barbara. 2006. *Diverse Communities: The Problem with Social Capital.* Cambridge: Cambridge University Press.

Asad, Talal. 1993. *Genealogies of Religion: Discipline and Reasons of Power in Christianity and Islam.* Baltimore: Johns Hopkins University Press.

————. 2003. *Formations of the Secular: Christianity, Islam, Modernity.* Stanford, CA: Stanford University Press.

Bachelard, Gaston. 1964. *The Poetics of Space.* Boston: Beacon Press.

Bakke, Ray. 1997. *A Theology as Big as the City.* Downers Grove, IL: InterVarsity Press.

Balmer, Randall H. 2006. *Mine Eyes Have Seen the Glory: A Journey into the Evangelical Subculture in America.* New York: Oxford University Press.

Barna, George. 2000. *Growing True Disciples.* Ventura, CA: Issachar Resources.

Barthes, Roland. 1972. *Mythologies.* New York: Noonday Press.

Bartkowski, John P. 2001. *Remaking the Godly Marriage: Gender Negotiation in Evangelical Families.* New Brunswick, NJ: Rutgers University Press.

Bartkowski, John P., and Helen A. Regis. 2003. *Charitable Choices: Religion, Race, and Poverty in the Post-Welfare Era.* New York: New York University Press.

Batteau, Allen. 1990. *The Invention of Appalachia.* Tucson: University of Arizona Press.

Beaver, Patricia D., and Helen M. Lewis. 1998. "Uncovering the Trail of Ethnic Denial: Ethnicity in Appalachia." In *Cultural Diversity in the U.S. South: Anthropological Contributions to a Region in Transition,* edited by Carole E. Hill and Patricia D. Beaver, 51–68. Athens: University of Georgia Press.

Bebbington, David W. 1989. *Evangelicalism in Modern Britain: A History from the 1730s to the 1980s.* London: Unwin Hyman.

Beidelman, T. O. 1982. *Colonial Evangelism: A Socio-Historical Study of an East African Mission at the Grassroots.* Bloomington: Indiana University Press.

———. 1993. *Moral Imagination in Kaguru Modes of Thought.* Washington, DC: Smithsonian Institution Press.

Bellah, Robert Neelly, Richard Madsen, William M. Sullivan, Ann Swidler, and Steven M. Tipton. 1985. *Habits of the Heart: Individualism and Commitment in American Life.* Berkeley: University of California Press.

Bender, Courtney. 2003. *Heaven's Kitchen: Living Religion at God's Love We Deliver.* Chicago: University of Chicago Press.

Berger, Peter L., and Richard John Neuhaus. 1977. *To Empower People: The Role of Mediating Structures in Public Policy.* Washington, DC: American Enterprise Institute for Public Policy Research.

Bialecki, Jon. 2008. "Between Stewardship and Sacrifice: Agency and Economy in a Southern California Charismatic Church." *Journal of the Royal Anthropological Institute* 14:372–390.

———. 2009. "Disjuncture, Continental Philosophy's New 'Political Paul,' and the Question of Progressive Christianity in a Southern California Third Wave Church." *American Ethnologist* 36(1):110–123.

Bialecki, Jon, Naomi Haynes, and Joel Robbins. 2008. "The Anthropology of Christianity." *Religion Compass* 2(6):1139–1158.

Bielo, James S. 2007. "'The Mind of Christ': Financial Success, Born-Again Personhood, and the Anthropology of Christianity." *Ethnos* 72(3):315–338.

———. 2009. *Words upon the Word: An Ethnography of Evangelical Bible Study.* New York: New York University Press.

Blau, Peter M. 1964. *Exchange and Power in Social Life.* New York: Wiley.

Bornstein, Erica. 2003. *The Spirit of Development: Protestant NGOs, Morality, and Economics in Zimbabwe.* New York: Routledge.

Bourdieu, Pierre. 1990. *The Logic of Practice.* Stanford, CA: Stanford University Press.

Brouwer, Steve, Paul Gifford, and Susan D. Rose. 1996. *Exporting the American Gospel: Global Christian Fundamentalism.* New York: Routledge.

Brown, Peter. 2005. "Remembering the Poor and the Aesthetic of Society." *Journal of Interdisciplinary History* 35(3):513–522.

Carle, Robert D., and Louis A. DeCaro Jr., eds. 1997. *Signs of Hope in the City: Ministries of Community Renewal.* Valley Forge, PA: Judson Press.

Carpenter, Joel A. 1997. *Revive Us Again: The Reawakening of American Fundamentalism.* New York: Oxford University Press.

Castelli, Elizabeth A. 2005. "Praying for the Persecuted Church: US Christian Activism in the Global Arena." *Journal of Human Rights* 4:1–31.

Chaves, Mark. 1999. "Religious Congregations and Welfare Reform: Who Will Take Advantage of 'Charitable Choice'?" *American Sociological Review* 64:836–846.

———. 2004. *Congregations in America*. Cambridge, MA: Harvard University Press.

Checker, Melissa, and Maggie Fishman, eds. 2004. *Local Actions: Cultural Activism, Power, and Public Life in America*. New York: Columbia University Press.

Chilton, David. 1981. *Productive Christians in an Age of Guilt-Manipulators*. Tyler, TX: Institute for Christian Economics.

Cnaan, Ram A., with Stephanie C. Boddie, Femida Handy, Gaynor Yancey, and Richard Schneider. 2002. *The Invisible Caring Hand: American Congregations and the Provision of Welfare*. New York: New York University Press.

Coleman, Simon. 2000. *The Globalisation of Charismatic Christianity: Spreading the Gospel of Prosperity*. Cambridge: Cambridge University Press.

———. 2004. "The Charismatic Gift." *Journal of the Royal Anthropological Institute* 10:421–442.

Coutin, Susan Bibler. 1993. *The Culture of Protest: Religious Activism and the U.S. Sanctuary Movement*. Boulder: Westview Press.

Crapanzano, Vincent. 2000. *Serving the Word: Literalism in America from the Pulpit to the Bench*. New York: New Press.

Cromartie, Michael, ed. 2003. *A Public Faith: Evangelicals and Civic Engagement*. Lanham, MD: Rowman & Littlefield.

Cruikshank, Barbara. 1999. *The Will to Empower: Democratic Citizens and Other Subjects*. Ithaca, NY: Cornell University Press.

Curtis, Susan. 2001. *A Consuming Faith: The Social Gospel and Modern American Culture*. Columbia: University of Missouri Press.

Dawson, John. 2001. *Taking Our Cities for God: How to Break Spiritual Strongholds*. Lake Mary, FL: Charisma House.

Deeb, Lara. 2006. *An Enchanted Modern: Gender and Public Piety in Shi'i Lebanon*. Princeton, NJ: Princeton University Press.

Derrida, Jacques. 2001. *On Cosmopolitanism and Forgiveness*. London: Routledge.

Dochuk, Darren. 2003. "'Praying for the Wicked City': Congregation, Community, and the Suburbanization of Fundamentalism." *Religion and American Culture* 13(2):167–203.

Dumont, Louis. 1986. *Essays on Individualism: Modern Ideology in Anthropological Perspective*. Chicago: University of Chicago Press.

Eiesland, Nancy L. 2000. *A Particular Place: Urban Restructuring and Religious Ecology in a Southern Exurb*. New Brunswick, NJ: Rutgers University Press.

Elisha, Omri. 2008a. "Faith beyond Belief: Evangelical Protestant Conceptions of Faith and the Resonance of Anti-humanism." *Social Analysis* 52(1): 56–78.

———. 2008b. "'You Can't Talk to an Empty Stomach': Faith-Based Activism, Holistic Evangelism, and the Publicity of Evangelical Engagement." In *Proselytization Revisited: Rights, Free Markets, and Culture Wars*, edited by Rosalind I. J. Hackett, 431–454. London: Equinox Press.

Emerson, Michael O., and Christian Smith. 2000. *Divided by Faith: Evangelical Religion and the Problem of Race in America.* New York: Oxford University Press.

Engelke, Matthew. 2007. *A Problem of Presence: Beyond Scripture in an African Church.* Berkeley: University of California Press.

Eppsteiner, Fred. 1988. *The Path of Compassion: Writing on Socially Engaged Buddhism.* Berkeley: Parallax Press.

Erzen, Tanya. 2006. *Straight to Jesus: Sexual and Christian Conversion in the Ex-Gay Movement.* Berkeley: University of California Press.

Fader, Ayala. 2009. *Mitzvah Girls: Bringing Up the Next Generation of Hasidic Girls in Brooklyn.* Princeton, NJ: Princeton University Press.

Fisher, Stephen L. 1993. *Fighting Back in Appalachia: Traditions of Resistance and Change.* Philadelphia: Temple University Press.

Frederick, Marla F. 2003. *Between Sundays: Black Women and Everyday Struggles of Faith.* Berkeley: University of California Press.

Fukuyama, Francis. 1999. *The Great Disruption: Human Nature and the Reconstitution of Social Order.* New York: Free Press.

Gallagher, Sally, and Christian Smith. 1999. "Symbolic Traditionalism and Pragmatic Egalitarianism: Contemporary Evangelicals, Families, and Gender." *Gender and Society* 13(2):211–233.

Galli, Mark. 2001. "Significance in a Small Package." *Christianity Today* 45(8): 97.

Garces-Foley, Kathleen. 2007. *Crossing the Ethnic Divide: The Multiethnic Church on a Mission.* New York: Oxford University Press.

Gifford, Paul. 1998. *African Christianity: Its Public Role.* Bloomington: Indiana University Press.

Ginsburg, Faye D. 1989. *Contested Lives : The Abortion Debate in an American Community.* Berkeley: University of California Press.

———. 1997. " 'From Little Things, Big Things Grow': Indigenous Media and Cultural Activism." In *Between Resistance and Revolution: Cultural Politics and Social Protest,* edited by Richard Fox and Orin Starn, 118–144. New Brunswick, NJ: Rutgers University Press.

Goldberg, Michelle. 2006. *Kingdom Coming: The Rise of Christian Nationalism.* New York: W. W. Norton & Co.

Goldfield, David. 1997. *Region, Race, and Cities: Interpreting the Urban South.* Baton Rouge: Louisiana State University Press.

Goldstein, Donna M. 2001. "Microenterprise Training Programs, Neoliberal Common Sense, and the Discourses of Self-Esteem." In *The New Poverty Studies: The Ethnography of Power, Politics, and Impoverished People in the United States,* edited by Judith Goode and Jeff Maskovsky, 236–272. New York: New York University Press.

Grantham, Dewey W. 1994. *The South in Modern America: A Region at Odds.* New York: HarperCollins.

Greenberg, Anna. 2000. "The Church and the Revitalization of Politics and Community." *Political Science Quarterly* 115(3):377–394.

Greenhouse, Carol J. 1986. *Praying for Justice: Faith, Order, and Community in an American Town.* Ithaca, NY: Cornell University Press.

Griffith, R. Marie. 1997. *God's Daughters: Evangelical Women and the Power of Submission*. Berkeley: University of California Press.

———. 2004. *Born Again Bodies: Flesh and Spirit in American Christianity*. Berkeley: University of California Press.

Guinness, Os. 1993. *Dining with the Devil: The Megachurch Movement Flirts with Modernity*. Grand Rapids, MI: Baker Book House.

Gunther, John. 1947. *Inside U.S.A*. New York: Harper & Brothers.

Gushee, David P. 2008. *The Future of Faith in American Politics: The Public Witness of the Evangelical Center*. Waco, TX: Baylor University Press.

Hackett, Rosalind I.J. 1995. "The Gospel of Prosperity in West Africa." In *Religion and the Transformations of Capitalism: Comparative Approaches*, edited by Richard H. Roberts, 199–214. New York: Routledge.

Haggard, Ted, and Jack Hayford, eds. 1997. *Loving Your City into the Kingdom*. Ventura, CA: Regal Books.

Hall, David D., ed. 1997. *Lived Religion in America: Toward a History of Practice*. Princeton, NJ: Princeton University Press.

Hall, Peter Dobkin. 1990. "The History of Religious Philanthropy in America." In *Faith and Philanthropy in America: Exploring the Role of Religion in America's Voluntary Sector*, edited by Robert Wuthnow, and Virginia A. Hodgkinson, 38–62. San Francisco, CA: Jossey-Bass Publishers.

Harding, Susan F. 2000. *The Book of Jerry Falwell: Fundamentalist Language and Politics*. Princeton, NJ: Princeton University Press.

Harrison, Faye V. 1998. "Rehistoricizing Race, Ethnicity, and Class in the U.S. Southeast." In *Cultural Diversity in the U.S. South: Anthropological Contributions to a Region in Transition*, edited by Carole E. Hill and Patricia D. Beaver, 179–189. Athens: University of Georgia Press.

Hart, D.G. 2000. "The Techniques of Church Growth." In *Modern Reformation*, special issue: *The Malling of Mission*, 9:20–25.

———. 2004. *Deconstructing Evangelicalism: Conservative Protestantism in the Age of Billy Graham*. Grand Rapids, MI: Baker Academic.

Hartigan, John. 2005. *Odd Tribes: Toward a Cultural Analysis of White People*. Durham, NC: Duke University Press.

Hedges, Chris. 2006. *American Fascists: The Christian Right and the War on America*. New York: Free Press.

Hefner, Robert W. 1993. "Introduction: World Building and the Rationality of Conversion." In *Conversion to Christianity: Historical and Anthropological Perspectives on a Great Transformation*, edited by Robert W. Hefner, 3–44. Berkeley: University of California Press.

———. 2000. *Civil Islam: Muslims and Democratization in Indonesia*. Princeton, NJ: Princeton University Press.

Hendershot, Heather. 2004. *Shaking the World for Jesus: Media and Conservative Evangelical Culture*. Chicago: University of Chicago Press.

Henry, Carl F. 1947. *The Uneasy Conscience of Fundamentalism*. Grand Rapids, MI: Eerdmans.

Heyrman, Christine Leigh. 1997. *Southern Cross: The Beginnings of the Bible Belt*. New York: Knopf.

Hill, Carole E. 1998. "Contemporary Issues in Anthropological Studies of the American South." In *Cultural Diversity in the U.S. South: Anthropological Contributions to a Region in Transition*, edited by Carole E. Hill and Patricia D. Beaver, 12–33. Athens: University of Georgia Press.

Hirschkind, Charles. 2006. *The Ethical Soundscape: Cassette Sermons and Islamic Counterpublics*. New York: Columbia University Press.

Hochschild, Arlie Russell. 1997. *The Time Bind: When Work Becomes Home and Home Becomes Work*. New York: Henry Holt.

Horton, Michael. 2000. "The Ethnocentricity of the American Church Growth Movement." In *Modern Reformation*, special issue: *The Malling of Mission*, 9:15–19.

Howell, Brian M. 2008. *Christianity in the Local Context: Southern Baptists in the Philippines*. New York: Palgrave Macmillan.

Jasper, James M. 1997. *The Art of Moral Protest: Culture, Biography, and Creativity in Social Movements*. Chicago: University of Chicago Press.

Jenkins, Philip. 2002. *The Next Christendom: The Coming of Global Christianity*. New York: Oxford University Press.

Jones, Ken. 2003. *The New Social Face of Buddhism: A Call to Action*. Boston: Wisdom Publications.

Kapferer, Bruce, ed. 1976. *Transaction and Meaning: Directions in the Anthropology of Exchange and Symbolic Behavior*. Philadelphia: Institute for the Study of Human Issues.

Katz, Michael B. 1986. *In the Shadow of the Poorhouse: A Social History of Social Welfare in America*. New York: Basic Books.

Keane, Webb. 2007. *Christian Moderns: Freedom and Fetish in the Mission Encounter*. Berkeley: University of California Press.

Keller, Timothy J. 1997. *Ministries of Mercy: The Call of the Jericho Road*. Phillipsburg, NJ: P&R Publishing.

Kintz, Linda. 1997. *Between Jesus and the Market: The Emotions That Matter in Right-Wing America*. Durham, NC: Duke University Press.

Kirby, Jack Temple. 1978. *Media-Made Dixie: The South in the American Imagination*. Baton Rouge: Louisiana State University Press.

Kreider, Larry. 2002. *Authority and Accountability: How to Respond to Leadership and Fellow Believers God Places in Our Lives*. Ephrata, PA: House to House Publications.

Lambert, Frank. 1999. *Inventing the "Great Awakening."* Princeton, NJ: Princeton University Press.

Lamont, Michèle, and Marcel Fournier. 1992. *Cultivating Differences: Symbolic Boundaries and the Making of Inequality*. Chicago: University of Chicago Press.

Lewis, Helen, Linda Johnson, and Don Askins, eds. 1978. *Colonialism in Modern America: The Appalachian Case*. Boone, NC: Appalachian Consortium Press.

Lichterman, Paul. 2005. *Elusive Togetherness: Church Groups Trying to Bridge America's Divisions*. Princeton, NJ: Princeton University Press.

Lindsay, D. Michael. 2007. *Faith in the Halls of Power: How Evangelicals Joined the American Elite*. Oxford: Oxford University Press.

Lindsay, D. Michael, and Conrad Hackett. 2008. "Measuring Evangelicalism: Consequences of Different Operationalization Strategies." *Journal for the Scientific Study of Religion* 47(3):499–514.

Lomnitz-Adler, Claudio. 1992. *Exits from the Labyrinth: Culture and Ideology in the Mexican National Space*. Berkeley: University of California Press.

Luhrmann, Tanya M. 2004. "Metakinesis: How God Becomes Intimate in Contemporary U.S. Christianity." *American Anthropologist* 106(3):518–528.

MacArthur, William J., Jr. 1978. *Knoxville's History: An Interpretation*. Knoxville: East Tennessee Historical Society.

Mahmood, Saba. 2005. *Politics of Piety: The Islamic Revival and the Feminist Subject*. Princeton, NJ: Princeton University Press.

Marsden, George M. 1987. *Reforming Fundamentalism: Fuller Seminary and the New Evangelicals*. Grand Rapids, MI: Eerdmans.

Martin, David. 2002. *Pentecostalism: The World Their Parish*. Oxford: Blackwell.

Mathews, Donald G. 1997. " 'Christianizing the South': Sketching a Synthesis." In *New Directions in American Religious History*, edited by Harry S. Stout and D. G. Hart, 84–115. New York: Oxford University Press.

Maxwell, David. 1998. "Delivered from the Spirit of Poverty? Pentecostalism, Prosperity and Modernity in Zimbabwe." *Journal of Religion in Africa* 28(3):350–373.

McCloud, Sean. 2007. *Divine Hierarchies: Class in American Religion and Religious Studies*. Chapel Hill: University of North Carolina Press.

McGirr, Lisa. 2001. *Suburban Warriors: The Origins of the New American Right*. Princeton, NJ: Princeton University Press.

McGuire, Meredith B. 2008. *Lived Religion: Faith and Practice in Everyday Life*. New York: Oxford University Press.

McRoberts, Omar M. 2003. *Streets of Glory: Church and Community in a Black Urban Neighborhood*. Chicago: University of Chicago Press.

Meyer, Birgit. 1999. *Translating the Devil: Religion and Modernity among the Ewe in Ghana*. Trenton, NJ: Africa World Press.

Miller, Daniel. 1998. *A Theory of Shopping*. Ithaca, NY: Cornell University Press.

Miller, Donald E. 1997. *Reinventing American Protestantism: Christianity in the New Millennium*. Berkeley: University of California Press.

Moeller, Susan D. 1999. *Compassion Fatigue: How the Media Sells Disease, Famine, War and Death*. New York: Routledge.

Moen, Matthew C. 1997. "The Changing Nature of Christian Right Activism: 1970s–1990s." In *Sojourners in the Wilderness: The Christian Right in Comparative Perspective*, edited by Corwin E. Smidt and James M. Penning, 21–37. Lanham, MD: Rowman & Littlefield.

Moore, R. Laurence. 1994. *Selling God: American Religion in the Marketplace of Culture*. New York: Oxford University Press.

Morley, Patrick. 1997. *The Man in the Mirror: Solving the 24 Problems Men Face*. Grand Rapids, MI: Zondervan.

Mosse, George. 1985. *Nationalism and Sexuality: Middle-Class Morality and Sexual Norms in Modern Europe*. Madison: University of Wisconsin Press.

Neely, Jack. 1995. *Knoxville's Secret History*. Knoxville, TN: Scruffy City Publishing.

Newman, Katherine S. 1988. *Falling from Grace: The Experience of Downward Mobility in the American Middle Class*. New York: Free Press.

Niebuhr, H. Richard. 1929. *The Social Sources of Denominationalism*. New York: Meridian.

———. 1988. *The Kingdom of God in America*. Middletown, CT: Wesleyan University Press.

Noll, Mark. 1994. *The Scandal of the Evangelical Mind*. Grand Rapids, MI: Eerdmans.

Nouwen, Henri. 1982. *Compassion: A Reflection on the Christian Life*. New York: Doubleday.

Odendahl, Teresa Jean. 1990. *Charity Begins at Home: Generosity and Self-Interest among the Philanthropic Elite*. New York: Basic Books.

Odum, Howard. 1947. *The Way of the South: Toward Regional Balance in America*. New York: Macmillan.

Olasky, Marvin. 1992. *The Tragedy of American Compassion*. Washington, DC: Regnery Publishing.

———. 1996. *Renewing American Compassion: How Compassion for the Needy Can Turn Ordinary Citizens into Heroes*. With an introduction by Newt Gingrich. New York: Free Press.

———. 2000. *Compassionate Conservatism: What It Is, What It Does, and How It Can Transform America*. With a foreword by George W. Bush. New York: Free Press.

O'Neill, Kevin Lewis. 2010. *City of God: Christian Citizenship in Postwar Guatemala*. Berkeley: University of California Press.

Orsi, Robert A. 2003. "Is the Study of Lived Religion Irrelevant to the World We Live In?" *Journal for the Scientific Study of Religion* 42(2): 169–174.

Ortner, Sherry B. 1999. *Life and Death on Mt. Everest: Sherpas and Himalayan Mountaineering*. Princeton, NJ: Princeton University Press.

Ownby, Ted. 1990. *Subduing Satan: Religion, Recreation, and Manhood in the Rural South, 1865–1920*. Chapel Hill: University of North Carolina Press.

Parry, Jonathan. 1986. "*The Gift*, the Indian Gift, and the 'Indian Gift.' " *Man* 21:453–473.

Perkins, John M. 1993. *Beyond Charity: The Call to Christian Community Development*. Grand Rapids, MI: Baker Books.

Phillips, Kevin. 2006. *American Theocracy: The Peril and Politics of Radical Religion, Oil, and Borrowed Money in the 21st Century*. New York: Viking.

Pressley, Calvin O., and Walter V. Collier. 1999. "Financing Historic Black Churches." In *Financing American Religion*, edited by Mark Chaves and Sharon L. Miller, 21–28. Walnut Creek, CA: AltaMira Press.

Pritchard, G.A. 1996. *Willow Creek Seeker Services: Evaluating a New Way of Doing Church*. Grand Rapids, MI: Baker Books.

Proudfoot, Merrill. 1990. *Diary of a Sit-In*. Urbana: University of Illinois Press.

Putnam, Robert D. 2000. *Bowling Alone: The Collapse and Revival of American Community*. New York: Simon & Schuster.

Putnam, Robert D., Lewis M. Feldstein, and Dan Cohen. 2003. *Better Together: Restoring the American Community.* New York: Simon & Schuster.

Rajagopal, Arvind. 2001. *Politics after Television: Hindu Nationalism and the Reshaping of the Public in India.* New York: Cambridge University Press.

Rauschenbusch, Walter. 1907. *Christianity and the Social Crisis.* New York: Macmillan.

Reed, John. 1972. *The Enduring South.* Lexington, MA: Lexington Books.

Robbins, Joel. 2004. *Becoming Sinners: Christianity and Moral Torment in a Papua New Guinea Society.* Berkeley: University of California Press.

———. 2007. "Between Reproduction and Freedom: Morality, Value, and Radical Cultural Change." *Ethnos* 72(3):293–314.

Rosenbaum, Susanna. 1999. "Embattled, Uncertain, and Exhausting: Motherhood and Work in the 1990s." Master's thesis, New York University.

Rozell, Mark J. 2003. "The Christian Right: Evolution, Expansion, Contraction." In *A Public Faith: Evangelicals and Civic Engagement,* edited by Michael Cromartie, 31–49. Lanham, MD: Rowman & Littlefield.

Sargeant, Kimon H. 2000. *Seeker Churches: Promoting Traditional Religion in a Nontraditional Way.* New Brunswick, NJ: Rutgers University Press.

Schaller, Lyle E. 1992. *The Seven-Day-a-Week Church.* Nashville: Abingdon Press.

———. 2000. *The Very Large Church.* Nashville: Abingdon Press.

Schervish, Paul G. 1990. "Wealth and the Spiritual Secret of Money." In *Faith and Philanthropy in America: Exploring the Role of Religion in America's Voluntary Sector,* edited by Robert Wuthnow and Virginia A. Hodgkinson, 63–90. San Francisco: Jossey-Bass.

Schieffelin, Bambi. 2002. "Marking Time: The Dichotomizing Discourse of Multiple Temporalities." *Current Anthropology* 43(supplement):S5–S17.

Schmidt, Leigh Eric. 2005. *Restless Souls: The Making of American Spirituality.* New York: HarperCollins.

Schneider, John R. 2002. *The Good of Affluence: Seeking God in a Culture of Wealth.* Grand Rapids, MI: Eerdmans.

Schulman, Bruce J. 1991. *From Cotton Belt to Sunbelt: Federal Policy, Economic Development, and the Transformation of the South, 1938–1980.* New York: Oxford University Press.

Sennett, Richard, and Jonathan Cobb. 1972. *The Hidden Injuries of Class.* New York: Knopf.

Shank, Harold, and Wayne Reed. 1995. "A Challenge to Suburban Evangelical Churches: Theological Perspectives on Poverty in America." *Journal of Interdisciplinary Studies* 7(1):119–134.

Shapiro, Henry D. 1977. *Appalachia on Our Minds: The Southern Mountains and Mountaineers in the American Consciousness, 1870–1920.* Chapel Hill: University of North Carolina Press.

Sharlet, Jeff. 2008. *The Family: The Secret Fundamentalism at the Heart of American Power.* New York: HarperCollins.

Shibley, Mark A. 1996. *Resurgent Evangelicalism in the United States: Mapping Cultural Change since 1970.* Columbia: University of South Carolina Press.

Sider, Ronald J. 1977. *Rich Christians in an Age of Hunger.* Downers Grove, IL.: InterVarsity Press.

———. 1999. *Just Generosity: A New Vision for Overcoming Poverty in America.* Grand Rapids, MI: Baker Books.

Silverman, Robert M. 2001. "CDCs and Charitable Organizations in the Urban South: Mobilizing Social Capital Based on Race and Religion for Neighborhood Revitalization." *Journal of Contemporary Ethnography* 30(2): 240–268.

Simmel, Georg. 1950. *The Sociology of Georg Simmel.* New York: Free Press.

Sjogren, Steve. 1993. *Conspiracy of Kindness: A Refreshing New Approach to Sharing the Love of Jesus with Others.* Ann Arbor, MI: Vine Books.

Smith, Christian. 1998. *American Evangelicalism: Embattled and Thriving.* Chicago: University of Chicago Press.

———. 2000. *Christian America? What Evangelicals Really Want.* Berkeley: University of California Press.

Spindler, George D., and Louis Spindler. 1983. "Anthropologists View American Culture." *Annual Review of Anthropology* 12:49–78.

Stack, Carol B. 1996. *Call to Home: African Americans Reclaim the Rural South.* New York: Basic Books.

Stewart, Kathleen. 1996. *A Space on the Side of the Road: Cultural Poetics in an "Other" America.* Princeton, NJ: Princeton University Press.

Stone, Jon R. 1997. *On the Boundaries of American Evangelicalism: The Postwar Evangelical Coalition.* New York: St. Martin's Press.

Stromberg, Peter G. 1986. *Symbols of Community: The Cultural System of a Swedish Church.* Tucson: University of Arizona Press.

Thumma, Scott. 1996. "The Kingdom, the Power, and the Glory: The Megachurch in Modern American Society." PhD dissertation, Emory University.

Thumma, Scott, and Dave Travis. 2007. *Beyond Megachurch Myths: What We Can Learn from America's Largest Churches.* San Francisco: Jossey-Bass.

Trueheart, Charles. 1996. "Welcome to the Next Church." *Atlantic Monthly,* August, 37–58.

Vaughan, John N. 1993. *Megachurches and America's Cities: How Churches Grow.* Grand Rapids, MI: Baker Books.

Verba, Sidney, Kay L. Schlozman, and Henry E. Brady. 1995. *Voice and Equality: Civic Voluntarism in American Politics.* Cambridge, MA: Harvard University Press.

Vygotsky, Lev S. 1978. *Mind and Society: The Development of Higher Psychological Processes.* Cambridge, MA: Harvard University Press.

Wanner, Catherine. 2007. *Communities of the Converted: Ukrainians and Global Evangelism.* Ithaca, NY: Cornell University Press.

Warner, R. Stephen. 1988. *New Wine in Old Wineskins: Evangelicals and Liberals in a Small-town Church.* Berkeley: University of California Press.

Watt, David H. 1991. *A Transforming Faith: Explorations of Twentieth-Century American Evangelicalism.* New Brunswick, NJ: Rutgers University Press.

Weber, Max. 1946a. *From Max Weber: Essays in Sociology.* Edited by H.H. Gerth and C. Wright Mills. New York: Oxford University Press.

————. 1946b. "The Protestant Sects and the Spirit of Capitalism." In *From Max Weber: Essays in Sociology*, edited by H.H. Gerth and C. Wright Mills, 302–322. New York: Oxford University Press.

Weber, Timothy. 1987. *Living in the Shadow of the Second Coming: American Premillennialism, 1875–1982*. Chicago: University of Chicago Press.

Weiner, Annette B. 1992. *Inalienable Possessions: The Paradox of Keeping-While-Giving*. Berkeley: University of California Press.

Wheeler, William Bruce. 2005. *Knoxville, Tennessee: A Mountain City in the New South*. 2nd edition. Knoxville: University of Tennessee Press.

Whisnant, David E. 1994. *Modernizing the Mountaineer: People, Power, and Planning in Appalachia*. Knoxville: University of Tennessee Press.

Wilcox, W. Bradford. 2004. *Soft Patriarchs, New Men: How Christianity Shapes Fathers and Husbands*. Chicago: University of Chicago Press.

Wilkinson, Bruce H. 2000. *The Prayer of Jabez: Breaking through to the Blessed Life*. Sisters, OR: Multnomah.

Williams, Rhys H. 1999. "Visions of the Good Society and the Religious Roots of American Political Culture." *Sociology of Religion* 60(1):1–34.

Wilson, Charles Reagan. 1980. *Baptized in Blood: The Religion of the Lost Cause, 1865–1920*. Athens: University of Georgia Press.

Winston, Diane. 1999. *Red-Hot and Righteous: The Urban Religion of the Salvation Army*. Cambridge, MA: Harvard University Press.

————, ed. 2009. *Small Screen, Big Picture: Television and Lived Religion*. Waco, TX: Baylor University Press.

Wolfe, Alan. 1998. *One Nation, after All*. New York: Viking.

————. 2000. "The Opening of the Evangelical Mind." *Atlantic Monthly*, October, 55–76.

Woodberry, Robert D., and Christian S. Smith. 1998. "Fundamentalism et al.: Conservative Protestants in America." *Annual Review of Sociology* 24:25–56.

Wuthnow, Robert. 1991. *Acts of Compassion: Caring for Others and Helping Ourselves*. Princeton, NJ: Princeton University Press.

————. 2004. *Saving America? Faith-Based Services and the Future of Civil Society*. Princeton, NJ: Princeton University Press.

Yancey, Philip. 1995. *The Jesus I Never Knew*. Grand Rapids, MI: Zondervan.

Yeuell, H. Davis, and Marcia Clark Myers. 1999. "The Presbyterians in Central Appalachia." In *Christianity in Appalachia: Profiles in Regional Pluralism*, edited by Bill J. Leonard, 189–207. Knoxville: University of Tennessee Press.

Young, Michael P. 2006. *Bearing Witness against Sin: The Evangelical Birth of the American Social Movement*. Chicago: University of Chicago Press.

Index

abolition, 14

abortion, 12–13, 17, 25, 105, 110, 170; and post-abortion programs, 39, 177; and pregnancy clinics, 102–3

accountability, 21, 29, 49, 142, 153–82, 184; "accountability groups," 171; horizontal accountability, 176, 236n7; ideology of, 108, 170–76, 236nn5–7; and inner-city outreach, 158–59, 200–203, 208–9; and nostalgia, 171–73; vertical accountability, 176, 180, 200–201, 236n7. *See also* compassion

activist orientations, 2, 24–27, 85, 119, 221, 227n14

adoption, 102

adult education classes, 101–2, 167–68, 188.

affluence, 13, 22, 29, 40, 58–59, 75; and class status, 126–27, 131, 135, 140, 144; and inner-city outreach, 183, 194–96; and megachurches, 3–4, 12, 29, 38, 123, 138; and outreach mobilization, 89, 140, 185, 189. *See also* wealth

Africa, 52, 234n6

African Americans, 75, 116–18, 158, 175–76, 202–4, 207, 215. *See also* black churches; race

Agee, James, 66

agency, 2, 19, 22–24, 86, 168, 170

AIDS ministry. *See* HIV/AIDS ministry

alcoholics, 106, 109, 113, 162–63, 179. *See also* substance abuse programs

Allahyari, Rebecca, 132

altruism, 8, 18, 29, 161, 177, 211–12, 222, 223–24n2, 236n8; and charitable giving, 180; and inner-city outreach, 195, 198, 208; and socially engaged evangelicals, 18, 25, 85, 111, 156

American Dream, 122, 146

Andrews, Raymond (pseud.), 148, 158, 175–76, 178

antimaterialism, 8, 29, 122–52, 233n2, 234n7; and busyness, 122, 139, 146–50, 234n7; and consumerism, 122, 127, 130, 135, 139–43; and gender ideology, 123–25, 127, 129–30, 140, 233–34nn2,4; and social mobility, 122–23, 126–27, 132, 139, 143–46, 232–33n1, 234n6

antimodernism, 138–39, 184

apocalypticism, 3, 15–16, 150, 186, 227n11. *See also* premillennialism

apostolic nostalgia, 171–73

Appalachia, 65, 67–71, 74, 183, 230nn2,3, 237n1; perceptions/stereotypes of, 67, 70, 74, 237n1

"Appalachian mentality," 70, 74

Appalachian Regional Commission, 230n2

Armageddon, battle of, 15

Asad, Talal, 211

Ashcroft, John, 225–26n8

253

progressivism: and black churches, 159; and conservative evangelicals, 8, 11, 16–17, 105–112, 187, 218–19; and local history, 65, 69, 71–72, 74; and the Social Gospel, 15; and socially engaged evangelicals, 34–35, 80, 105–12, 206, 218, 221
proselytization, 9, 29–30, 35, 47–48, 91, 133, 170, 215, 231–32n2
prosperity theology, 122, 137, 145, 234n6
prostitutes, 103, 114, 203
pseudonyms, 223n1
Putnam, Robert, 210, 239n11

race, 4, 8, 57, 183–213; and local history/regionalism, 65, 67–69, 75–77, 80, 230n3; racial alienation/tension, 65, 75–76, 79–80, 159–60, 192–93, 198–99, 200–202; racial reconciliation, 44, 184, 192, 199–202, 205, 207, 209; and segregation, 75, 154–55, 159, 185, 190, 237–38n2. See also black churches
racism, 159, 189, 199, 201–4, 238–39n7
Rajagopal, Arvind, 227–28n14
Ramsey, Dave, 137
Rauschenbusch, Walter, 15
real-estate development, 54, 128, 194, 200, 204–5, 239n8
reciprocity, 155–56, 169, 176, 179–80, 210
Reconstruction, 69, 77
redemption, 9, 15, 20, 79, 86, 115, 141–43, 160, 162; redemptive relationships, 20, 48, 103, 118, 159; and stewardship, 141; transactional logic of, 165, 176–77, 181–82;
redistributive practices, 205–6
Reed, Ralph, 226n9
reflexive critique, 26–27, 29, 56, 119–20, 190, 217, 221, 239n10; and class status, 52, 121–24, 127, 130–31, 133–37, 139, 151; and consumerism, 139–41; and family, 130, 148–150. See also antimaterialism
Reformed theology, 77, 228n1
refugee families, 8, 51, 90–93, 134–35; sponsorships for, 91–93, 164, 231–32n2
regional culture, 61–68, 77, 84; and U.S. South, 67, 230nn2,3
relationalism, 20–22, 156, 170–171, 201; and compassion/accountability, 158–61, 163–64, 170–71, 180; one-on-one,

26, 93, 96, 108–10, 218; redemptive relationships, 20, 48, 103, 118, 159; and social outreach, 94, 96, 107–9, 117–19, 142–43, 148, 192, 198–99
Renewing American Compassion (Olasky), 236n6
repentance, 30, 77, 115, 201
Republican Party, 12, 68, 172, 226n9
revivalism, Christian, 2, 8, 11, 54, 63–64, 77–79, 82–84, 185, 220, 237n9; and socially engaged evangelicals, 8, 26, 28, 37, 86, 119, 153, 191; in U.S. history, 14, 77, 86, 238n4, 229n3
Richards, Damien (pseud.), 194–98
right-wing politics, 17, 131, 138–39, 211, 213, 217–20; and welfare reform, 172–73, 236n6. See also Christian Right; fundamentalism, Christian
Robbins, Joel, 19, 237n9
Robertson, Pat, 12, 13, 17
Roosevelt, Franklin D., 71

sacrifice, 9, 22, 26, 77, 93, 98, 115, 119; and class status, 122–23, 127–28, 136, 139, 141, 143–44, 149, 151–52; and compassion/accountability, 155, 161, 164, 166–67, 178–79; female domestic, 98, 123, 129–30, 149; of Jesus Christ, 143, 166, 176
Saddleback Church (Orange County, Calif.), 13, 45, 53, 210
salvation, 8, 14–15, 30–31, 77, 217; and compassion/accountability, 156, 165, 170, 176–77; theology of, 10, 19–20, 24, 46, 222, 225n7, 231n1
Salvation Army, 78, 113, 226–27n10
Samaritans of Knoxville (pseud.), 7, 50, 89–98, 106, 114, 208; and class status, 140–41, 147; and compassion/accountability, 157–61, 166–69, 174–76, 181, 192; and domestic violence shelters, 93–98; and refugee families, 90–93
sanctuary movement (1980s), 25
Satan, 15, 49, 58, 225n7
Schuller, Robert, 53
Scientology, Church of, 12
Scofield Reference Bible (1909), 15
self-criticism, evangelical. See reflexive critique
selflessness, 29, 123, 128, 133, 148–49, 161, 173, 179–80, 239n8
Sennett, Richard, 122–23, 232–33n1
separatism, 8, 16, 149, 185, 197
September 11 terrorist attacks, 12, 83

TEXT
10/13 Sabon
DISPLAY
Sabon
COMPOSITOR
Toppan Best-set Premedia Limited
INDEXER
Sharon Sweeney
PRINTER AND BINDER
Maple-Vail Book Manufacturing Group